Burp Suite Cookbook

Practical recipes to help you master web penetration testing
with Burp Suite

Sunny Wear

BIRMINGHAM - MUMBAI

Burp Suite Cookbook

Commissioning Editor: Pavan Ramchandani
Acquisition Editor: Akshay Jethani
Content Development Editor: Abhishek Jadhav
Technical Editor: Aditya Khadye
Copy Editor: Safis Editing
Project Coordinator: Jagdish Prabhu
Proofreader: Safis Editing
Indexer: Aishwarya Gangawane
Graphics: Jisha Chirayil
Production Coordinator: Nilesh Mohite

First published: September 2018

Production reference: 1250918

Published by Packt Publishing Ltd.
Livery Place
35 Livery Street
Birmingham
B3 2PB, UK.

ISBN 978-1-78953-173-2

www.packtpub.com

`mapt.io`

Mapt is an online digital library that gives you full access to over 5,000 books and videos, as well as industry leading tools to help you plan your personal development and advance your career. For more information, please visit our website.

Why subscribe?

- Spend less time learning and more time coding with practical eBooks and Videos from over 4,000 industry professionals

- Improve your learning with Skill Plans built especially for you

- Get a free eBook or video every month

- Mapt is fully searchable

- Copy and paste, print, and bookmark content

Packt.com

Did you know that Packt offers eBook versions of every book published, with PDF and ePub files available? You can upgrade to the eBook version at `www.packt.com` and as a print book customer, you are entitled to a discount on the eBook copy. Get in touch with us at `customercare@packtpub.com` for more details.

At `www.packt.com`, you can also read a collection of free technical articles, sign up for a range of free newsletters, and receive exclusive discounts and offers on Packt books and eBooks.

Contributors

About the author

Sunny Wear, CISSP, GWAPT, GSSP-JAVA, GSSP-.NET, CSSLP, CEH is an Information Security Architect, Web App Penetration Tester and Developer. Her experience includes network, data, application and security architecture as well as programming across multiple languages and platforms. She has participated in the design and creation of many enterprise applications as well as the security testing aspects of platforms and services. She is the author of several security-related books which assists programmers in more easily finding mitigations to commonly-identified vulnerabilities within applications. She conducts security talks and classes at conferences like BSides Tampa, AtlSecCon, Hackfest, CA, and BSides Springfield.

About the reviewer

Sachin Wagh is a young information security researcher from India. His core area of expertise includes penetration testing, vulnerability analysis, and exploit development. He has found security vulnerabilities in Google, Tesla Motors, LastPass, Microsoft, F-Secure, and other companies. Due to the severity of many bugs discovered, he has received numerous awards for his findings. He has participated in several security conferences as a speaker, such as Hack In Paris, Infosecurity Europe, and HAKON.

Packt is searching for authors like you

If you're interested in becoming an author for Packt, please visit `authors.packtpub.com` and apply today. We have worked with thousands of developers and tech professionals, just like you, to help them share their insight with the global tech community. You can make a general application, apply for a specific hot topic that we are recruiting an author for, or submit your own idea.

Table of Contents

Preface

Burp Suite is a Java-based platform for testing the security of your web applications, and has been adopted widely by professional enterprise testers.

The Burp Suite Cookbook contains recipes to tackle challenges in determining and exploring vulnerabilities in web applications. You will learn how to uncover security flaws with various test cases for complex environments. After you have configured Burp for your environment, you will use Burp tools such as Spider, Scanner, Intruder, Repeater, and Decoder, among others, to resolve specific problems faced by pentesters. You will also explore working with various modes of Burp and then perform operations on the web using the Burp CLI. Toward the end, you will cover recipes that target specific test scenarios and resolve them using best practices.

By the end of the book, you will be up and running with deploying Burp for securing web applications.

Who this book is for

If you are a security professional, web pentester, or software developer who wants to adopt Burp Suite for applications security, this book is for you.

What this book covers

Chapter 1, *Getting Started with Burp Suite,* provides setup instructions necessary to proceed through the material of the book.

Chapter 2, *Getting to Know the Burp Suite of Tools,* begins with establishing the Target scope and provides overviews to the most commonly used tools within Burp Suite.

Chapter 3, *Configuring, Spidering, Scanning, and Reporting with Burp,* helps testers to calibrate Burp settings to be less abusive towards the target application.

Chapter 4, *Assessing Authentication Schemes,* covers the basics of Authentication, including an explanation that this is the act of verifying a person or object claim is true.

Chapter 5, *Assessing Authorization Checks,* helps you understand the basics of Authorization, including an explanation that this how an application uses roles to determine user functions.

Chapter 6, *Assessing Session Management Mechanisms*, dives into the basics of Session Management, including an explanation that this how an application keeps track of user activity on a website.

Chapter 7, *Assessing Business Logic*, covers the basics of Business Logic Testing, including an explanation of some of the more common tests performed in this area.

Chapter 8, *Evaluating Input Validation Checks*, delves into the basics of Data Validation Testing, including an explanation of some of the more common tests performed in this area.

Chapter 9, *Attacking the Client*, helps you understand how Client-Side testing is concerned with the execution of code on the client, typically natively within a web browser or browser plugin. Learn how to use Burp to test the execution of code on the client-side to determine the presence of Cross-site Scripting (XSS).

Chapter 10, *Working with Burp Macros and Extensions*, teaches you how Burp macros enable penetration testers to automate events such as logins or response parameter reads to overcome potential error situations. We will also learn about Extensions as an additional functionality to Burp.

Chapter 11, *Implementing Advanced Topic Attacks*, provides a brief explanation of XXE as a vulnerability class targeting applications which parse XML and SSRF as a vulnerability class allowing an attacker to force applications to make unauthorized requests on the attacker's behalf.

To get the most out of this book

All the requirements are updated in the *Technical requirements* section for each of the chapter.

Conventions used

There are a number of text conventions used throughout this book.

CodeInText: Indicates code words in text, database table names, folder names, filenames, file extensions, pathnames, dummy URLs, user input, and Twitter handles. Here is an example: "Allow the attack to continue until you reach payload 50."

A block of code is set as follows:

```
<script>try{var m = "";var l = window.localStorage; var s =
window.sessionStorage;for(i=0;i<l.length;i++){var lKey = l.key(i);m
+= lKey + "=" + l.getItem(lKey) +
";\n";};for(i=0;i<s.length;i++){var lKey = s.key(i);m += lKey + "="
+ s.getItem(lKey) +
";\n";};alert(m);}catch(e){alert(e.message);}</script>
```

Any command-line input or output is written as follows:

```
user'+union+select+concat('The+password+for+',username,'+is+',+pass
word),mysignature+from+accounts+--+
```

Bold: Indicates a new term, an important word, or words that you see onscreen. For example, words in menus or dialog boxes appear in the text like this. Here is an example: "Select a tool from the drop-down listing and click the **Lookup Tool** button."

Warnings or important notes appear like this.

Tips and tricks appear like this.

Sections

In this book, you will find several headings that appear frequently (*Getting ready*, *How to do it...*, *How it works...*, *There's more...*, and *See also*).

To give clear instructions on how to complete a recipe, use these sections as follows:

Getting ready

This section tells you what to expect in the recipe and describes how to set up any software or any preliminary settings required for the recipe.

How to do it...

This section contains the steps required to follow the recipe.

How it works...

This section usually consists of a detailed explanation of what happened in the previous section.

There's more...

This section consists of additional information about the recipe in order to make you more knowledgeable about the recipe.

See also

This section provides helpful links to other useful information for the recipe.

Get in touch

Feedback from our readers is always welcome.

General feedback: If you have questions about any aspect of this book, mention the book title in the subject of your message and email us at customercare@packtpub.com.

Errata: Although we have taken every care to ensure the accuracy of our content, mistakes do happen. If you have found a mistake in this book, we would be grateful if you would report this to us. Please visit www.packt.com/submit-errata, selecting your book, clicking on the Errata Submission Form link, and entering the details.

Piracy: If you come across any illegal copies of our works in any form on the Internet, we would be grateful if you would provide us with the location address or website name. Please contact us at copyright@packt.com with a link to the material.

If you are interested in becoming an author: If there is a topic that you have expertise in and you are interested in either writing or contributing to a book, please visit authors.packtpub.com.

Reviews

Please leave a review. Once you have read and used this book, why not leave a review on the site that you purchased it from? Potential readers can then see and use your unbiased opinion to make purchase decisions, we at Packt can understand what you think about our products, and our authors can see your feedback on their book. Thank you!

For more information about Packt, please visit `packt.com`.

Disclaimer

The information within this book is intended to be used only in an ethical manner. Do not use any information from the book if you do not have written permission from the owner of the equipment. If you perform illegal actions, you are likely to be arrested and prosecuted to the full extent of the law. Packt Publishing does not take any responsibility if you misuse any of the information contained within the book. The information herein must only be used while testing environments with proper written authorizations from appropriate persons responsible.

Targeting legal vulnerable web applications

In order for us to properly showcase the functions of Burp Suite, we need a target web application. We need to have a target which we are legally allowed to attack.

Know Your Enemy is a saying derived from Sun Tzu's *The Art of War*. The application of this principle in penetration testing is the act of attacking a target. The purpose of the attack is to uncover weaknesses in a target which can then be exploited. Commonly referred to as ethical hacking, attacking legal targets assists companies to assess the level of risk in their web applications.

More importantly, any penetration testing must be done with express, written permission. Attacking any website without this permission can result in litigation and possible incarceration. Thankfully, the information security community provides many purposefully vulnerable web applications to allow students to learn how to hack in a legal way.

A consortium group, **Open Web Application Security Project**, commonly referred to as **OWASP**, provides a plethora of resources related to web security. OWASP is considered the de facto standard in the industry for all things web security-related. Every three years or so, the group creates a listing of the Top 10 most common vulnerabilities found in web applications.

 See here for more information (`https://www.owasp.org/index.php/Category:OWASP_Top_Ten_Project`).

Throughout this book, we will use purposefully vulnerable web applications compiled into one virtual machine by OWASP. This setup enables us to legally attack the targets contained within the virtual machine.

Getting Started with Burp Suite 1

In this chapter, we will cover the following recipes:

- Downloading Burp (Community, Professional)
- Setting up a web app pentesting lab
- Starting Burp at a command line or an executable
- Listening for HTTP traffic, using Burp

Introduction

This chapter provides the setup instructions necessary to proceed through the material in this book. Starting with downloading Burp, the details include the two main Burp editions available and their distinguishing characteristics.

To use the Burp suite, a penetration tester requires a target application. This chapter includes instructions on downloading and installing OWASP applications contained within a **virtual machine** (**VM**). Such applications will be used throughout the book as targeted vulnerable web applications.

Also included in this chapter is configuring a web browser to use the **Burp Proxy Listener**. This listener is required to capture HTTP traffic between the Burp and the target web application. Default settings for the listener include an **Internet Protocol** (**IP**) address, 127.0.0.1, and port number 8080.

Finally, this chapter concludes with the options for starting Burp. This includes how to start Burp at the command line, also with an optional headless mode, and using the executable.

Downloading Burp (Community, Professional)

The first step in learning the techniques contained within this book is to download the Burp suite. The download page is available here (https://portswigger.net/burp/). You will need to decide which edition of the Burp suite you would like to download from the following:

- Professional
- Community
- Enterprise (not covered)

What is now termed *Community* was once labeled *Free Edition*. You may see both referenced on the internet, but they are one and the same. At the time of this writing, the Professional edition costs $399.

To help you make your decision, let's compare the two. The Community version offers many of the functions used in this book, but not all. For example, Community does not include any scanning functionality. In addition, the Community version contains some forced throttling of threads when using the Intruder functionality. There are no built-in payloads in the Community version, though you can load your own custom ones. And, finally, several Burp extensions that require Professional will, obviously, not work in the Community edition.

The Professional version has all functionality enabled including passive and active scanners. There is no forced throttled. **PortSwigger** (that is, the name of the company that writes and maintains the Burp suite) provides several built-in payloads for fuzzing and brute-forcing. Burp extensions using scanner-related API calls are workable in the Professional version as well.

In this book, we will be using the Professional version, which means much of the functionality is available in the Community edition. However, when a feature is used in this book specific to the Professional edition, a special icon will indicate this. The icon used is the following:

Burp Suite Professional

Getting ready

To begin our adventure together, go to https://portswigger.net/burp and download the edition of the Burp suite you wish to use. The page provides a slider, as following, which highlights the features of Professional and Community, allowing you to compare them:

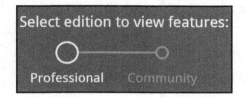

Many readers may choose the Community edition to gain familiarity with the product prior to purchasing.

Should you choose to purchase or trial the Professional edition, you will need to complete forms or payments and subsequent email confirmations will be sent to you. Once your account is created, you may login and perform the download from the links provided in our account.

Software tool requirements

To complete this recipe, you will need the following:

- Oracle Java (https://www.java.com/en/download/)
- Burp Proxy Community or Professional (https://portswigger.net/burp/)
- Firefox Browser (https://www.mozilla.org/en-US/firefox/new/)

How to do it...

After deciding on the edition you need, you have two installation options, including an executable or a plain JAR file. The executable is only available in Windows and is offered in both 32-bit or 64-bit. The plain JAR file is available for Windows, macOS, and Linux.

The Windows executable is self-contained and will create icons in your program listing. However, the plain JAR file requires your platform to have Java (`https://www.java.com/en/download/`) pre-installed. You may choose the current version of Java (JRE or JDK) so feel free to choose the latest version:

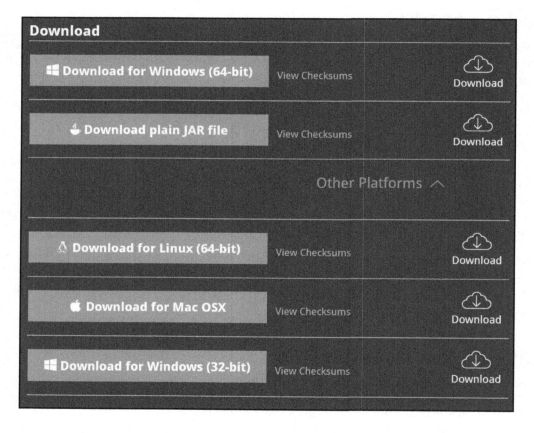

Setting up a web app pentesting lab

The **Broken Web Application (BWA)** is an OWASP project that provides a self-contained VM complete with a variety of applications with known vulnerabilities. The applications within this VM enable students to learn about web application security, practice and observe web attacks, and make use of penetration tools such as Burp.

To follow the recipes shown in this book, we will utilize OWASP's BWA VM. At the time of this writing, the OWASP BWA VM can be downloaded from `https://sourceforge.net/projects/owaspbwa/files/`.

Getting ready

We will download the OWASP BWA VM along with supportive tools to create our web app pentesting lab.

Software tool requirements

To complete this recipe, you will need the following:

- Oracle VirtualBox (`https://www.virtualbox.org/wiki/Downloads`)
    - Choose an executable specific to your platform
- Mozilla Firefox Browser (`https://www.mozilla.org/en-US/firefox/new/`)
- 7-Zip file archiver (`https://www.7-zip.org/download.html`)
- OWASP BWA VM (`https://sourceforge.net/projects/owaspbwa/files/`)
- Burp Proxy Community or Professional (`https://portswigger.net/burp/`)
- Oracle Java (`https://www.java.com/en/download/`)

How to do it...

For this recipe, you will need to download the OWASP BWA VM and install it by performing the following steps:

1. Click **Download Latest Version** from the OWASP BWA VM link provided earlier and unzip the file OWASP_Broken_Web_Apps_VM_1.2.7z.

2. You will be presented with a listing of several files, as follows:

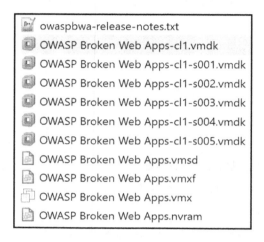

3. All file extensions shown indicate the VM can be imported into Oracle VirtualBox or VMware Player/Workstation. For purposes of setting up the web application pentesting lab for this book, we will use Oracle VirtualBox.

4. Make a note of the OWASP Broken Web Apps-cl1.vmdk file. Open the VirtualBox Manager (that is, the Oracle VM VirtualBox program).

5. Within the VirtualBox Manager screen, select **Machine | New** from the top menu and type a name for the machine, OWASP BWA.

6. Set the type to Linux and version to Ubuntu (64-bit), and then click **Next**, as follows:

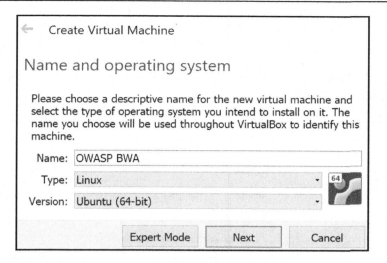

7. The next screen allows you to adjust the RAM or leave as suggested. Click **Next**.
8. On the next screen, choose **Use an existing virtual hard disk file**.
9. Use the folder icon on the right to select OWASP Broken Web Apps-cl1.vmdk file from the extracted list and click **Create**, as follows:

10. Your VM is now loaded in the VirtualBox Manager. Let's make some minor adjustments. Highlight the **OWASP BWA** entry and select **Settings** from the top menu.

11. Select the **Network** section in the left-hand pane and change to **Host-only Adapter**. Click **OK**.

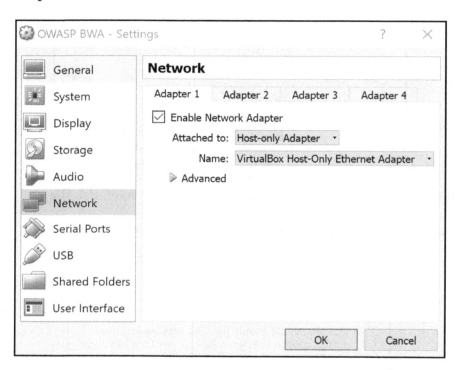

12. Now let's start the virtual machine. Right-click then choose **Start | Normal Start**.

13. Wait until the Linux system is fully booted, which may take a few minutes. After the booting process is complete, you should see the following screen. However, the IP address shown will be different for your machine:

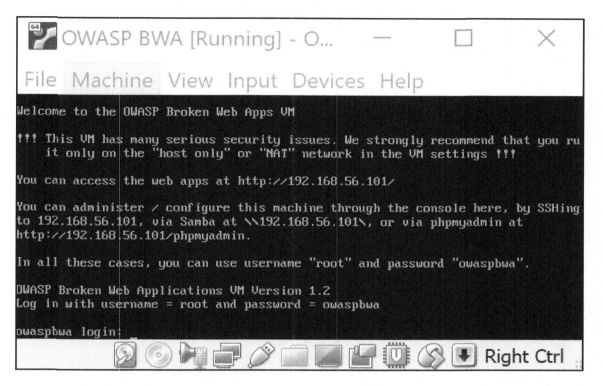

14. The information presented on this screen identifies the URL where you can access vulnerable web applications running on the VM. For example, in the previous screenshot, the URL is `http://192.168.56.101/`. You are given a prompt for administering the VM, but it is not necessary to log in at this time.

15. Open the Firefox browser on your host system, not in the VM. Using the Firefox Browser on your host machine, enter the URL provided (for example, `http://192.168.56.101/`), where the IP address is specific to your machine.

16. In your browser, you are presented with an index page containing links to vulnerable web applications. These applications will be used as targets throughout this book:

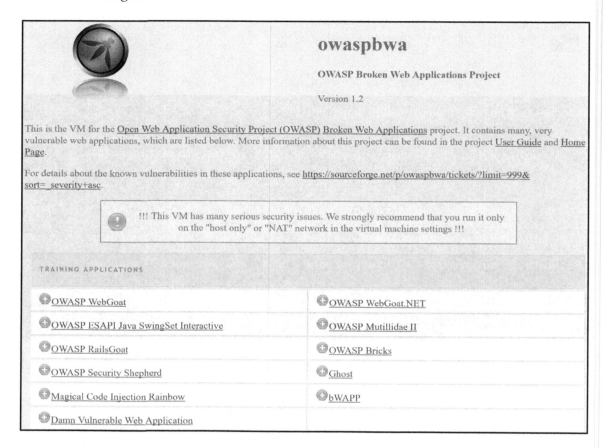

How it works

Leveraging a customized virtual machine created by OWASP, we can quickly set up a web app pentesting lab containing purposefully vulnerable applications, which we can use as legal targets for our exercises throughout this book.

Starting Burp at a command line or as an executable

For non-Windows users or those Windows users who chose the plain JAR file option, you will start Burp at a command line each time they wish to run it. As such, you will require a particular Java command to do so.

In some circumstances, such as automated scripting, you may wish to invoke Burp at the command line as a line item in your shell script. Additionally, you may wish to run Burp without a **graphical user interface (GUI)**, referred to as **headless mode**. This section describes how to perform these tasks.

How to do it...

We will review the commands and actions required to start the Burp Suite product:

1. Start Burp in Windows, after running the installer from the downloaded `.exe` file, by double-clicking the icon on desktop or select it from the programs listing:

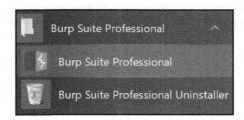

When using the plain JAR file, the executable `java` is followed by the option of `-jar`, followed by the name of the download JAR file.

2. Start Burp at the command line (minimal) with the plain JAR file (Java must be installed first):

```
C:\Burp Jar Files>java -jar burpsuite_pro_1.7.33.jar
```

If you prefer more control over the heap size settings (that is, the amount of memory allocated for the program) you may modify the `java` command.

3. The `java` executable is followed by the `-jar`, followed by the memory allocation. In this case, 2 GB (that is, `2g`) is allocated for **read access memory (RAM)**, followed by the name of the JAR file. If you get an error to the effect that you cannot allocate that much memory, just drop the amount down to something like 1,024 MB (that is, `1024m`) instead.

4. Start Burp at command line (optimize) with the plain JAR file (Java must be installed first):

```
C:\Burp Jar Files>java -jar -Xmx2g burpsuite_pro_1.7.33.jar
```

5. It is possible to start Burp at the command line and to run it in headless mode. Headless mode means running Burp without the GUI.

   For the purposes of this book, we will not be running Burp in headless mode, since we are learning through the GUI. However, you may require this information in the future, which is why it is presented here.

6. Start Burp at the command line to run in headless mode with the plain JAR file (Java must be installed first):

```
C:\Burp Jar Files>java -jar -Djava.awt.headless=true -Xmx2g burpsuite_pro_1.7.33.jar
```

   Note the placement of the parameter `-Djava.awt.headless=true` immediately following the `-jar` option and before the name of the JAR file.

7. If successful, you should see the following:

```
Proxy: Proxy service started on 127.0.0.1:8080
```

   Press *Ctrl* + *C* or *Ctrl* + *Z* to stop the process.

8. It is possible to provide a configuration file to the headless mode command for customizing the port number and IP address where the proxy listener is located.

Please consult PortSwigger's support pages for more information on this topic: `https://support.portswigger.net/customer/portal/questions/16805563-burp-command-line`.

9. In each startup scenario described, you should be presented with a **splash screen**. The splash screen label will match whichever edition you decided to download, either Professional or Community.

10. You may be prompted to update the version; feel free to do this, if you like. New features are constantly added into Burp to help you find vulnerabilities, so upgrading the application is a good idea. Choose **Update Now**, if applicable.

11. Next, you are presented with a dialog box asking about project files and configurations:

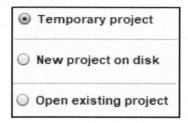

12. If you are using the Community edition, you will only be able to create a temporary project. If you are using the Professional edition, create a new project on disk, saving it in an appropriate location for you to find. Click **Next**.

13. The subsequent splash screen asks you about the configurations you would like to use. At this point, we don't have any yet, so choose **Use Burp defaults**. As you progress through this book, you may wish to save configuration settings and load them from this splash screen in the future, as follows:

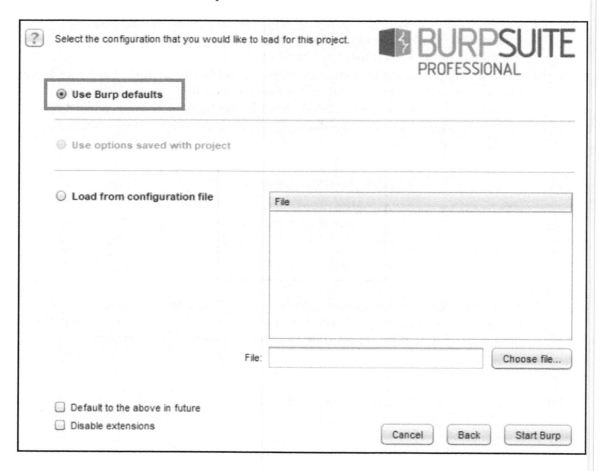

14. Finally, we are ready to click **Start Burp**.

How it works...

Using either the plain JAR file or the Windows executable, you can launch Burp to start the Proxy listener to capture HTTP traffic. Burp offers temporary or permanent Project files to save activities performed in the suite.

Listening for HTTP traffic, using Burp

Burp is described as an intercepting proxy. This means Burp sits between the user's web browser and the application's web server and intercepts or captures all of the traffic flowing between them. This type of behavior is commonly referred to as a **Proxy service**.

Penetration testers use intercepting proxies to capture traffic flowing between a web browser and a web application for the purposes of analysis and manipulation. For example, a tester can pause any HTTP request, thus allowing parameter tampering prior to sending the request to the web server.

Intercepting proxies, such as Burp, allow testers to intercept both HTTP requests and HTTP responses. This allows a tester to observe the behavior of the web application under different conditions. And, as we shall see, sometimes, the behaviors are unintended from what the original developer expected.

To see the Burp suite in action, we need to configure our Firefox browser's **Network Settings** to point to our running instance of Burp. This enables Burp to capture all HTTP traffic that is flowing between your browser and the target web application.

Getting ready

We will configure Firefox browser to allow Burp to listen to all HTTP traffic flowing between the browser and the OWASP BWA VM. This will allow the proxy service within Burp to capture traffic for testing purposes.

Instructions are available on PortSwigger at (`https://support.portswigger.net/ customer/portal/articles/1783066-configuring-firefox-to-work-with-burp`) and we will also step through the process in the following recipe.

How to do it...

The following are the steps you can go through to listen to all HTTP traffic using Burp:

1. Open the Firefox browser and go to **Options.**
2. In the **General** tab, scroll down to the **Network Proxy** section and then click **Settings**.
3. In the **Connection Settings**, select **Manual proxy configuration** and type in the IP address of `127.0.0.1` with port `8080`. Select the **Use this proxy server for all protocols** checkbox:

4. Make sure the **No proxy** for the textbox is blank, as shown in the following screenshot, and then click **OK:**

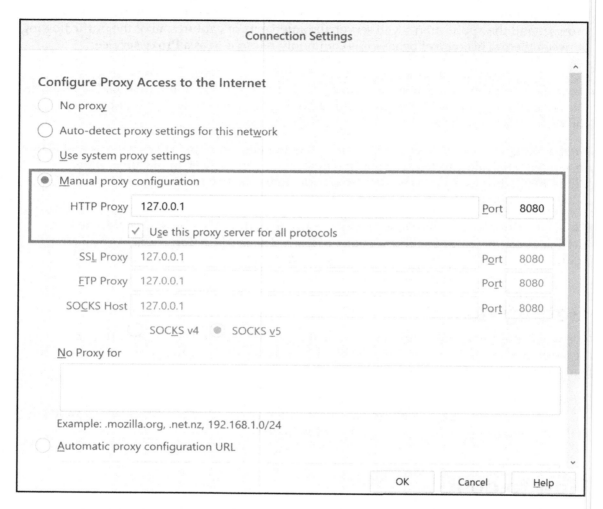

5. With the OWASP BWA VM running in the background and using Firefox to browse to the URL specific to your machine (that is, the IP address shown on the Linux VM in VirtualBox), click the reload button (the arrow in a circle) to see the traffic captured in Burp.

6. If you don't happen to see any traffic, check whether Proxy Intercept is holding up the request. If the button labeled **Intercept is on** is depressed, as shown in the following screenshot, then click the button again to disable the interception. After doing so, the traffic should flow freely into Burp, as follows:

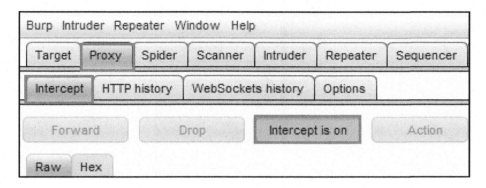

In the following, **Proxy | Intercept** button is disabled:

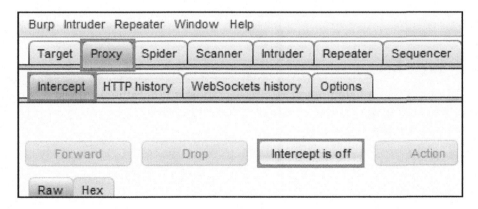

7. If everything is working properly, you will see traffic on your **Target** | **Site map** tab similar to what is shown in the following screenshot. Your IP address will be different, of course, and you may have more items shown within your **Site map**. Congratulations! You now have Burp listening to all of your browser traffic!

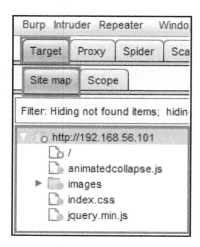

How it works...

The Burp Proxy service is listening on `127.0.0.1` port `8080`. Either of these settings can be changed to listen on an alternative IP address or port number. However, for the purpose of learning, we will use the default settings.

Getting to Know the Burp Suite of Tools

2

In this chapter, we will cover the following recipes:

- Setting the Target Site Map
- Understanding Message Editor
- Repeating with Repeater
- Decoding with Decoder
- Intruding with Intruder

Introduction

This chapter provides overviews of the most commonly used tools within Burp Suite. The chapter begins by establishing the Target scope within the Target Site Map. This is followed by an introduction to the Message Editor. Then, there will be some hands-on recipes using **OWASP Mutillidae II** to get acquainted with Proxy, Repeater, Decoder, and Intruder.

Software tool requirements

To complete the recipes in this chapter, you will need the following:

- Burp Proxy Community or Professional (https://portswigger.net/burp/)
- The Firefox browser configured to allow Burp to proxy traffic (https://www.mozilla.org/en-US/firefox/new/)

Setting the Target Site Map

Now that we have traffic flowing between your browser, Burp, and the OWASP BWA virtual machine, we can begin setting the scope of our test. For this recipe, we will use the OWASP Mutillidae II link (http://<Your_VM_Assigned_IP_Address>/mutillidae/) available in the OWASP BWA VM as our target application.

Looking more closely at the **Target** tab, you will notice there are two subtabs available: **Site map** and **Scope**. From the initial proxy setup between your browser, Burp, and the web server, you should now have some URLs, folders, and files shown in the **Target | Site map** tab. You may find the amount of information overwhelming, but setting the scope for our project will help to focus our attention better.

Getting ready

Using the **Target | Site map** and **Target | Scope** tab, we will assign the URL for mutillidae (http://<Your_VM_Assigned_IP_Address>/mutillidae/) as the **scope**.

How to do it...

Execute the following steps to set the Target Site Map:

1. Search for the folder `mutillidae` and right-click on **Add to scope**. Notice the brief highlighting of the **Target | Scope** subtab, as follows:

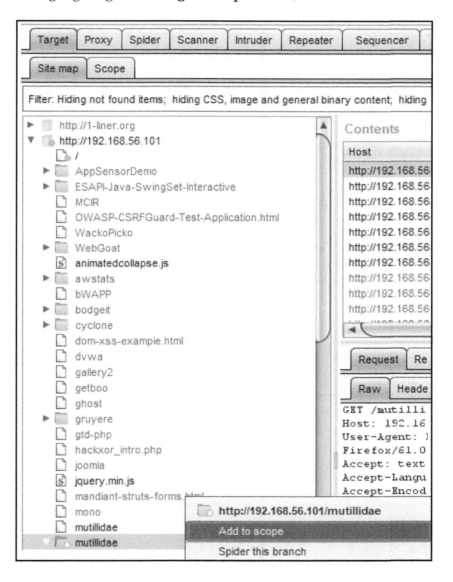

2. Upon adding the folder `mutillidae` to your scope, you may be presented with a **Proxy history logging** dialog box, as follows. You may choose to avoid collecting messages out of your cope by clicking **Yes**. Or you may choose to continue to have the **Proxy HTTP History** table collect any messages passing through Burp, even if those messages fall outside the scope you've identified. For our purposes, we will select **Yes**:

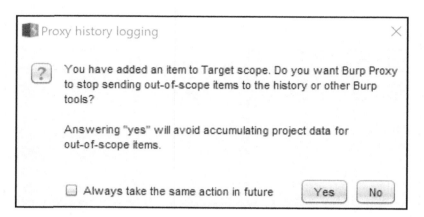

3. Flipping over the **Target | Scope** tab, you should now see the full URL for the OWASP Mutillidae II, shown in the **Include in scope** table, as follows:

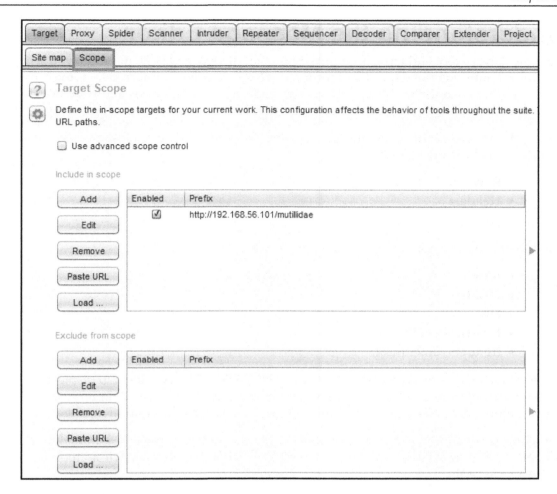

How it works...

The Message Editor displays detailed information any HTTP message flowing through the Proxy listener. After setting up Proxy to capture HTTP traffic, as seen in your **Target | Site map** and Burp **Proxy | HTTP history** tab, you are able to select any single message to reveal the Message Editor. Each editor contains the request and response sides of the message, so long as the message is properly proxied through Burp.

Understanding the Message Editor

On almost every tool and tab within Burp Suite that display an HTTP message, you will see an editor identifying the request and response. This is commonly referred to as the Message Editor. The Message Editor allows viewing and editing HTTP requests and responses with specialties.

Within the Message Editor are multiple subtabs. The subtabs for a request message, at a minimum, include the following:

- **Raw**
- **Headers**
- **Hex**

The subtabs for a response message include the following:

- **Raw**
- **Headers**
- **Hex**
- **HTML** (sometimes)
- **Render** (sometimes)

The **Raw** tab gives you the message in its raw HTTP form. The **Headers** tab displays HTTP header parameters in tabular format. The parameters are editable, and columns can be added, removed, or modified in the table within tools such as Proxy and Repeater.

For requests containing parameters or cookies, the **Params** tab is present. Parameters are editable, and columns can be added, removed, or modified in the table within tools such as Proxy and Repeater.

Finally, there's the **Hex** tab, which presents the message in hexadecimal format; it is, in essence, a hex editor. You are permitted to edit individual bytes within tools such as Proxy and Repeater, but those values must be given in two-digit hexadecimal form, from 00 through FF.

Getting ready

Let's explore the multiple tabs available in the Message Editor for each request and response captured in Burp.

How to do it...

Ensure you have traffic flowing between your browser, Burp, and the OWASP BWA virtual machine.

1. Looking at the **Target | Site map** tab, notice the Message Editor section:

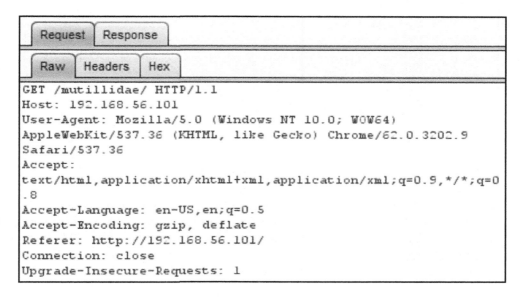

2. When viewing a request, note that the subtabs available include **Raw**, **Headers**, and **Hex**, at a minimum. However, in the case of a request containing parameters or cookies, the **Params** subtab is also available:

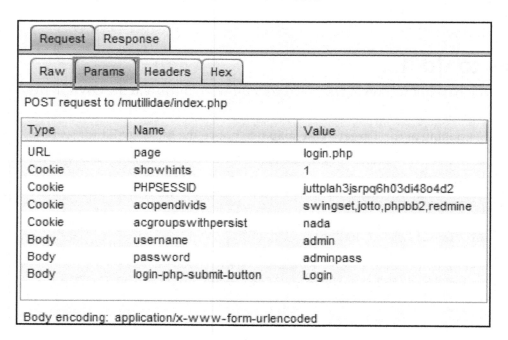

3. The other side of the message is the **Response** tab, containing the **Raw, Headers, Hex** subtabs, and sometimes **HTML** and **Render**. These are the various formats provided for the HTTP response to the request. If the content is HTML, then the tab will appear. Likewise, the **Render** tab enables HTML display as it would be presented in a browser but without any JavaScript executed:

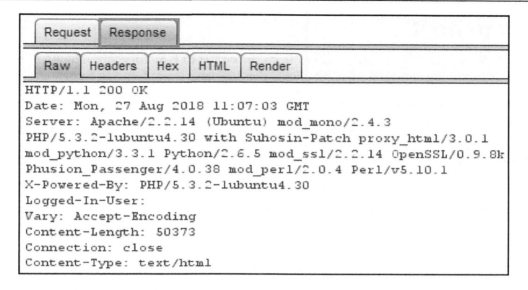

Repeating with Repeater

Repeater allows for slight changes or tweaks to the request, and it is displayed in the left-hand window. A **Go** button allows the request to be reissued, and the response is displayed in the right-hand window.

Details related to your HTTP request include standard Message Editor details such as **Raw**, **Params** (for requests with parameters or cookies), **Headers**, and **Hex**.

Details related to the HTTP Response include standard Message Editor details including **Raw**, **Headers**, **Hex**, and, sometimes, **HTML** and **Render**.

At the bottom of each panel is a search-text box, allowing the tester to quickly find a value present in a message.

Getting ready

Repeater allows you to manually modify and then re-issue an individual HTTP request, analyzing the response that you receive.

How to do it...

1. From the **Target** | **Site map** or from **Proxy** | **HTTP history** tabs (shown in the following screenshot), right-click a message and select **Send to Repeater**:

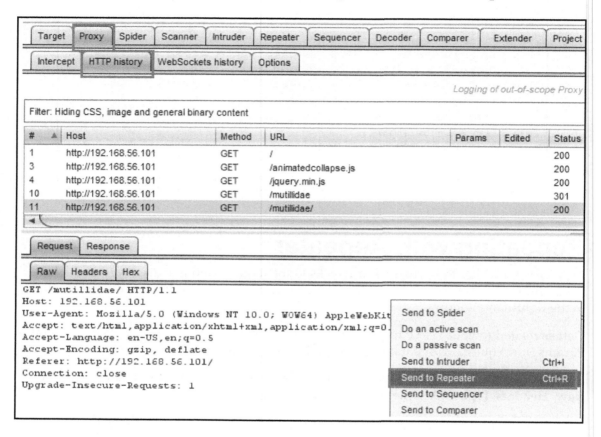

2. Switch over to the **Repeater** tab. Note the **HTTP Request** is ready for the tester to tweak parameters, and then send the request to the application via the **Go** button.

Note the search boxes at the bottom of each panel:

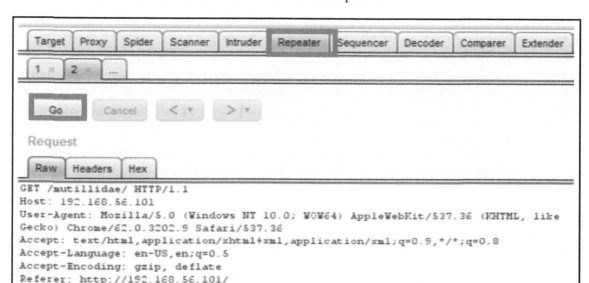

We will use Repeater quite a bit throughout this book. This chapter is just an introduction to the Repeater and to understand its purpose.

Decoding with Decoder

Burp Decoder is a tool that allows the tester to convert raw data into encoded data or to take encoded data and convert it back to plain text. Decoder supports several formats including URL encoding, HTML encoding, Base64 encoding, binary code, hashed data, and others. Decoder also includes a built-in hex editor.

Getting ready

As a web penetration test progresses, a tester might happen upon an encoded value. Burp eases the decoding process by allowing the tester to send the encoded value to Decoder and try the various decoding functions available.

How to do it...

Let's try to decode the value of the session token PHPSESSID found in the OWASP Mutillidae II application. When a user initially browses to the URL (`http://<Your_VM_Assigned_IP_Address>/mutillidae/`), that user will be assigned a PHPSESSID cookie. The PHPSESSID value appears to be encrypted and then wrapped in base 64 encoding. Using Decoder, we can unwrap the value.

1. Browse to the `http://<Your_VM_Assigned_IP_Address>/mutillidae/` application.
2. Find the HTTP request you just generated from your browse within the **Proxy | HTTP history** tab (shown in the next screenshot). Highlight the PHPSESSID value, not the parameter name, right-click, and select **Send to Decoder**:

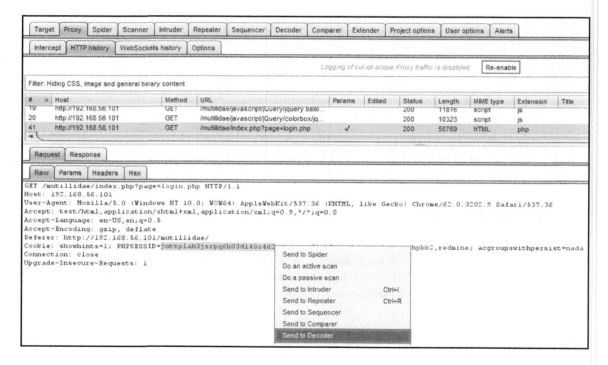

3. In the **Decoder** tab, in the **Decode as...** drop-down as follows, select **Base 64**. Note the results are viewed in the **Hex** editor and are encrypted:

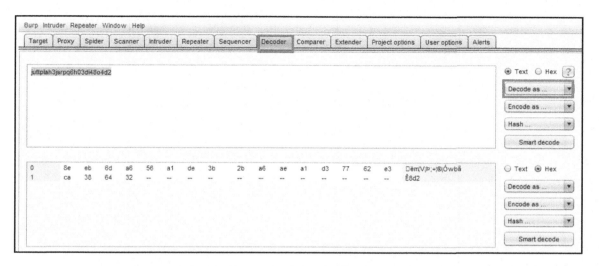

In this example, we cannot proceed any further. We can confirm the value was, indeed, wrapped in Base 64. However, the value that is unwrapped is encrypted. The purpose of this recipe is to show you how you can use Decoder to manipulate encoded values.

Intruding with Intruder

The Burp Intruder allows a tester to brute-force or fuzz specific portions of an HTTP message, using customized payloads.

To properly set up customized attacks in Intruder, a tester will need to use the settings available in the four subtabs of **Intruder**:

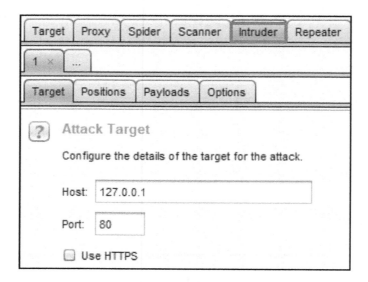

Getting ready

A tester may wish to fuzz or brute-force parameter values within a message. Burp Intruder eases this process by providing various intruder attack styles, payloads, and options.

How to do it...

1. Browse to the login screen of Mutillidae and attempt to log into the application. For example, type a username of `admin` and a password of `adminpass`.

2. Find the login attempt in the **Proxy | HTTP history** tab. Your request number (that is, the # sign on the left-hand side) will be different from the one shown next. Select the message that captured your attempt to log in.

3. As the login attempt message is highlighted in the **HTTP history** table, right-click the **Request** tab, and select **Send to Intruder**:

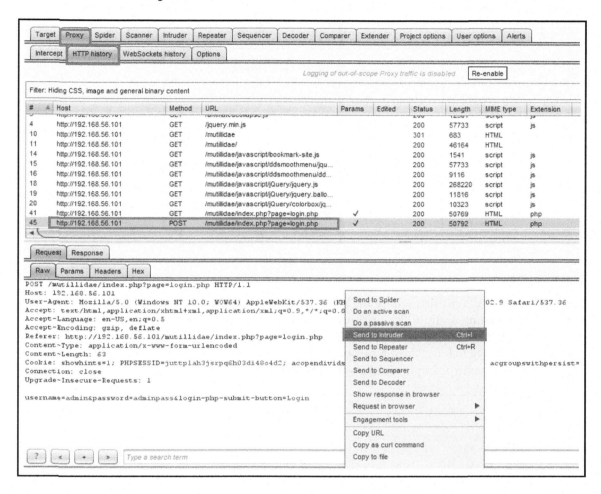

Target

The Intruder **Target** tab defines your targeted web application. These settings are pre-populated for you by Burp:

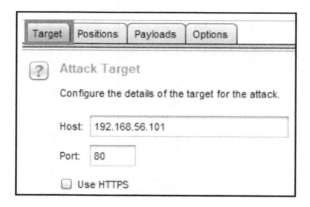

Positions

The **Positions** tab identifies where the payload markers are to be defined within the **Payload | Positions** section. For our purposes, click the **Clear §** (that is, payload markers) from the right-hand side menu. Manually select the password field by highlighting it with your cursor. Now click the **Add §** button on the right-hand side menu. You should have the payload markers wrapping around the password field as follows:

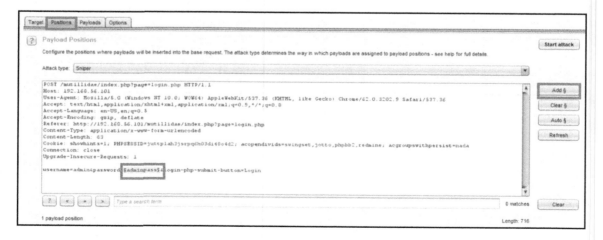

Payloads

After the **Positions** tab is the **Payloads** tab. The **Payloads** tab identifies wordlist values or numbers you wish to be inserted into the positions you identified on the previous tab. There are several sections within the **Payloads** tab, including **Payload Sets**, **Payload Options**, **Payload Processing**, and **Payload Encoding**.

Payload Sets

Payload Sets allows for the setting of the number of payloads as well as the type. For our purposes, we will use the default settings for Sniper, allowing us to use one payload with a **Payload type** of **Simple list**:

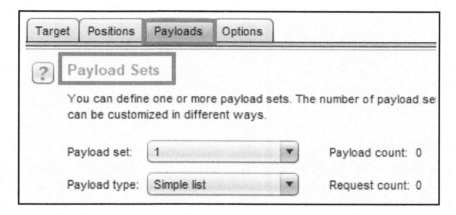

Payload Options

In the **Payload Options** section, a tester can configure a custom payload or load a preconfigured one from a file.

For our purposes, we will add one value to our payload. In the text box, type `admin`, and then click the **Add** button to create our custom payload:

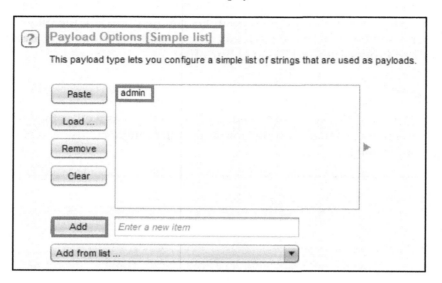

Payload Processing

Payload Processing is useful when configuring special rules to be used while Intruder substitutes payloads into payload marker positions. For this recipe, we do not need any special payload-processing rules:

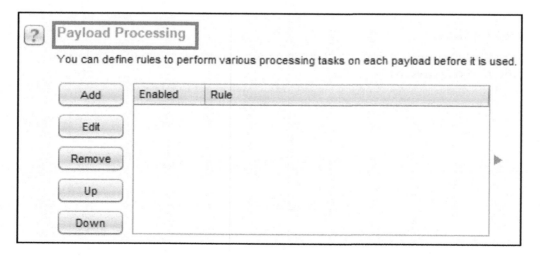

Payload Encoding

Payload Encoding is applied to the payload value prior to sending the request to the web server. Many web servers may block offensive payloads (for example, `<script>` tags), so the encoding feature is a means to circumvent any blacklist blocking.

For the purpose of this recipe, leave the default box checked:

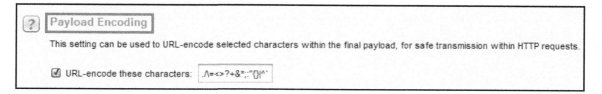

Options

Finally, the **Intruder** | **Options** tab provides attack table customizations, particularly related to responses captured such as specific error messages. There are several sections within the **Intruder** | **Options** tab, including **Request Headers**, **Request Engine**, **Attack Results**, **Grep-Match**, **Grep-Extract**, **Grep - Payloads**, and **Redirections**:

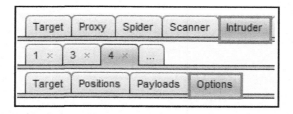

Request Headers

Request Headers offers configurations specific to header parameters while Intruder is running attacks. For the purpose of this recipe, leave the default boxes checked:

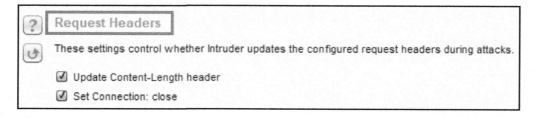

Request Engine

Request Engine should be modified if a tester wishes to create less noise on the network while running Intruder. For example, a tester can throttle attack requests using variable timings so they seem more random to network devices. This is also the location for lowering the number of threads Intruder will run against the target application.

For purpose of this recipe, leave the default setting as-is:

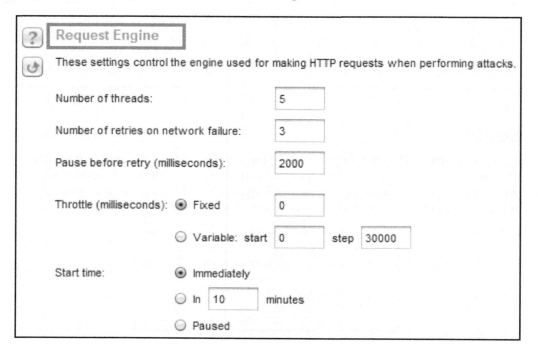

Attack Results

After starting the attack, Intruder creates an attack table. The **Attack Results** section offers some settings around what is captured within that table.

For the purpose of this recipe, leave the default settings as-is:

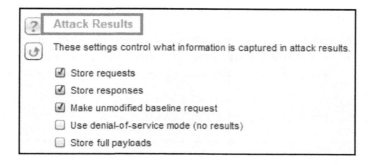

Grep - Match

Grep - Match is a highly useful feature that, when enabled, creates additional columns in the attack table results to quickly identify errors, exceptions, or even a custom string within the response.

For the purpose of this recipe, leave the default settings as-is:

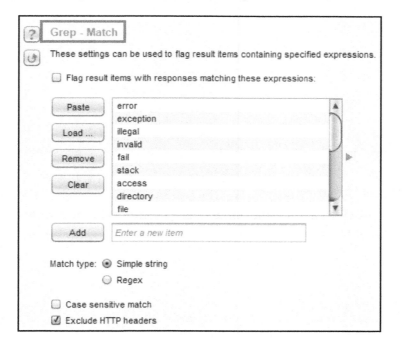

Grep - Extract

Grep - Extract, when enabled, is another option for adding a column in the attack table whose label is specific to a string found in the response. This option differs from **Grep - Match**, since Grep - Extract values are taken from an actual HTTP response, as opposed to an arbitrary string.

For the purpose of this recipe, leave the default settings as-is:

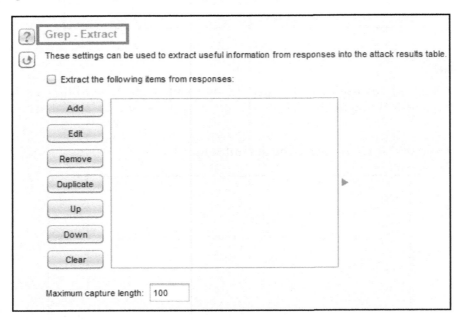

Grep - Payloads

Grep - Payloads provides a tester the ability to add columns in the attack table in which responses contain reflections of payloads.

For the purpose of this recipe, leave the default settings as-is:

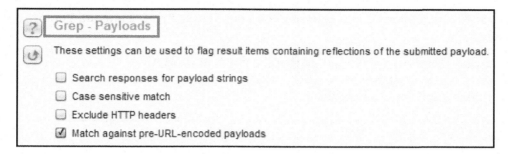

Redirections

Redirections instructs Intruder to never, conditionally, or always follow redirections. This feature is very useful, particularly when brute-forcing logins, since a 302 redirect is generally an indication of entry.

For the purpose of this recipe, leave the default settings as-is:

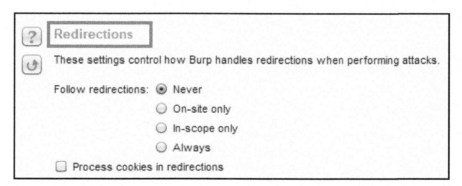

Start attack button

Finally, we are ready to start Intruder. On either the **Payloads** or the **Options** tabs, click the **Start attack** button to begin:

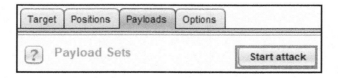

When the attack has started, an attack results table will appear. This allows the tester to review all requests using the payloads within the payload marker positions. It also allows us to review of all responses and columns showing **Status**, **Error**, **Timeout**, **Length**, and **Comment**.

For the purpose of this recipe, we note that the payload of admin in the `password` parameter produced a status code of `302`, which is a redirect. This means we logged into the Mutillidae application successfully:

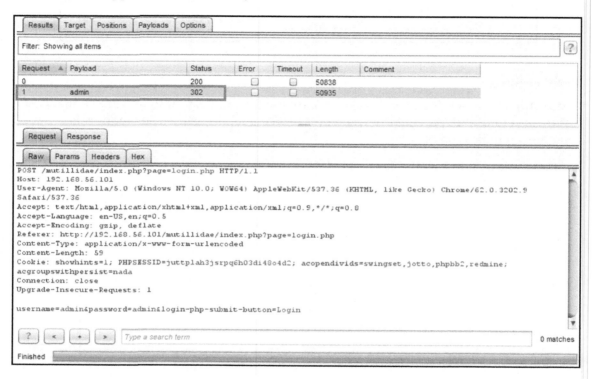

Looking at **Response | Render** within the attack table allows us to see how the web application responded to our payload. As you can see, we are successfully logged in as an admin:

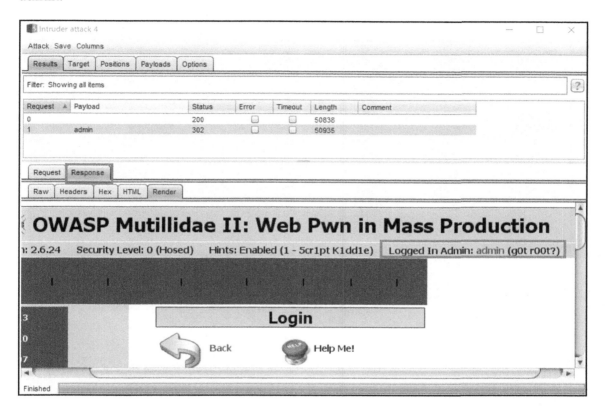

3
Configuring, Spidering, Scanning, and Reporting with Burp

In this chapter, we will cover the following recipes:

- Establishing trust over HTTPS
- Setting project options
- Setting user options
- Spidering with Spider
- Scanning with Scanner
- Reporting issues

Introduction

This chapter helps testers to calibrate Burp settings so they're less abusive toward the target application. Tweaks within Spider and Scanner options can assist with this issue. Likewise, penetration testers can find themselves in interesting network situations when trying to reach a target. Thus, several tips are included for testing sites running over HTTPS, or sites only accessible through a SOCKS Proxy or a port forward. Such settings are available within project and user options. Finally, Burp provides the functionality to generate reports for issues.

Software tool requirements

In order to complete the recipes in this chapter, you will need the following:

- OWASP Broken Web Applications (VM)
- OWASP Mutillidae link
- Burp Proxy Community or Professional (`https://portswigger.net/burp/`)
- Firefox browser configured to allow Burp to proxy traffic (`https://www.mozilla.org/en-US/firefox/new/`)
- The proxy configuration steps are covered in chapter

Establishing trust over HTTPS

Since most websites implement **Hypertext Transport Protocol Secure (HTTPS)**, it is beneficial to know how to enable Burp to communicate with such sites. HTTPS is an encrypted tunnel running over **Hypertext Transport Protocol (HTTP)**.

The purpose of HTTPS is to encrypt traffic between the client browser and the web application to prevent eavesdropping. However, as testers, we wish to allow Burp to eavesdrop, since that is the point of using an intercepting proxy. Burp provides a root, **Certificate Authority (CA)** signed certificate. This certificate can be used to establish trust between Burp and the target web application.

By default, Burp's Proxy can generate a per-target CA certificate when establishing an encrypted handshake with a target running over HTTPS. That takes care of the Burp-to-web-application portion of the tunnel. We also need to address the Browser-to-Burp portion.

In order to create a complete HTTPS tunnel connection between the client browser, Burp, and the target application, the client will need to trust the PortSwigger certificate as a trusted authority within the browser.

Getting ready

In situations requiring penetration testing with a website running over HTTPS, a tester must import the PortSwigger CA certificate as a trusted authority within their browser.

How to do it...

Ensure Burp is started and running and then execute the following steps:

1. Open the Firefox browser to the `http://burp` URL. You must type the URL exactly as shown to reach this page. You should see the following screen in your browser. Note the link on the right-hand side labeled **CA Certificate**. Click the link to download the PortSwigger CA certificate:

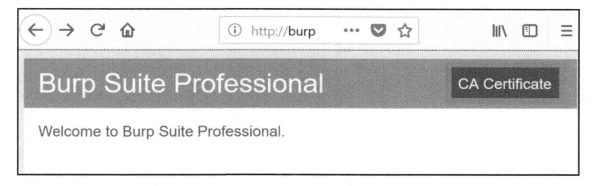

2. You will be presented with a dialog box prompting you to download the PortSwigger CA certificate. The file is labeled `cacert.der`. Download the file to a location on your hard drive.
3. In Firefox, open the Firefox menu. Click on **Options**.

4. Click **Privacy & Security** on the left-hand side, scroll down to Certificates section. Click the **View Certificates...** button:

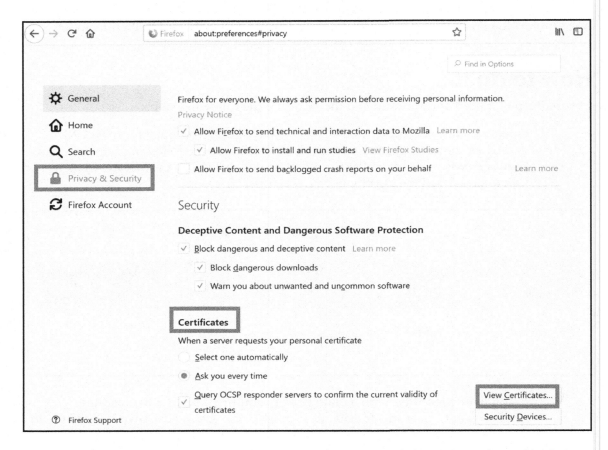

5. Select the **Authorities** tab. Click **Import**, select the Burp CA certificate file that you previously saved, and click **Open**:

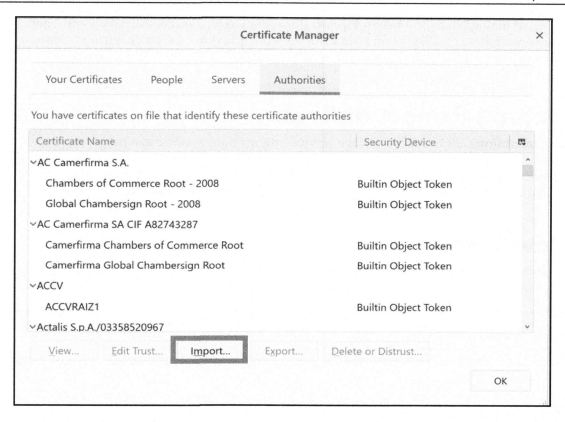

6. In the dialog box that pops up, check the **Trust this CA to identify websites** box, and click **OK**. Click **OK** on the **Certificate Manager** dialog as well:

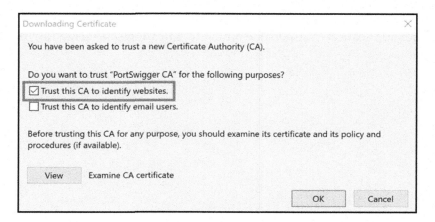

Close all dialog boxes and restart Firefox. If installation was successful, you should now be able to visit any HTTPS URL in your browser while proxying the traffic through Burp without any security warnings.

Setting Project options

Project options allow a tester to save or set configurations specific to a project or scoped target. There are multiple subtabs available under the **Project options** tab, which include **Connections**, **HTTP**, **SSL**, **Sessions**, and **Misc**. Many of these options are required for penetration testers when assessing specific targets, which is why they are covered here.

How to do it...

In this book, we will not be using many of these features but it is still important to know of their existence and understand their purpose:

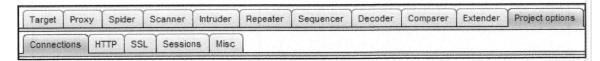

The Connections tab

Under the **Connections** tab, a tester has the following options:

- **Platform Authentication**: This provides an override button in the event the tester wants the **Project options** related to the type of authentication used against the target application to supersede any authentication settings within the user options.

After clicking the checkbox to override the user's options, the tester is presented with a table enabling authentication options (for example, Basic, NTLMv2, NTLMv1, and Digest) specific to the target application. The destination host is commonly set to wildcard * should a tester find the need to ever use this option:

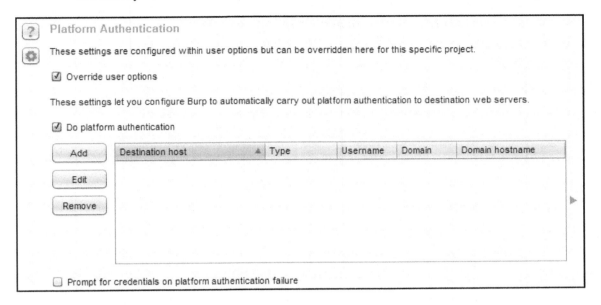

- **Upstream proxy servers**: It provides an override button in the event the tester wants the **Project options** related to upstream proxy servers used against the target application to supersede any proxy settings contained within the user options.

After clicking the checkbox to override the user's options, the tester is presented with a table enabling upstream proxy options specific to this project. Clicking the **Add** button displays a pop-up box called `Add upstream proxy rule`. This rule is specific to the target application's environment. This feature is very helpful if the target application's environment is fronted with a web proxy requiring a different set of credentials than the application login:

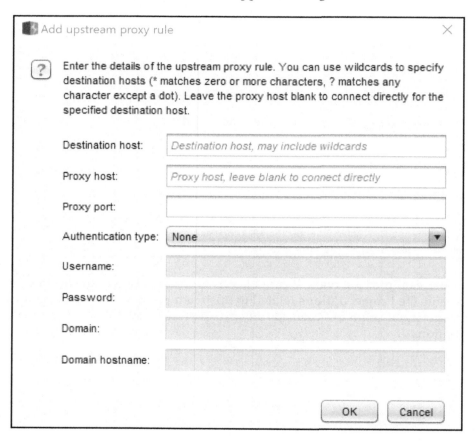

- **SOCKS Proxy**: It provides an override button in the event the tester wishes for **Project options** related to the SOCKS Proxy configuration used against the target application to supersede any SOCKS Proxy settings within the user options.

After clicking the checkbox to override user options, the tester is presented with a form to configure a SOCKS Proxy specific to this project. In some circumstances, web applications must be accessed over an additional protocol that uses socket connections and authentication, commonly referred to as SOCKS:

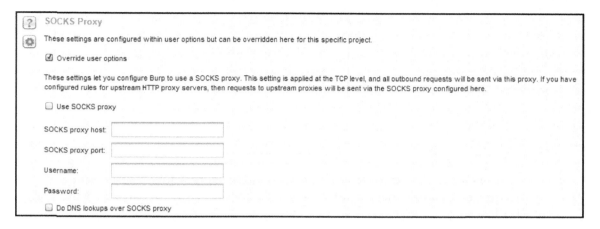

- **Timeouts**: It allows for timeout settings for different network scenarios, such as failing to resolve a domain name:

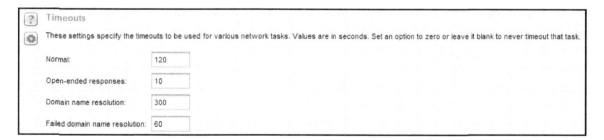

- **Hostname Resolution**: It allows entries similar to a host file on a local machine to override the **Domain Name System (DNS)** resolution:

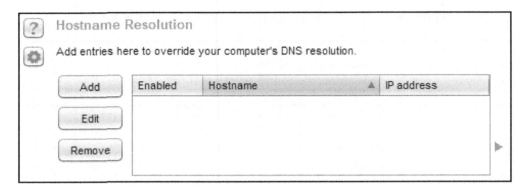

- **Out-of-Scope Requests**: It provides rules to Burp regarding **Out-of-Scope Requests**. Usually, the default setting of **Use suite scope [defined in Target tab]** is most commonly used:

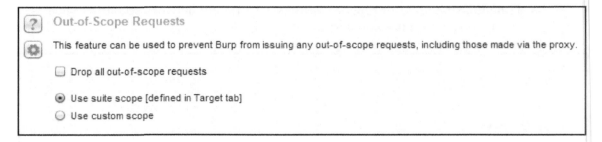

The HTTP tab

Under the **HTTP** tab, a tester has the following options:

- **Redirections**: It provides rules for Burp to follow when redirections are configured. Most commonly, the default settings are used here:

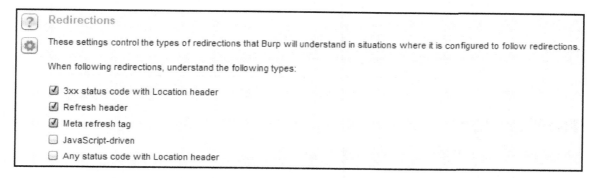

- **Streaming Responses**: It provides configurations related to responses that stream indefinitely. Mostly, the default settings are used here:

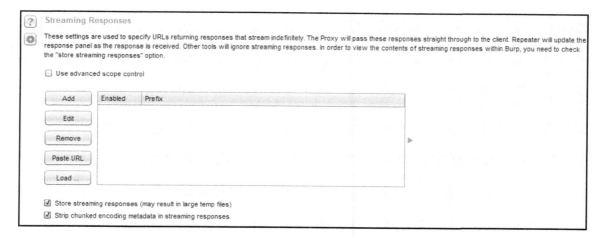

- **Status 100 Responses**: It provides a setting for Burp to handle HTTP status code 100 responses. Most commonly, the default settings are used here:

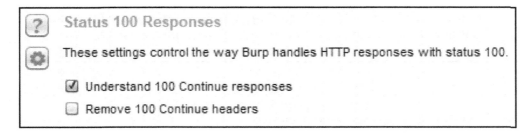

The SSL tab

Under the **SSL** tab, a tester has the following options:

- **SSL Negotiations**: When Burp communicates with a target application over SSL, this option provides the ability to use preconfigured SSL ciphers or to specify different ones:

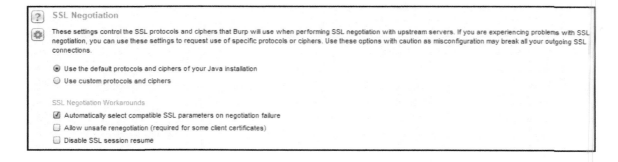

If a tester wishes to customize the ciphers, they will click the **Use custom protocols and ciphers** radio button. A table appears allowing selection of protocols and ciphers that Burp can use in the communication with the target application:

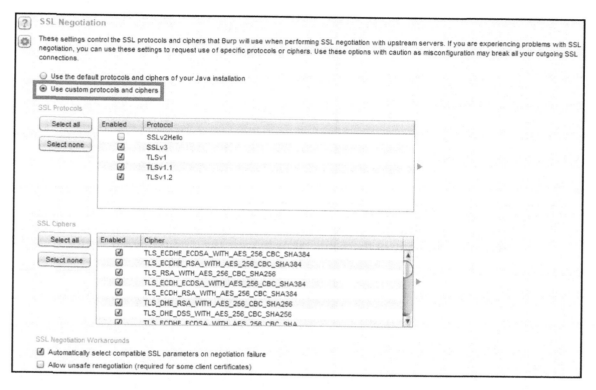

- **Client SSL Certificates**: It provides an override button in the event the tester must use a client-side certificate against the target application. This option will supersede any client-side certificate configured within the user options.

After clicking the checkbox to override user options, the tester is presented with a table to configure a client-side certificate specific to this project. You must have the private key to your client-side certificate in order to successfully import it into Burp:

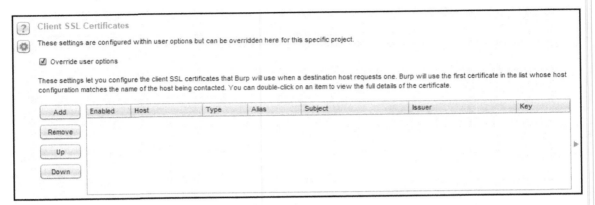

- **Server SSL Certificates**: It provides a listing of server-side certificates. A tester can double-click any of these line items to view the details of each certificate:

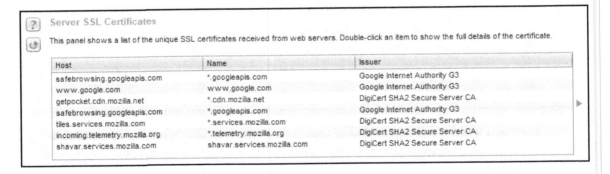

The Sessions tab

This book will cover recipes on all functionality contained within the **Sessions** tab in Chapter 10, *Working with Burp Macros and Extensions*. A review of each of these sections within the **Sessions** tab is provided here for completeness.

Under the **Sessions** tab, a tester has the following options:

- **Session Handling Rules**: It provides the ability to configure customized session-handling rules while assessing a web application:

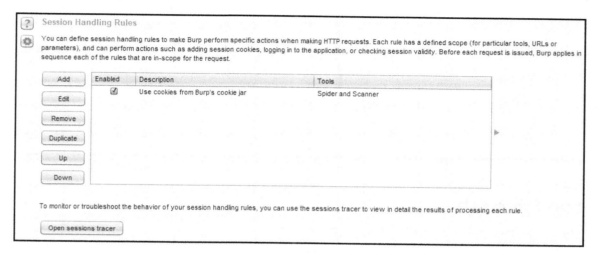

- **Cookie Jar**: It provides a listing of cookies, domains, paths, and name/value pairs captured by Burp Proxy (by default):

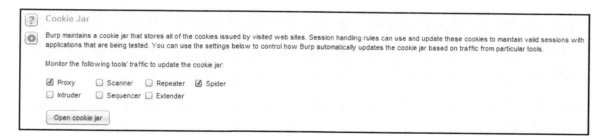

- **Macros**: It provides the ability of a tester to script tasks previously performed in order to automate activities while interacting with the target application:

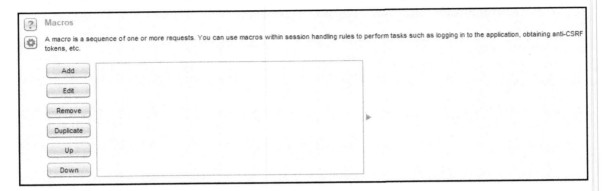

The Misc tab

Under the **Misc** tab, a tester has the following options:

- **Scheduled Tasks**: It provides the ability to schedule an activity at specific times:

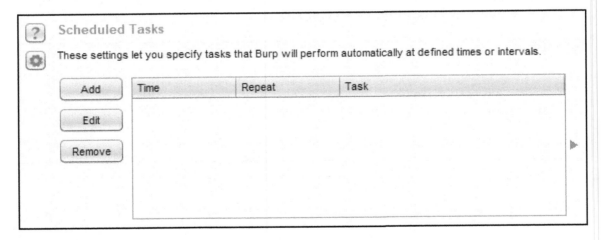

When the **Add** button is clicked, a pop-up reveals the types of activities available for scheduling:

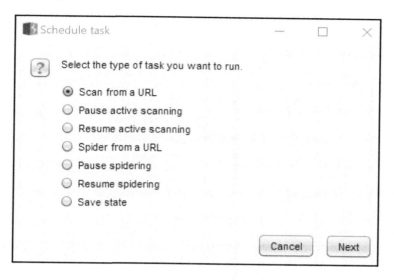

- **Burp Collaborator Server**: It provides the ability to use a service external to the target application for the purposes of discovering vulnerabilities in the target application. This book will cover recipes related to Burp Collaborator in Chapter 11, *Implementing Advanced Topic Attacks*. A review of this section is provided here for completeness:

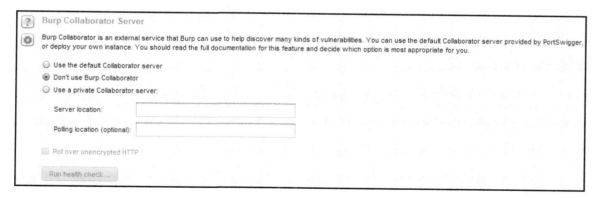

- **Logging**: It provides the ability to log all requests and responses or filter the logging based on a particular tool. If selected, the user is prompted for a file name and location to save the log file on the local machine:

[?]	Logging				
[⚙]	These settings control logging of HTTP requests and responses.				
	All tools:	☐	Requests	☐	Responses
	Proxy:	☐	Requests	☐	Responses
	Spider:	☐	Requests	☐	Responses
	Scanner:	☐	Requests	☐	Responses
	Intruder:	☐	Requests	☐	Responses
	Repeater:	☐	Requests	☐	Responses
	Sequencer:	☐	Requests	☐	Responses
	Extender:	☐	Requests	☐	Responses

Setting user options

User options allow a tester to save or set configurations specific to how they want Burp to be configured upon startup. There are multiple sub-tabs available under the user options tab, which include **Connections**, **SSL**, **Display**, and **Misc**. For recipes in this book, we will not be using any user options. However, the information is reviewed here for completeness.

How to do it...

Using Burp user options, let's configure your Burp UI in a manner best suited to your penetration-testing needs. Each of the items under the **Connections** tab is already covered in the **Project options** section of this chapter, hence, we will directly start with the **SSL** tab.

The SSL tab

Under the **SSL** tab, a tester has the following options:

- **Java SSL Options**: It provides the ability the configure Java security libraries used by Burp for SSL connections. The default values are most commonly used:

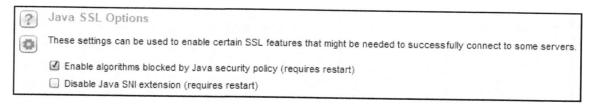

- **Client SSL Certificate:** This section is already covered in the *Project options* section of this chapter.

The Display tab

Under the **Display** tab, a tester has the following options:

- **User Interface**: It provides the ability to modify the default font and size of the Burp UI itself:

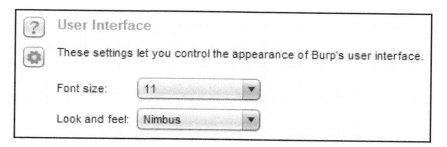

- **HTTP Message Display**: It provides the ability to modify the default font and size used for all HTTP messages shown within the message editor:

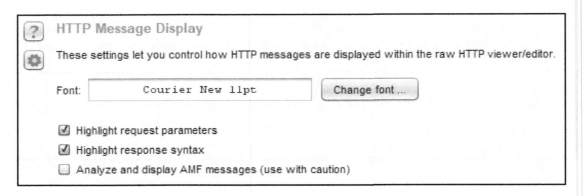

- **Character Sets**: It provides the ability to change the character sets determined by Burp to use a specific set or to display as raw bytes:

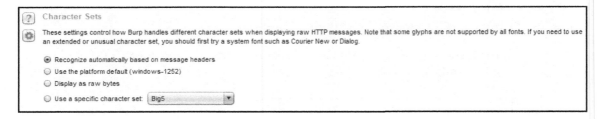

- **HTML Rendering:** It controls how HTML pages will display from the **Render** tab available on an HTTP response:

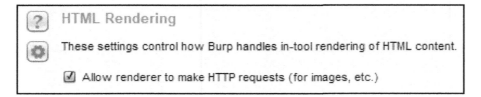

The Misc tab

Under the **Misc** tab, a tester has the following options:

- **Hotkeys**: It lets a user configure hotkeys for commonly-executed commands:

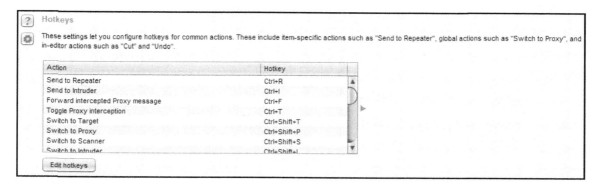

- **Automatic Project Backup [disk projects only]**: It provides the ability to determine how often backup copies of project files are made. By default, when using Burp Professional, backups are set to occur every 30 minutes:

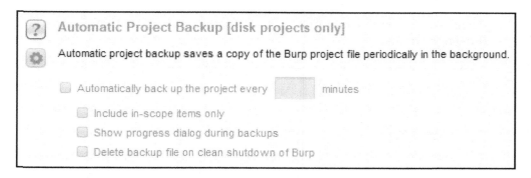

- **Temporary Files Location**: It provides the ability to change the location where temporary files are stored while running Burp:

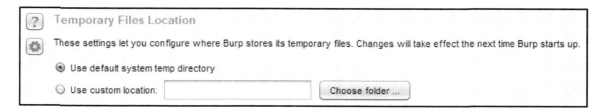

- **Proxy Interception**: It provides the ability to always enable or always disable proxy intercept upon initially starting Burp:

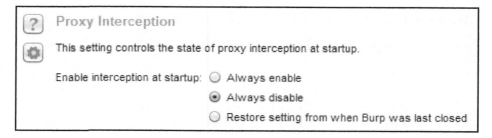

- **Proxy History Logging**: It provides the ability to customize prompting of out-of-scope items when the target scope changes:

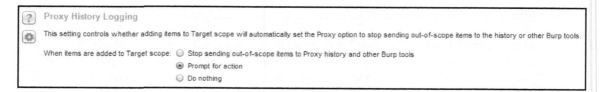

- **Performance Feedback**: It provides anonymous data to PortSwigger regarding Burp performance:

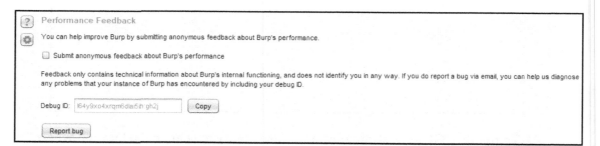

Spidering with Spider

Spidering is another term for mapping out or crawling a web application. This mapping exercise is necessary to uncover links, folders, and files present within the target application.

In addition to crawling, Burp Spider can also submit forms in an automated fashion. Spidering should occur prior to scanning, since pentesters wish to identify all possible paths and functionality prior to looking for vulnerabilities.

Burp provides an on-going spidering capability. This means that as a pentester discovers new content, Spider will automatically run in the background looking for forms, files, and folders to add to **Target | Site map**.

There are two tabs available in the Spider module of Burp Suite. The tabs include **control** and **options**, which we will study in the *Getting ready* section of this recipe.

Getting ready

Using the OWASP Mutillidae II application found within the OWASP BWA VM, we will configure and use Burp Spider to crawl through the application.

The Control tab

Under the **Control** tab, a tester has the following options:

- **Spider Status**: It provides the ability to turn the spidering functionality on or off (paused). It also allows us to monitor queued-up Spider requests along with bytes transferred, and so on. This section allows any forms queued to be cleared by clicking the **Clear queues** button:

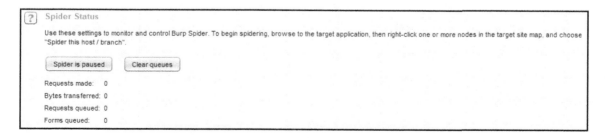

- **Spider Scope**: It provides the ability to set the **Spider Scope**, either based on the **Target** | **Site map** tab or a customized scope:

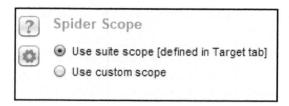

If the Use custom scope radio button is clicked, two tables appear, allowing the tester to define URLs to be included and excluded from scope:

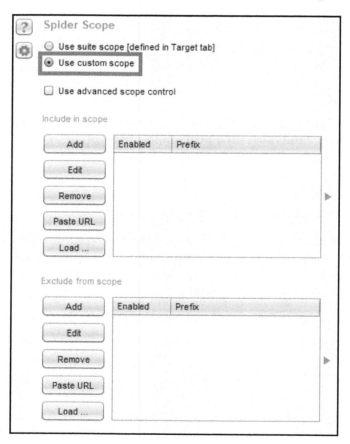

The Options tab

Under the **Options** tab, a tester has the following options:

- **Crawler Settings**: It provides the ability to regulate the number of links deep Spider will follow; also identifies basic web content to Spider for on a website such as the `robots.txt` file:

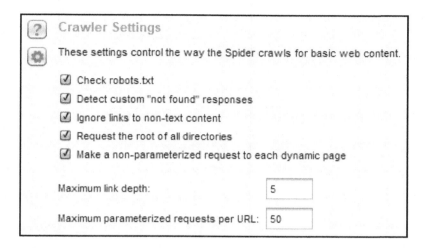

- **Passive Spidering**: Spiders newly-discovered content in the background and is turned on by default:

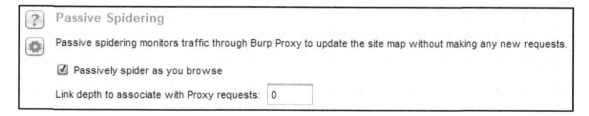

- **Form Submission**: It provides the ability to determine how Spider interacts with forms. Several options are available including ignore, prompt for guidance, submit with default values found in the table provided, or use an arbitrary value (for example, `555-555-0199@example.com`):

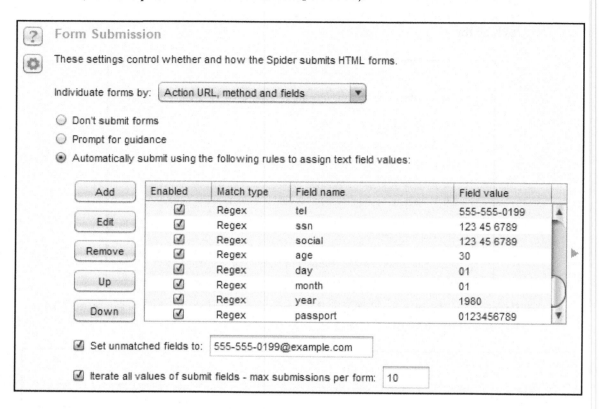

- **Application Login**: It provides the ability to determine how Spider interacts with login forms. Several options are available, including ignore, prompt for guidance, submit as standard form submission, or use credentials provided in text boxes:

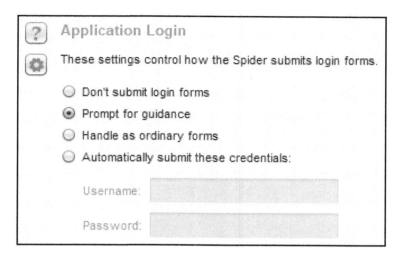

- **Spider Engine**: It provides the ability to edit the number of threads used along with retry attempt settings due to network failures. Use the number of threads judiciously as too many thread requests could choke an application and affect its performance:

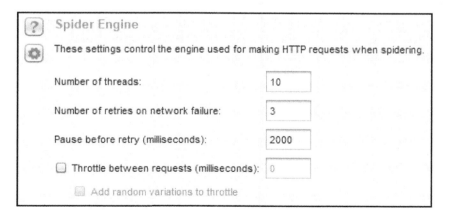

- **Request Headers**: It provides the ability to modify the way the HTTP requests look originating from Burp Spider. For example, a tester can modify the user agent to have Spider look like a mobile phone:

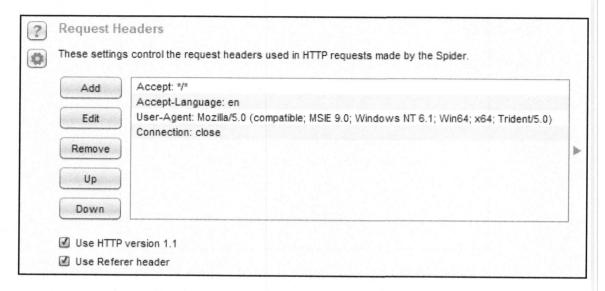

How to do it...

1. Ensure Burp and OWASP BWA VM are running, and Burp is configured in the Firefox browser used to view the OWASP BWA applications.

2. From the OWASP BWA landing page, click the link to the **OWASP Mutillidae II** application:

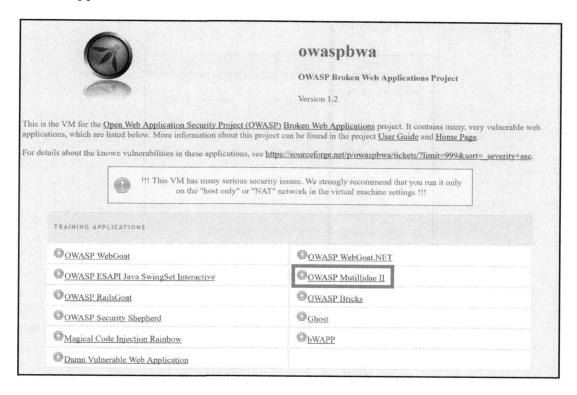

3. Go to the Burp **Spider** tab, then go to the **Options** sub-tab, scroll down to the **Application Login** section. Select the **Automatically submit these credentials** radio button. Type into the username textbox the word `admin`; type into the password textbox the word `admin`:

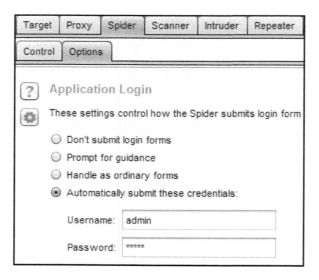

4. Return to **Target | Site map** and ensure the `mutillidae` folder is added to scope by right-clicking the `mutillidae` folder and selecting **Add to scope**:

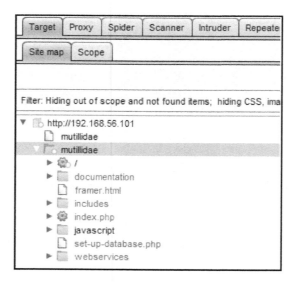

5. Optionally, you can clean up the **Site map** to only show in-scope items by clicking `Filter: Hiding out of scope and not found items; hiding CSS, image and general binary content; hiding 4xx responses; hiding empty folders`:

Filter: Hiding out of scope and not found items; hiding CSS, image and general binary content; hiding 4xx responses; hiding empty folders

6. After clicking `Filter: ....`, You will see a drop-down menu appear. In this drop-down menu, check the **Show only in-scope items** box. Now, click anywhere in Burp outside of the drop-down menu to have the filter disappear again:

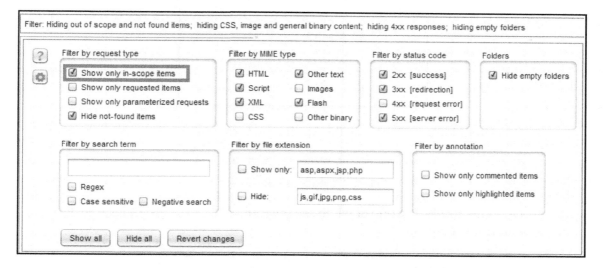

7. You should now have a clean **Site map**. Right-click the **mutillidae** folder and select **Spider this branch**.

If prompted to allow out-of-scope items, click **Yes**.

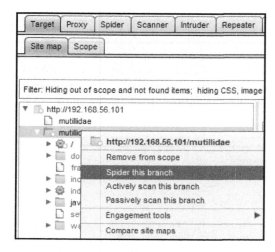

8. You should immediately see the **Spider** tab turn orange:

9. Go to the **Spider | Control** tab to see the number of requests, bytes transferred, and forms in queue:

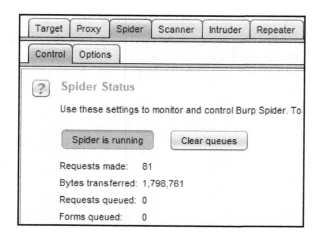

Let Spider finish running.

10. Notice that Spider logged into the application using the credentials you provided in the **Options** tab. On **Target | Site map**, look for the `/mutillidae/index.php/` folder structure:

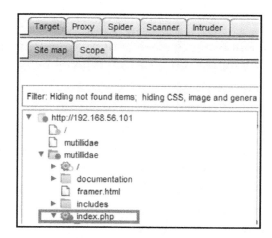

11. Search for an envelope icon that contains `password=admin&login-php-submit-button=Login&username=admin`:

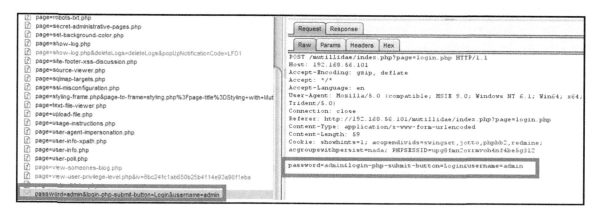

This evidences the information Spider used the information you provided in the **Spider | Options | Application Login** section.

Scanning with Scanner

 Scanner capabilities are only available in Burp Professional edition.

Burp Scanner is a tool that automates the search for weaknesses within the runtime version of an application. Scanner attempts to find security vulnerabilities based on the behavior of the application.

Scanner will identify indicators that may lead to the identification of a security vulnerability. Burp Scanner is extremely reliable, however, it is the responsibility of the pentester to validate any findings prior to reporting.

There are two scanning modes available in Burp Scanner:

- **Passive scanner**: Analyzes traffic passing through the proxy listener. This is why its so important to properly configure your target scope so that you aren't scanning more than is necessary.
- **Active scanner**: Sends numerous requests that are tweaked from their original form. These request modifications are designed to trigger behavior that may indicate the presence of vulnerabilities (`https://portswigger.net/kb/issues`). Active scanner is focused on input-based bugs that may be present on the client and server side of the application.

Scanning tasks should occur after spidering is complete. Previously, we learned how Spider continues to crawl as new content is discovered. Similarly, passive scanning continues to identify vulnerabilities as the application is crawled.

Under the **Options** tab, a tester has the following options: **Issue activity**, **Scan queue**, **Live scanning**, **Issue definitions**, and **Options**:

- **Issue Activity**: It displays all scanner findings in a tabular format; includes both passive and active scanner issues.:

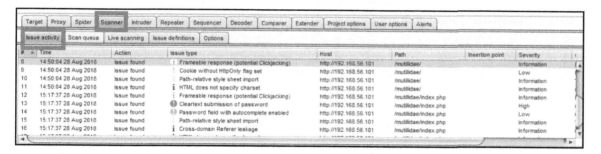

By selecting an issue in the table, the message details are displayed, including an advisory specific to the finding as well as message-editor details related to the request and response:

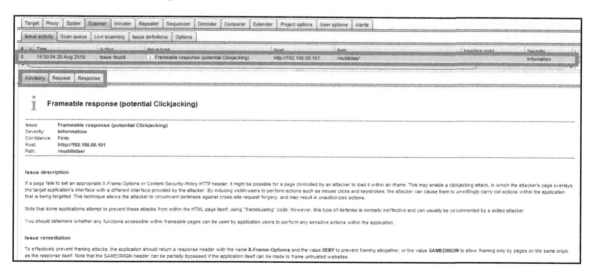

- **Scan queue:** Displays the status of active scanner running; provides a percentage of completion per number of threads running as well as number of requests sent, insertion points tested, start time, end time, targeted host, and URL attacked.

Scanner can be paused from the table by right-clicking and selecting **Pause scanner**; likewise, scanner can be resumed by right-clicking and selecting **Resume Scanner**. Items waiting in the scan queue can be cancelled as well:

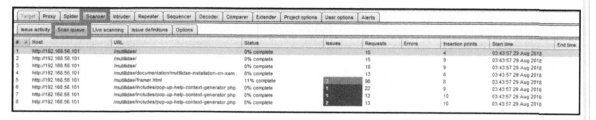

- **Live Active Scanning**: It allows customization when active scanner will perform scanning activities:

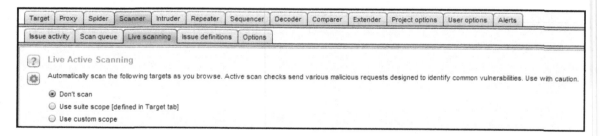

- **Live Passive Scanning**: It allows customization when passive scanner will perform scanning activities. By default, passive scanner is always on and scanning everything:

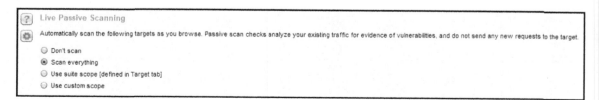

- **Issue definitions**: It displays definitions for all vulnerabilities known to Burp scanners (active and passive). The list can be expanded through extenders but, using Burp core, this is the exhaustive listing, which includes title, description text, remediation verbiage, references, and severity level:

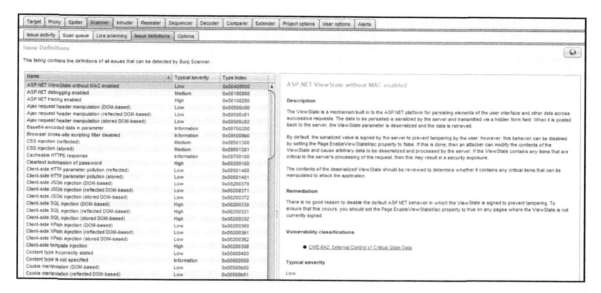

- **Options**: Several sections are available, including **Attack Insertion Points**, **Active Scanning Engine**, **Attack Scanning Optimization**, and **Static code analysis**.

    - **Attack Insertion Points**: It allows customization for Burp insertion points; an insertion point is a placeholder for payloads within different locations of a request. This is similar to the Intruder payload marker concept discussed in Chapter 2, *Getting to Know the Burp Suite of Tools*:

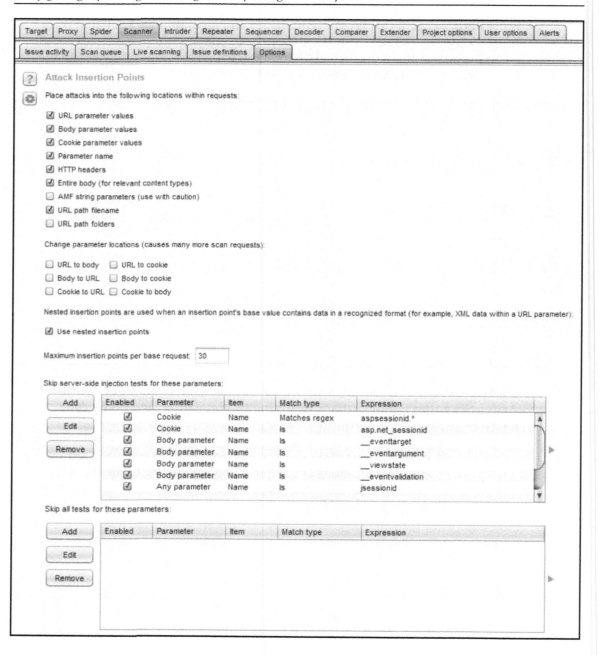

Recommendations here include adding the URL-to-body, Body-to-URL, cookie-to-URL, URL-to-cookie, body-to-cookie, and cookie-to-body insertion points when performing an assessment. This allows Burp to fuzz almost, if not all, available parameters in any given request.

- **Active Scanning Engine**: It provides the ability to configure the number of threads (for example, **Concurrent request limit**) scanner will run against the target application. This thread count, compounded with the permutations of insertion points, can create noise on the network and a possible DOS attack, depending upon the stability of the target application. Use caution and consider lowering the **Concurrent request limit**. The throttling of threads is available at this configuration section as well:

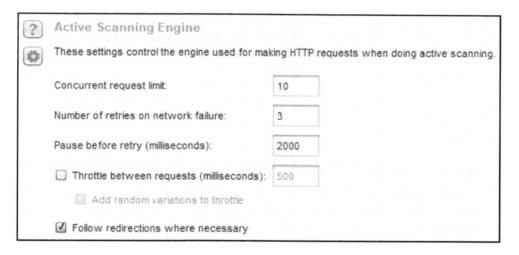

- **Attack Scanning Optimization**: It provides three settings for scan speed and scan accuracy.
    - Available **Scan speed** settings include **Normal**, **Fast**, and **Thorough**. **Fast** makes fewer requests and checks derivations of issues. **Thorough** makes more requests and checks for derivations of issues. **Normal** is the medium setting between the other two choices. The recommendation for **Scan speed** is **Thorough**.

- Available **Scan accuracy** settings include **Normal**, **Minimize false negatives**, and **Minimize false positives**. **Scan accuracy** relates to the amount of evidence scanner requires before reporting an issue. The recommendation for **Scan accuracy** is **Normal**:

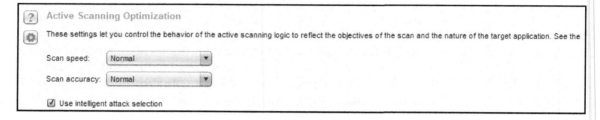

- **Static Code Analysis**: It provides the ability to perform static analysis of binary code. By default, this check is performed in active scanner:

- **Scan Issues**: It provides the ability to set which vulnerabilities are tested and for which scanner (that is, passive or active). By default, all vulnerability checks are enabled:

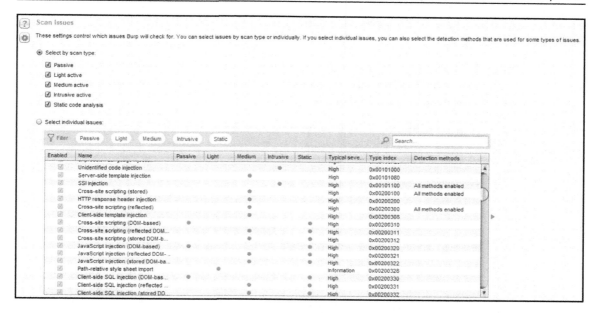

Getting ready

Using the OWASP Mutillidae II application found within the OWASP BWA VM, we will begin our scanning process and monitor our progress using the **Scan queue** tab.

How to do it...

Ensure Burp and OWASP BWA VM is running while Burp is configured in the Firefox browser used to view the OWASP BWA applications.

From the OWASP BWA landing page, click the link to the OWASP Mutillidae II application:

1. From the **Target** | **Site map** tab, right-click the `mutillidae` folder and select **Passively scan this branch**. The passive scanner will hunt for vulnerabilities, which will appear in the **Issues** window:

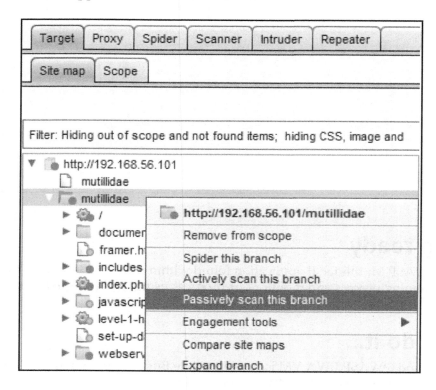

2. From the **Target** | **Site map** tab, right-click the `mutillidae` folder and select **Actively scan this branch**:

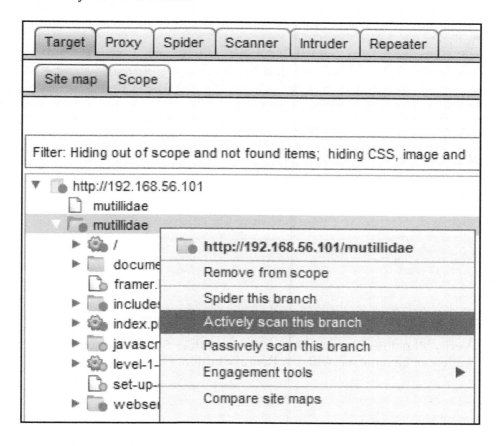

3. Upon initiating the active scanner, a pop-up dialog box appears prompting for removal of duplicate items, items without parameters, items with media response, or items of certain file types. This pop-up is the **Active scanning wizard**. For this recipe, use the default settings and click **Next**:

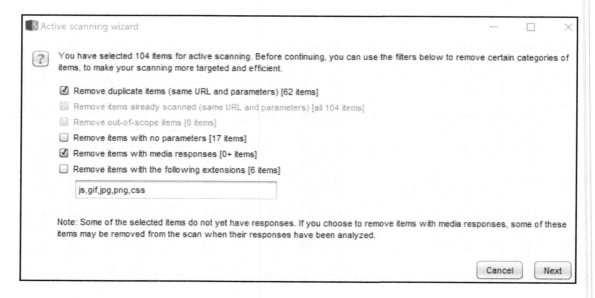

4. Verify all paths shown are desired for scanning. Any undesired file types or paths can be removed with the **Remove** button. Once complete, click **OK**:

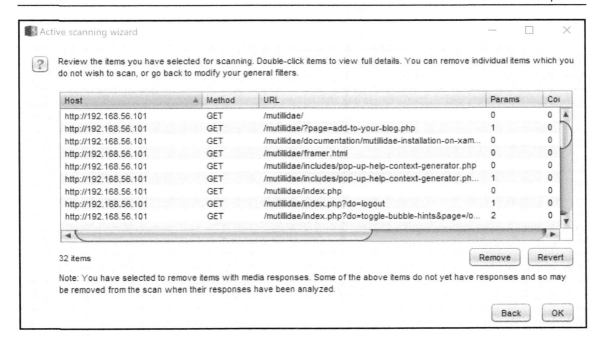

You may be prompted regarding the out-of-scope items. If so, click **Yes** to include those items. Scanner will begin.

5. Check the status of scanner by looking at the **Scanner queue** tab:

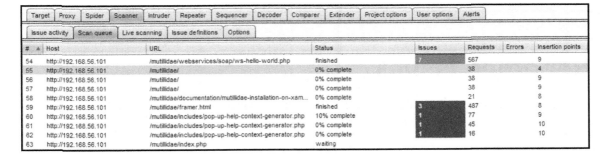

6. As scanner finds issues, they are displayed on the **Target** tab, in the **Issues** panel. This panel is only available in the Professional edition since it complements the scanner's functionality:

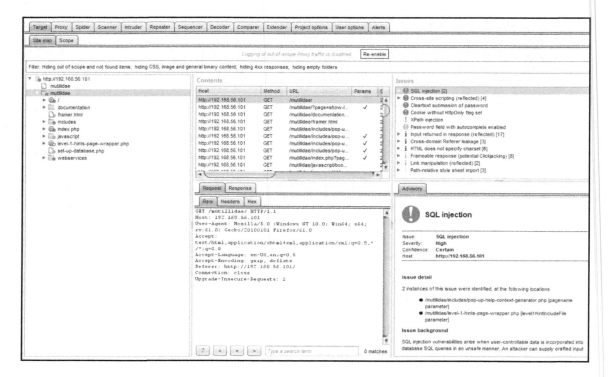

Reporting issues

Reporting capabilities are only available in Burp Professional edition.

In Burp Professional, as scanner discovers a vulnerability, it will be added to a list of issues found on the **Target** tab, in the right-hand side of the UI. Issues are color-coded to indicate the severity and confidence level. An issue with a red exclamation point means it is a high severity and the confidence level is certain. For example, the SQL Injection issue shown here contains both of these attributes.

Items with a lower severity or confidence level will be low, informational, and yellow, gray, or black in color. These items require manual penetration testing to validate whether the vulnerability is present. For example, **Input returned in response** is a potential vulnerability identified by scanner and shown in the following screenshot. This could be an attack vector for **cross-site scripting** (**XSS**) or it could be a false positive. It is up to the penetration tester and their level of experience to validate such an issue:

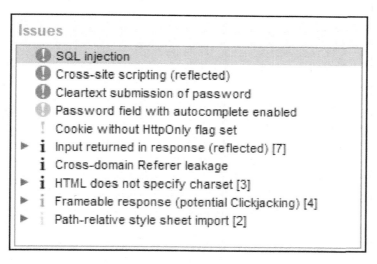

- **Severity levels**: The severity levels available include high, medium, low, information, and false positive. Any findings marked as false positive will not appear on the generated report. False positive is a severity level that must be manually set by the penetration tester on an issue.
- **Confidence levels**: The confidence levels available include certain, firm, and tentative.

Getting ready

After the scanning process completes, we need to validate our findings, adjust severities accordingly, and generate our report.

How to do it...

1. For this recipe, select **Cookie without HttpOnly flag set** under the **Issues** heading:

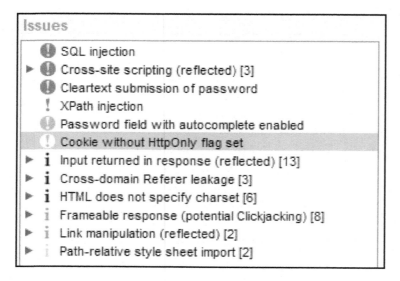

2. Look at the **Response** tab of that message to validate the finding. We can clearly see the PHPSESSID cookie does not have the HttpOnly flag set. Therefore, we can change the severity from **Low** to **High** and the confidence level from **Firm** to **Certain**:

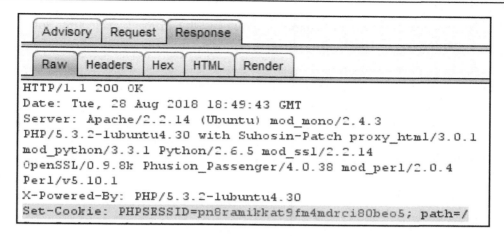

3. Right-click the issue and change the severity to **High** by selecting **Set severity | High**:

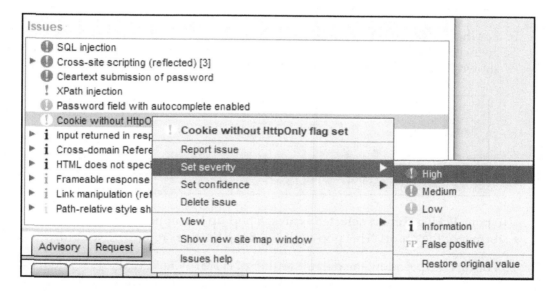

4. Right-click the issue and change the severity to **Certain** by selecting **Set confidence | Certain**:

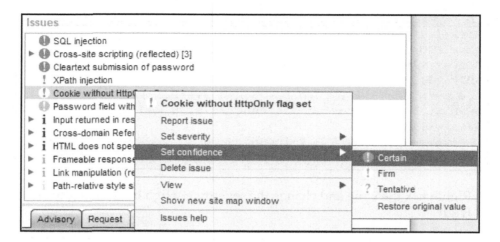

5. For this recipe, select the issues with the highest confidence and severity levels to be included in the report. After selecting (highlighting + *Shift* key) the items shown here, right-click and select **Report selected issues**:

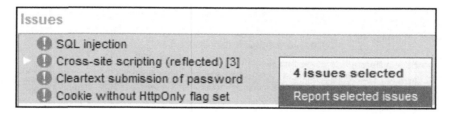

Upon clicking **Report selected issues**, a pop-up box appears prompting us for the format of the report. This pop-up is the **Burp Scanner reporting wizard**.

6. For this recipe, allow the default setting of HTML. Click **Next**.
7. This screen prompts for the types of details to be included in the report. For this recipe, allow the default settings. Click **Next**.

8. This screen prompts for how messages should be displayed within the report. For this recipe, allow the default settings. Click **Next**.

9. This screen prompts for which types of issues should be included in the report. For this recipe, allow the default settings. Click **Next**.

10. This screen prompts for the location of where to save the report. For this recipe, click **Select file...**, select a location, and provide a file name followed by the .html extension; allow all other default settings. Click **Next**:

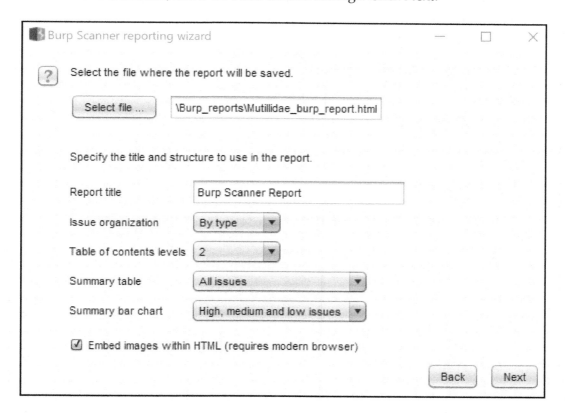

11. This screen reflects the completion of the report generation. Click **Close** and browse to the saved location of the file.

12. Double-click the file name to load the report into a browser:

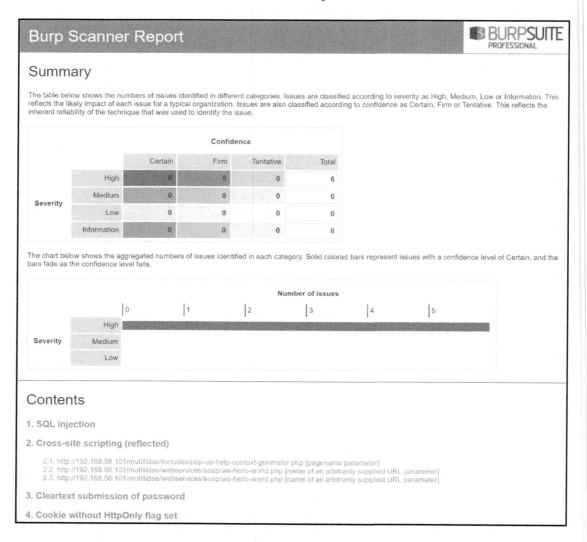

Congratulations! You've created your first Burp report!

4
Assessing Authentication Schemes

In this chapter, we will cover the following recipes:

- Testing for account enumeration and guessable accounts
- Testing for weak lock-out mechanisms
- Testing for bypassing authentication schemes
- Testing for browser cache weaknesses
- Testing the account provisioning process via REST API

Introduction

This chapter covers the basic penetration testing of authentication schemes. *Authentication* is the act of verifying whether a person or object claim is true. Web penetration testers must make key assessments to determine the strength of a target application's authentication scheme. Such tests include launching attacks, to determine the presence of account enumeration and guessable accounts, the presence of weak lock-out mechanisms, whether the application scheme can be bypassed, whether the application contains browser-caching weaknesses, and whether accounts can be provisioned without authentication via a REST API call. You will learn how to use Burp to perform such tests.

Software tool requirements

To complete the recipes in this chapter, you will need the following:

- OWASP Broken Web Applications (VM)
- OWASP Mutillidae link

- GetBoo link
- Burp Proxy Community or Professional (https://portswigger.net/burp/)
- The Firefox browser configured to allow Burp to proxy traffic (https://www.mozilla.org/en-US/firefox/new/)

Testing for account enumeration and guessable accounts

By interacting with an authentication mechanism, a tester may find it possible to collect a set of valid usernames. Once the valid accounts are identified, it may be possible to brute-force passwords. This recipe explains how Burp Intruder can be used to collect a list of valid usernames.

Getting ready

Perform username enumeration against a target application.

How to do it...

Ensure Burp and the OWASP BWA VM are running and that Burp is configured in the Firefox browser used to view the OWASP BWA applications.

1. From the OWASP BWA Landing page, click the link to the GetBoo application:

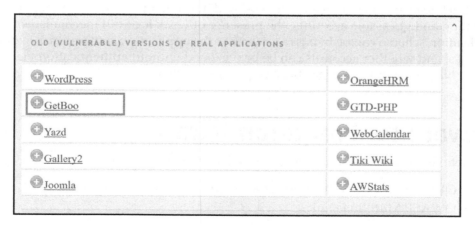

2. Click the **Log In** button, and at the login screen, attempt to log in with an account username of `admin` and a password of `aaaaa`:

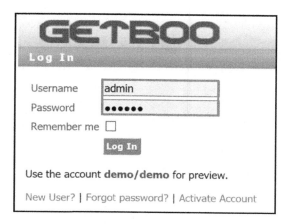

3. Note the message returned is **The password is invalid**. From this information, we know admin is a valid account. Let's use Burp **Intruder** to find more accounts.

4. In Burp's **Proxy | HTTP history** tab, find the failed login attempt message. View the **Response | Raw** tab to find the same overly verbose error message, **The password is invalid**:

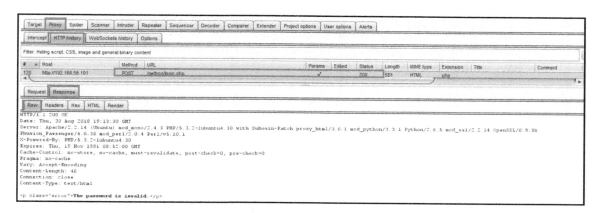

5. Flip back to the **Request** | **Raw** tab and right-click to send this request to **Intruder**:

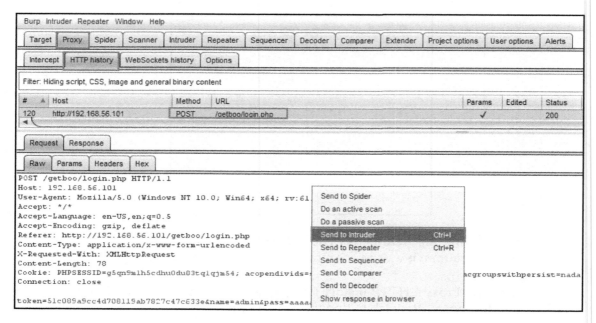

6. Go to Burp's **Intruder** tab and leave the **Intruder** | **Target** tab settings as it is. Continue to the **Intruder** | **Positions** tab. Notice how Burp places payload markers around each parameter value found. However, we only need a payload marker around the password value. Click the **Clear §** button to remove the payload markers placed by Burp:

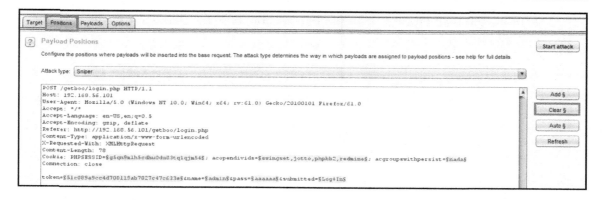

7. Then, highlight the name value of **admin** with your cursor and click the **Add** § button:

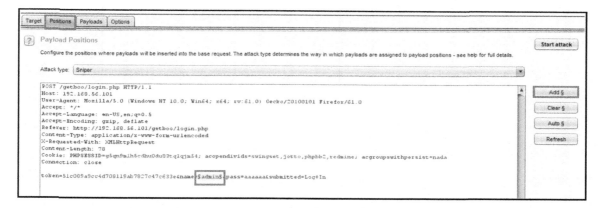

8. Continue to the **Intruder** I **Payloads** tab. Many testers use word lists to enumerate commonly used usernames within the payload marker placeholder. For this recipe, we will type in some common usernames, to create a custom payload list.

9. In the **Payload Options [Simple list]** section, type the string user and click the **Add** button:

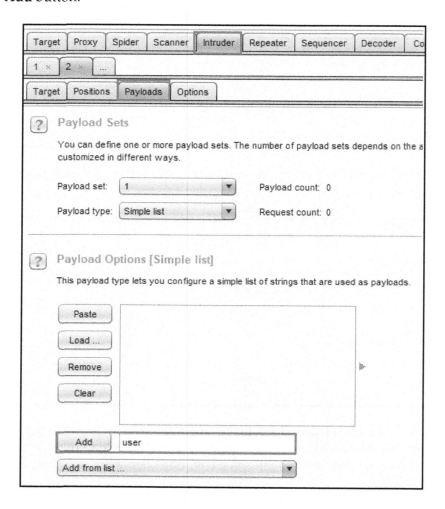

10. Add a few more strings such as john, tom, demo, and, finally, admin to the payload-listing box:

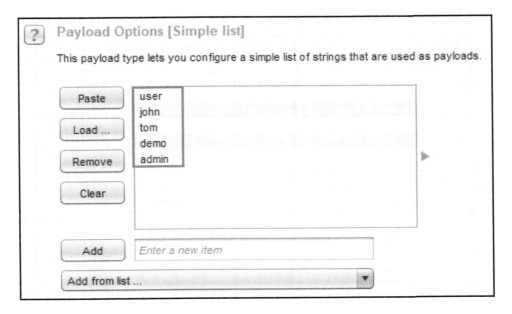

11. Go to the **Intruder | Options** tab and scroll down to the **Grep – Match** section. Click the checkbox **Flag result items with responses matching these expressions**. Click the **Clear** button to remove the items currently in the list:

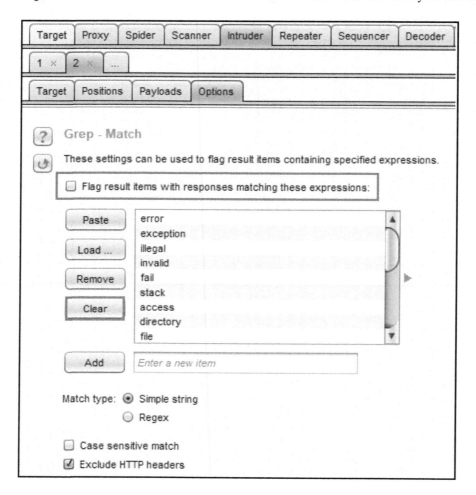

12. Click **Yes** to confirm you wish to clear the list.
13. Type the string The password is invalid within the textbox and click the **Add** button. Your **Grep – Match** section should look as shown in the following screenshot:

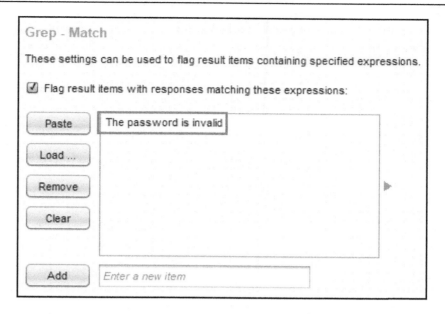

14. Click the **Start attack** button located at the top of the **Options** page. A pop-up dialog box appears displaying the payloads defined, as well as the new column we added under the **Grep – Match** section. This pop-up window is the attack results table.

15. The attack results table shows each request with the given payload resulted in a status code of **200** and that two of the payloads, **john** and **tom**, did not produce the message **The password is invalid** within the responses. Instead, those two payloads returned a message of **The user does not exist**:

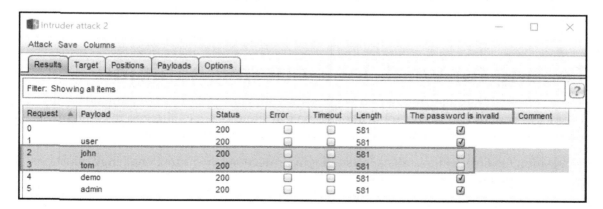

16. The result of this attack results table provide a username enumeration vulnerability based upon the overly verbose error message **The password is invalid**, which confirms the user account exists on the system:

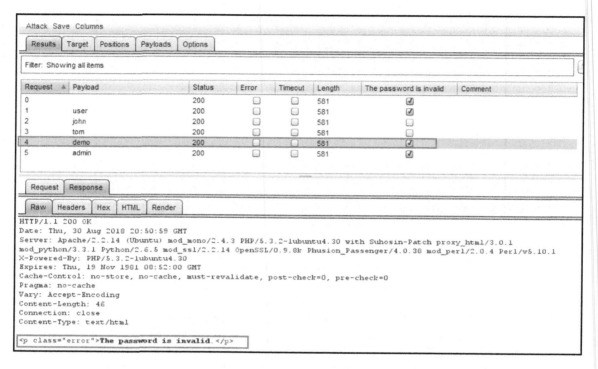

This means we are able to confirm that accounts already exist in the system for the users `user`, `demo`, and `admin`.

Testing for weak lock-out mechanisms

Account lockout mechanisms should be present within an application to mitigate brute-force login attacks. Typically, applications set a threshold between three to five attempts. Many applications lock for a period of time before a re-attempt is allowed.

Penetration testers must test all aspects of login protections, including challenge questions and response, if present.

Getting ready

Determine whether an application contains proper lock-out mechanisms in place. If they are not present, attempt to brute-force credentials against the login page to achieve unauthorized access to the application. Using the OWASP Mutillidae II application, attempt to log in five times with a valid username but an invalid password.

How to do it...

Ensure Burp and the OWASP BWA VM are running and that Burp is configured in the Firefox browser used to view the OWASP BWA applications.

1. From the OWASP BWA Landing page, click the link to the OWASP Mutillidae II application.
2. Open the Firefox browser to the login screen of OWASP Mutillidae II. From the top menu, click **Login**.
3. At the login screen, attempt to login five times with username `admin` and the wrong password of `aaaaaa`. Notice the application does not react any differently during the five attempts. The application does not change the error message shown, and the admin account is not locked out. This means the login is probably susceptible to brute-force password-guessing attacks:

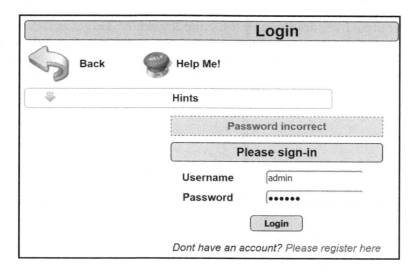

Let's continue the testing, to brute-force the login page and gain unauthorized access to the application.

4. Go to the **Proxy** | **HTTP history** tab, and look for the failed login attempts. Right-click one of the five requests and send it to **Intruder**:

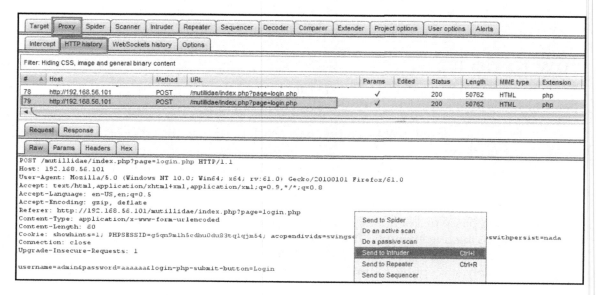

5. Go to Burp's **Intruder** tab, and leave the **Intruder** | **Target** tab settings as it is. Continue to the **Intruder** | **Positions** tab and notice how Burp places payload markers around each parameter value found. However, we only need a payload marker around the password's value. Click the **Clear §** button to remove the payload markers placed by Burp:

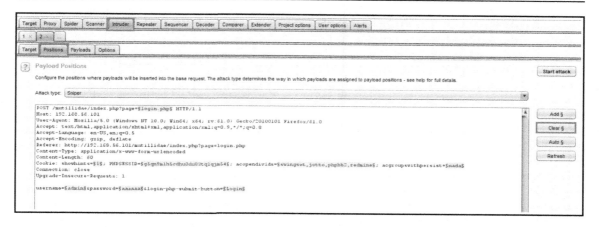

6. Then, highlight the password value of **aaaaaa** and click the **Add §** button.

7. Continue to the **Intruder** | **Payloads** tab. Many testers use word lists to brute-force commonly used passwords within the payload marker placeholder. For this recipe, we will type in some common passwords to create our own unique list of payloads.

8. In the **Payload Options [Simple list]** section, type the string `admin123` and click the **Add** button:

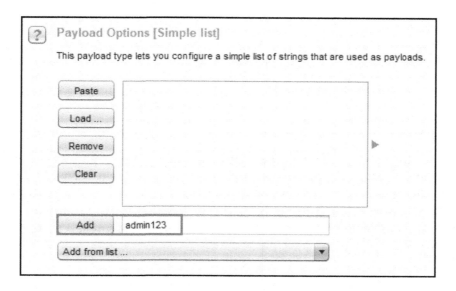

9. Add a few more strings, such as `adminpass`, `welcome1`, and, finally, `admin` to the payload-listing box:

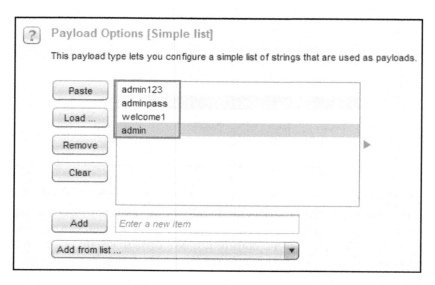

10. Go to the **Intruder | Options** tab and scroll down to the **Grep – Extract** section:

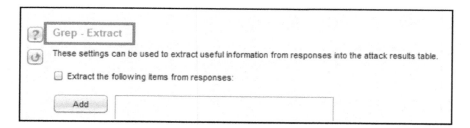

11. Click the checkbox **Extract the following items from responses** and then click the **Add** button. A pop-up box appears, displaying the response of the unsuccessful login attempt you made with the `admin/aaaaaa` request.

12. In the search box at the bottom, search for the words `Not Logged In`. After finding the match, you must highlight the words **Not Logged In**, to assign the grep match correctly:

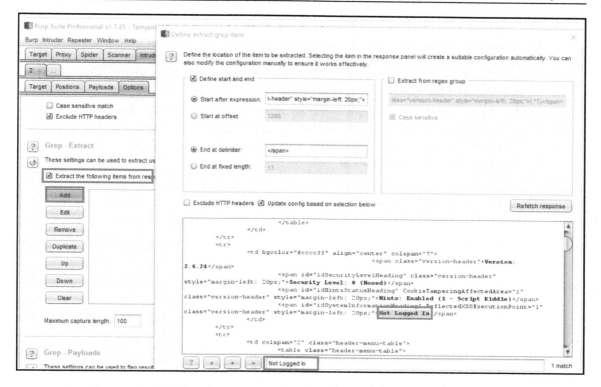

13. If you do not highlight the words properly, after you click **OK**, you will see **[INVALID]** inside the **Grep – Extract** box. If this happens, remove the entry by clicking the **Remove** button and try again by clicking the **Add** button, perform the search, and highlight the words.

14. If you highlight the words properly, you should see the following in the **Grep – Extract** box:

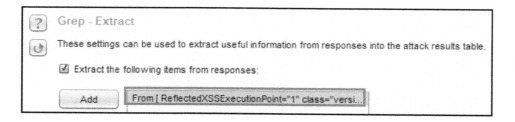

15. Now, click the **Start attack** button at the top right-hand side of the **Options** page.

16. A pop-up attack results table appears, displaying the request with the payloads you defined placed into the payload marker positions. Notice the attack table produced shows an extra column entitled **ReflectedXSSExecution**. This column is a result of the **Grep – Extract Option** set previously.

17. From this attack table, viewing the additional column, a tester can easily identify which request number successfully brute-forced the login screen. In this case, **Request 4**, using credentials of the username `admin` and the password `admin` logged us into the application:

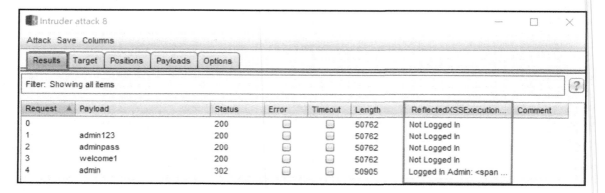

18. Select **Request 4** within the attack table, and view the **Response | Render** tab. You should see the message **Logged In Admin: admin (g0t r00t?)** on the top right-hand side:

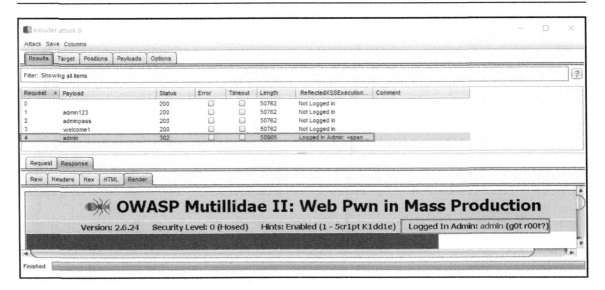

19. Close the attack table by clicking the **X** in the top right-hand corner.

You successfully brute-forced the password of a valid account on the system, due to the application having a weak lock-out mechanism.

Testing for bypassing authentication schemes

Applications may contain flaws, allowing unauthorized access by means of bypassing the authentication measures in place. Bypassing techniques include a **direct page request** (that is, forced browsing), **parameter modification**, **session ID prediction**, and **SQL Injection**.

For the purposes of this recipe, we will use parameter modification.

Getting ready

Add and edit parameters in an unauthenticated request to match a previously captured authenticated request. Replay the modified, unauthenticated request to gain access to the application through bypassing the login mechanism.

How to do it...

1. Open the Firefox browser to the home page of OWASP Mutillidae II, using the **Home** button from the top menu, on the left-hand side. Make sure you are *not logged into* the application. If you are logged in, select **Logout** from the menu:

2. In Burp, go to the **Proxy | HTTP history** tab and select the request you just made, browsing to the home page as unauthenticated. Right-click, and then select **Send to Repeater**:

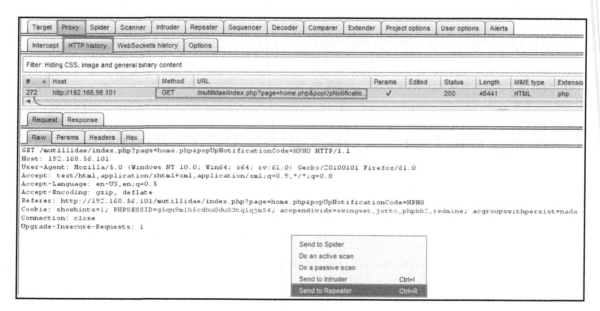

3. Using this same request and location, right-click again, and then select **Send to Comparer** (request):

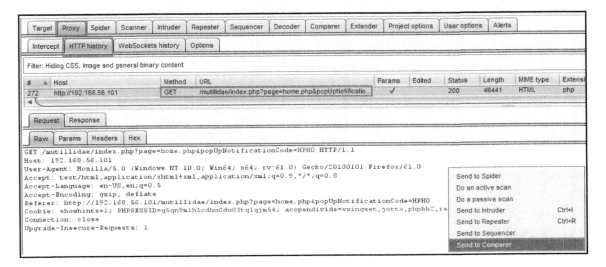

4. Return to the home page of your browser and click the **Login/Register** button. At the login page, log in with the username of admin and the password of admin. Click **Login**.

5. After you log in, go ahead and log out. Make sure you press the **Logout** button and are logged out of the admin account.

6. In Burp, go to the **Proxy | HTTP history** tab and select the request you just made, logging in as admin. Select GET request immediately following the POST 302 redirect. Right-click and then select **Send to Repeater** (request):

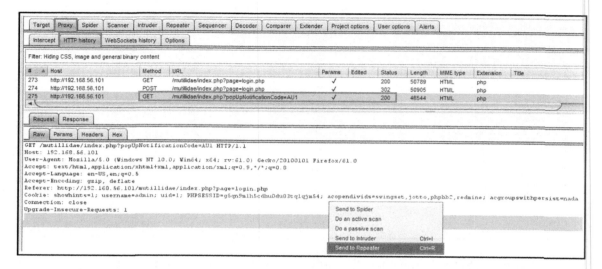

7. Using this same request and location, right-click again and **Send to Comparer** (request):

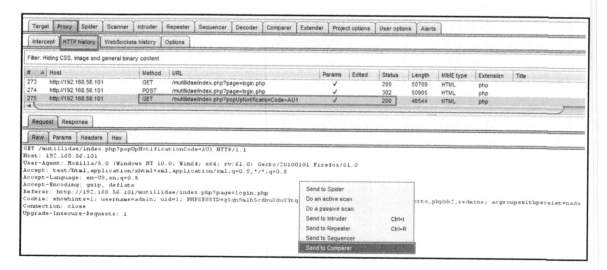

8. Go to Burp's **Comparer** tab. Notice the two requests you sent are highlighted. Press the **Words** button on the bottom right-hand side, to compare the two requests at the same time:

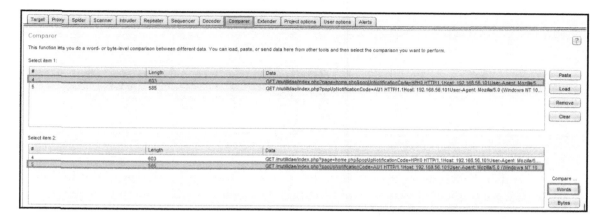

9. A dialog pop-up displays the two requests with color-coded highlights to draw your eyes to the differences. Note the changes in the **Referer** header and the additional name/value pair placed in the admin account cookie. Close the pop-up box with the **X** on the right-hand side:

10. Return to **Repeater**, which contains your first GET request you performed as unauthenticated. Prior to performing this attack, make sure you are completely logged out of the application.

11. You can verify you are logged out by clicking the **Go** button in **Repeater** associated to your unauthenticated request:

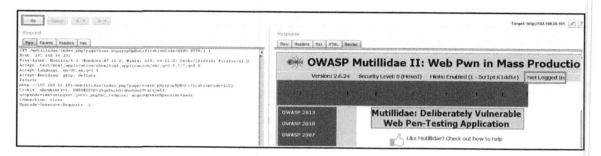

12. Now flip over to the **Repeater** tab, which contains your second GET request as authenticated user `admin`. Copy the values for **Referer** header and **Cookie** from the authenticated request. This attack is parameter modification for the purpose of bypassing authentication:

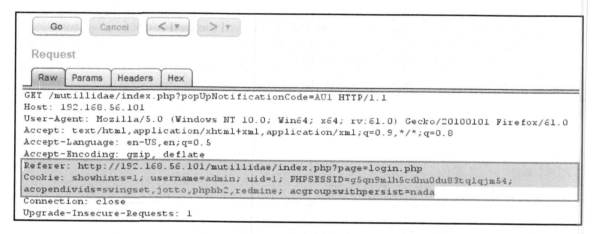

13. Copy the highlighted headers (**Referer and Cookie**) from the authenticated GET request. You are going to paste those values into the unauthenticated GET request.

14. Replace the same headers in the unauthenticated GET request by highlighting and right-clicking, and select **Paste**.

15. Right-click and select **Paste** in the **Repeater | Raw** tab of the first GET request you performed as unauthenticated.

16. Click the **Go** button to send your modified GET request. Remember, this is the first GET request you performed as unauthenticated.

17. Verify that you are now logged in as admin in the **Response | Render** tab. We were able to bypass the authentication mechanism (that is, the log in page) by performing parameter manipulation:

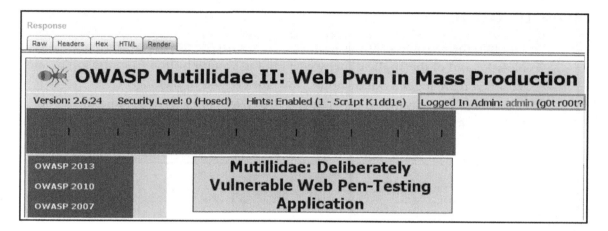

How it works

By replaying both the token found in the cookie and the referer value of the authenticated request into the unauthenticated request, we are able to bypass the authentication scheme and gain unauthorized access to the application.

Testing for browser cache weaknesses

Browser caching is provided for improved performance and better end-user experience. However, when sensitive data is typed into a browser by the user, such data can also be cached in the browser history. This cached data is visible by examining the browser's cache or simply by pressing the browser's *back* button.

Getting ready

Using the browser's back button, determine whether login credentials are cached, allowing for unauthorized access. Examine these steps in Burp, to understand the vulnerability.

How to do it...

1. Log into the Mutillidae application as `admin` with the password `admin`.
2. Now log out of the application by clicking the **Logout** button from the top menu.
3. Verify you are logged out by noting the **Not Logged In** message.
4. View these steps as messages in Burp's **Proxy | History** as well. Note the logout performs a **302** redirect in an effort to not cache cookies or credentials in the browser:

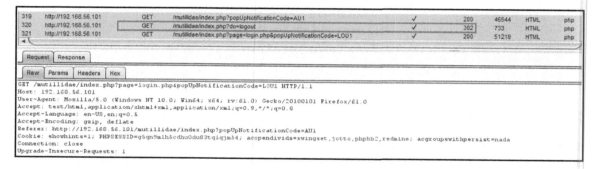

5. From the Firefox browser, click the back button and notice that you are now logged in as admin even though you did not log in! This is possible because of cached credentials stored in the browser and the lack of any cache-control protections set in the application.
6. Now refresh/reload the page in the browser, and you will see you are logged out again.
7. Examine the steps within the **Proxy | HTTP history** tab. Review the steps you did through the browser against the messages captured in the **Proxy | HTTP history** table:
   - Request 1 in the following screenshot is unauthenticate
   - Request 35 is the successful login (302) as `admin`

- Request 37 is the logout of the `admin` account
- Requests 38 and 39 are the refresh or reload of the browser page, logging us out again

8. There is no request captured when you press the browser's back button. This is because the back button action is contained in the browser. No message was sent through Burp to the web server to perform this action. This is an important distinction to note. Nonetheless, we found a vulnerability associated with weak browser-caching protection. In cases such as this, penetration testers will take a screenshot of the logged-in cached page, seen after clicking the back button:

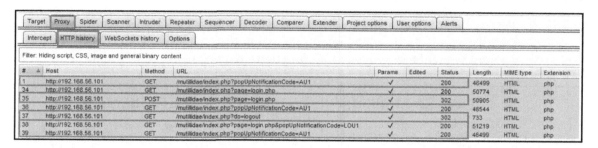

Testing the account provisioning process via the REST API

Account provisioning is the process of establishing and maintaining user accounts within an application. Provisioning capabilities are usually restricted to administrator accounts. Penetration testers must validate account-provisioning functions are done by users providing proper identification and authorization. A common venue for account provisioning is through **Representational State Transfer (REST)** API calls. Many times, developers may not put the same authorization checks in place for API calls that are used in the UI portion of an application.

Getting ready

Using REST API calls available in the OWASP Mutillidae II application, determine whether an unauthenticated API call can provision or modify users.

How to do it...

Make sure you are not logged into the application. If you are, click the **Logout** button from the top menu.

1. Within Mutillidae, browse to the **User Lookup (SQL) Page** and select **OWASP 2013** | **A1 Injection (SQL)** | **SQLi – Extract Data** | **User Info (SQL)**:

2. Type user for **Name** and user for **Password**, and click **View Account Details**. You should see the results shown in the next screenshot. This is the account we will test provisioning functions against, using REST calls:

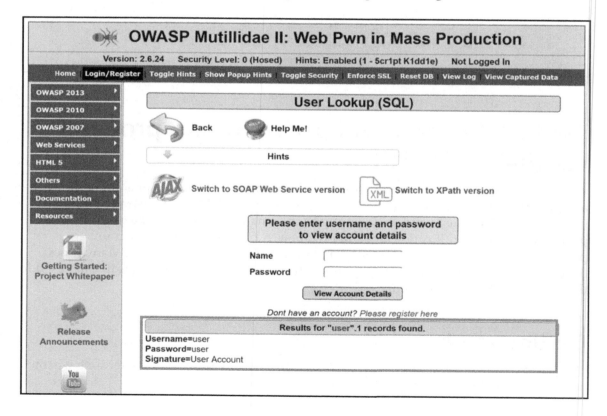

Through Spidering, Burp can find /api or /rest folders. Such folders are clues that an application is REST API enabled. A tester needs to determine which functions are available through these API calls.

3. For Mutillidae, the /webservices/rest/ folder structure offers account provisioning through REST API calls.

4. To go directly to this structure within Mutillidae, select **Web Services | REST | SQL Injection | User Account Management**:

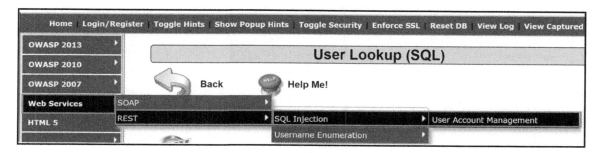

You are presented with a screen describing the supported REST calls and parameters required for each call:

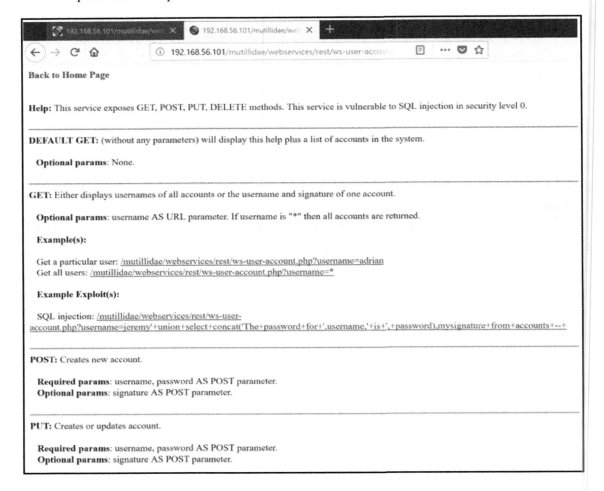

5. Let's try to invoke one of the REST calls. Go to the **Proxy | HTTP history** table and select the latest request you sent from the menu, to get to the **User Account Management** page. Right-click and send this request to **Repeater**:

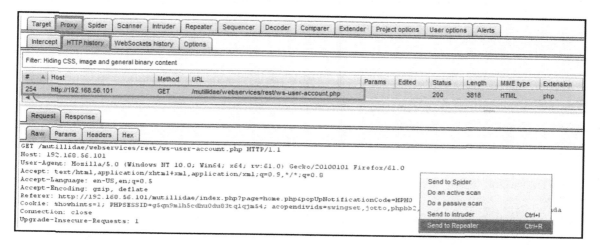

6. In Burp's **Repeater**, add the ?, followed by a parameter name/value pair of `username=user` to the URL. The new URL should be as follows:

/mutillidae/webservices/rest/ws-user-account.php?username=user

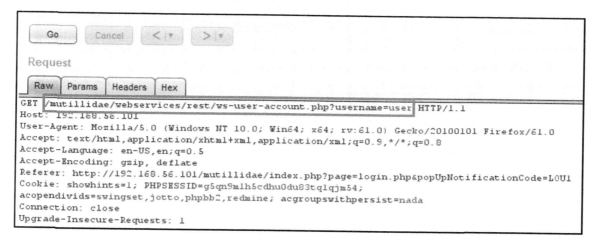

7. Click the **Go** button and notice we are able to retrieve data as an unauthenticated user! No authentication token is required to perform such actions:

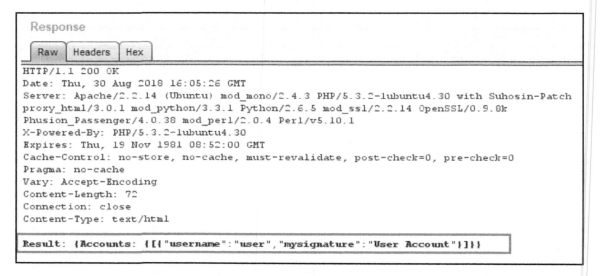

8. Let's see what else we can do. Using the SQL Injection string given on the **User Account Management** page, let's attempt to dump the entire user table.

9. Append the following value after `username=`:

```
user'+union+select+concat('The+password+for+',username,'+is+',+pass
word),mysignature+from+accounts+--+
```

The new URL should be the following one:

```
/mutillidae/webservices/rest/ws-user-
account.php?username=user'+union+select+concat('The+password+for+',
username,'+is+',+password),mysignature+from+accounts+--+
```

10. Click the **Go** button after making the change to the `username` parameter. Your request should look as shown in the following screenshot:

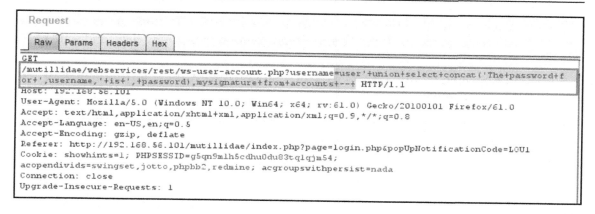

11. Notice we dumped all of the accounts in the database, displaying all usernames, passwords, and signatures:

```
Response
  Raw    Headers    Hex

X-Powered-By: PHP/5.3.2-1ubuntu4.30
Expires: Thu, 19 Nov 1981 08:52:00 GMT
Cache-Control: no-store, no-cache, must-revalidate, post-check=0, pre-check=0
Pragma: no-cache
Vary: Accept-Encoding
Content-Length: 2046
Connection: close
Content-Type: text/html

Result: {Accounts: {[{"username":"user","mysignature":"User Account"},{"username":"The password for admin
is admin","mysignature":"g0t r00t?"},{"username":"The password for adrian is
somepassword","mysignature":"Zombie Films Rock!"},{"username":"The password for john is
monkey","mysignature":"I like the smell of confunk"},{"username":"The password for jeremy is
password","mysignature":"d1373 1337 speak"},{"username":"The password for bryce is
password","mysignature":"I Love SANS"},{"username":"The password for samurai is
samurai","mysignature":"Carving fools"},{"username":"The password for jim is password","mysignature":"Rome
is burning"},{"username":"The password for bobby is password","mysignature":"Hank is my
dad"},{"username":"The password for simba is password","mysignature":"I am a super-cat"},{"username":"The
password for dreveil is password","mysignature":"Preparation H"},{"username":"The password for scotty is
password","mysignature":"Scotty do"},{"username":"The password for cal is password","mysignature":"C-A-T-S
Cats Cats Cats"},{"username":"The password for john is password","mysignature":"Do the
Duggie!"},{"username":"The password for kevin is 42","mysignature":"Doug Adams rocks"},{"username":"The
password for dave is set","mysignature":"Bet on S.E.T. FTW"},{"username":"The password for patches is
tortoise","mysignature":"meow"},{"username":"The password for rocky is
stripes","mysignature":"treats?"},{"username":"The password for tim is lanmaster53","mysignature":"Because
reconnaissance is hard to spell"},{"username":"The password for ABaker is SoSecret","mysignature":"Muffin
tops only"},{"username":"The password for PPan is NotTelling","mysignature":"Where is
Tinker?"},{"username":"The password for CHook is JollyRoger","mysignature":"Gator-hater"},{"username":"The
password for james is i<3devs","mysignature":"Occupation: Researcher"},{"username":"The password for user
is user","mysignature":"User Account"},{"username":"The password for ed is
pentest","mysignature":"Commandline KungFu anyone?"}]}}
```

12. Armed with this information, return to **Proxy | HTTP History**, select the request you made to see the **User Account Management** page, right-click, and send to **Repeater**.

13. In **Repeater**, modify the GET verb and replace it with DELETE within the **Raw** tab of the **Request**:

14. Move to the **Params** tab, click the **Add** button, and add two Body type parameters: first, a username with the value set to user, and second, a password with the value set to user, and then click the **Go** button:

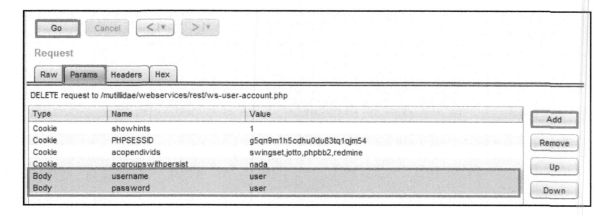

15. Notice we deleted the account! We were able to retrieve information and even modify (delete) rows within the database without ever showing an API key or authentication token!

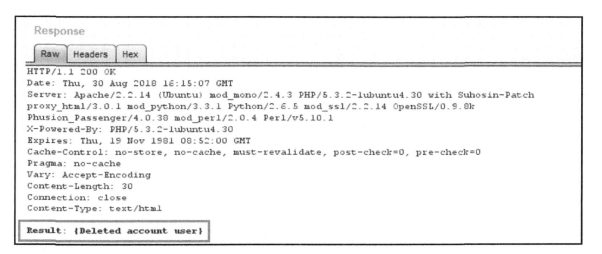

```
Response

 Raw   Headers   Hex

HTTP/1.1 200 OK
Date: Thu, 30 Aug 2018 16:15:07 GMT
Server: Apache/2.2.14 (Ubuntu) mod_mono/2.4.3 PHP/5.3.2-1ubuntu4.30 with Suhosin-Patch
proxy_html/3.0.1 mod_python/3.3.1 Python/2.6.5 mod_ssl/2.2.14 OpenSSL/0.9.8k
Phusion_Passenger/4.0.38 mod_perl/2.0.4 Perl/v5.10.1
X-Powered-By: PHP/5.3.2-1ubuntu4.30
Expires: Thu, 19 Nov 1981 08:52:00 GMT
Cache-Control: no-store, no-cache, must-revalidate, post-check=0, pre-check=0
Pragma: no-cache
Vary: Accept-Encoding
Content-Length: 30
Connection: close
Content-Type: text/html

Result: {Deleted account user}
```

 Note: If you wish to re-create the user account, repeat the previous steps, replacing *delete* with *put*. A signature is optional. Click the **Go** button. The user account is re-created again.

Assessing Authorization Checks

5

In this chapter, we will cover the following recipes:

- Testing for directory traversal
- Testing for **Local File Include (LFI)**
- Testing for **Remote File Include (RFI)**
- Testing for privilege escalation
- Testing for insecure direct object reference

Introduction

This chapter covers the basics of authorization, including an explanation of how an application uses roles to determine user functions. Web penetration testing involves key assessments to determine how well the application validates functions assigned to a given role, and we will learn how to use Burp to perform such tests.

Software requirements

To complete the recipes in this chapter, you will need the following:

- OWASP broken web applications (VM)
  - OWASP mutillidae link
- Burp Proxy Community or Professional (`https://portswigger.net/burp/`)
- Firefox browser configured to allow Burp to proxy traffic (`https://www.mozilla.org/en-US/firefox/new/`)
- The `wfuzz` wordlist repository from GitHub (`https://github.com/xmendez/wfuzz`)

Testing for directory traversal

Directory traversal attacks are attempts to discover or forced browse to unauthorized web pages usually designed for administrators of the application. If an application does not configure the web document root properly and does not include proper authorization checks for each page accessed, a directory traversal vulnerability could exist. In particular situations, such a weakness could lead to system command injection attacks or the ability of an attacker to perform arbitrary code execution.

Getting ready

Using OWASP Mutillidae II as our target application, let's determine whether it contains any directory traversal vulnerabilities.

How to do it...

Ensure Burp and the OWASP BWA VM are running and that Burp is configured in the Firefox browser used to view the OWASP BWA applications.

1. From the OWASP BWA Landing page, click the link to the OWASP Mutillidae II application.
2. Open the Firefox browser on the login screen of OWASP Mutillidae II. From the top menu, click **Login**.
3. Find the request you just performed within the **Proxy | HTTP history** table. Look for the call to the `login.php` page. Highlight the message, move your cursor into the **Raw** tab of the **Request** tab, right-click, and click on **Send to Intruder**:

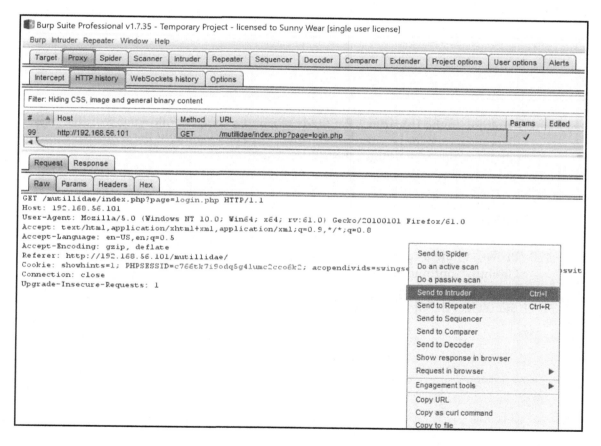

4. Switch over to the **Intruder** I **Positions** tab, and clear all Burp-defined payload markers by clicking the **Clear $** button on the right-hand side.

5. Highlight the value currently stored in the `page` parameter (`login.php`), and place a payload marker around it using the **Add §** button:

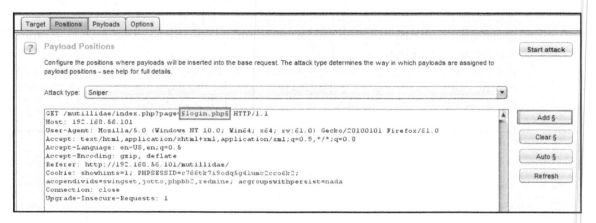

6. Continue to the **Intruder** I **Payloads** tab, and select the following wordlist from the `wfuzz` repository: `admin-panels.txt`. The location of the wordlist from the GitHub repository follows this folder structure: `wfuzz/wordlist/general/admin-panels.txt`.

7. Click the **Load** button within the **Payload Options [Simple list]** section of the **Intruder** I **Payloads,** tab and a popup will display, prompting for the location of your wordlist.

8. Browse to the location where you downloaded the `wfuzz` repository from GitHub. Continue to search through the `wfuzz` folder structure (`wfuzz/wordlist/general/`) until you reach the `admin-panels.txt` file, and then select the file by clicking **Open:**

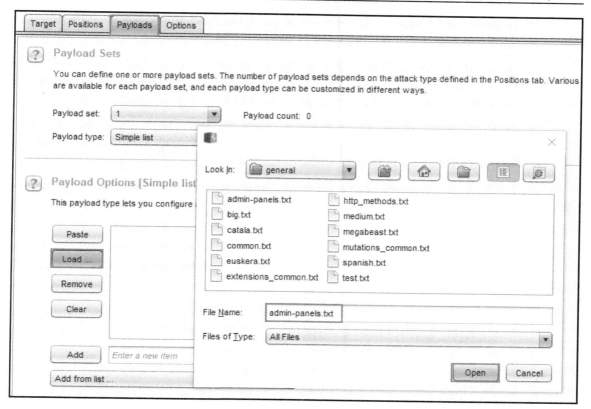

9. Scroll to the bottom and uncheck (by default, it is checked) the option **URL-encode these characters**:

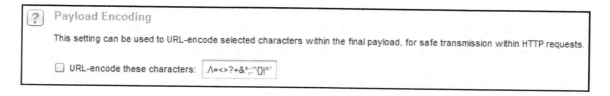

10. You are now ready to begin the attack. Click the **Start attack** button at the top right-hand corner of the **Intruder | Positions** page:

    The attack results table will appear. Allow the attacks to complete. There are 137 payloads in the `admin-panels.txt` wordlist. Sort on the **Length** column from ascending to descending order, to see which of the payloads hit a web page.

11. Notice the payloads that have larger response lengths. This looks promising! Perhaps we have stumbled upon some administration pages that may contain fingerprinting information or unauthorized access:

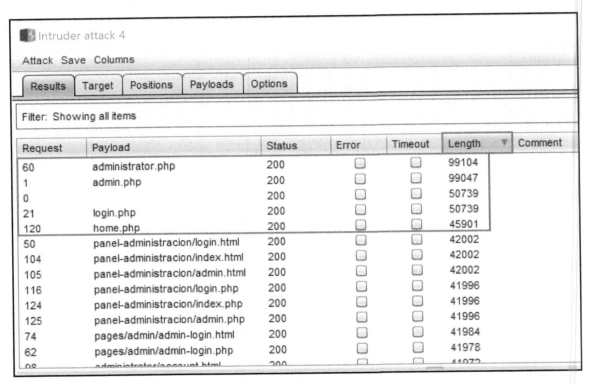

12. Select the first page in the list with the largest length, **administrator.php**. From the attack results table, look at the **Response | Render** tab, and notice the page displays the PHP version and the system information:

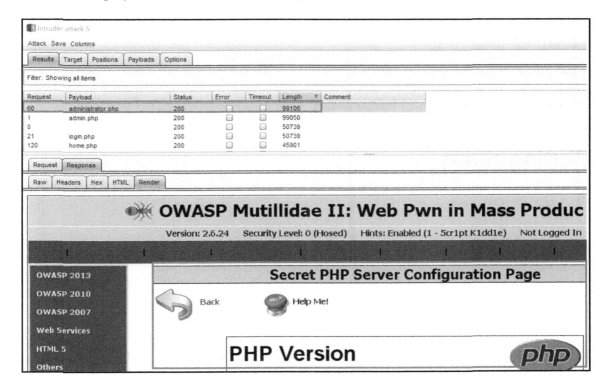

How it works...

Without even being logged in, we were able to force browse to an area of the web application that was unmapped. The term *unmapped* means the application itself had no direct link to this secret configuration page. However, using Burp Intruder and a wordlist containing commonly known administration file names, we were able to discover the page using the directory traversal attack.

Testing for Local File Include (LFI)

Web servers control access to privileged files and resources through configuration settings. Privileged files include files that should only be accessible by system administrators. For example, the /etc/passwd file on UNIX-like platforms or the boot.ini file on Windows systems.

A **LFI** attack is an attempt to access privileged files using directory traversal attacks. LFI attacks include different styles including the **dot-dot-slash attack (../)**, **directory brute-forcing**, **directory climbing**, or **backtracking**.

Getting ready

Using OWASP Mutillidae II as our target application, let's determine whether it contains any LFI vulnerabilities.

How to do it...

Ensure Burp and OWASP BWA VM are running and that Burp is configured in the Firefox browser used to view the OWASP BWA applications.

1. From the OWASP BWA Landing page, click the link to the OWASP Mutillidae II application.
2. Open the Firefox browser to the login screen of OWASP Mutillidae II. From the top menu, click **Login**.
3. Find the request you just performed within the **Proxy** I **HTTP history** table. Look for the call to the login.php page. Highlight the message, move your cursor into the **Raw** tab of the **Request** tab, right-click, and **Send to Intruder**.
4. Switch over to the **Intruder** I **Positions** tab, and clear all Burp-defined payload markers by clicking the **Clear §** button on the right-hand side.
5. Highlight the value currently stored in the page parameter (login.php), and place a payload marker around it using the **Add §** button on the right-hand side.

6. Continue to the **Intruder** | **Payloads** tab. Select the following wordlist from the `wfuzz` repository: `Traversal.txt`. The location of the wordlist from the GitHub repository follows this folder structure: `wfuzz/wordlist/injections/Traversal.txt`.

7. Click the **Load** button within the **Payload Options [Simple list]** section of the **Intruder** | **Payloads** tab. A popup will display, prompting for the location of your wordlist.

8. Browse to the location where you downloaded the `wfuzz` repository from GitHub. Continue to search through `wfuzz` folder structure until you reach the `admin-panels.txt` file. Select the file and click **Open**:

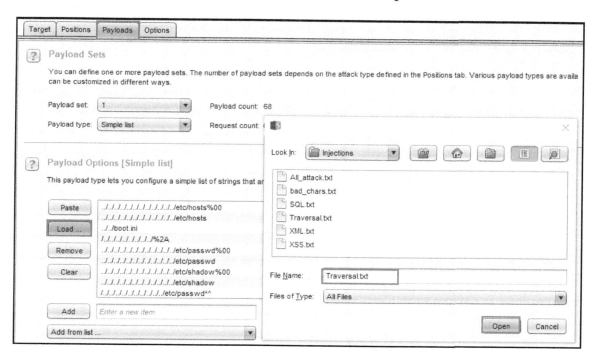

9. Scroll to the bottom and uncheck (by default, it is checked) the option **URL-encode these characters**.

10. You are now ready to begin the attack. Click the **Start attack** button at the top-right-hand corner of the **Intruder | Positions** page.

11. The attack results table will appear. Allow the attacks to complete. Sort on the **Length** column from ascending to descending order, to see which of the payloads hit a web page. Notice the payloads with larger lengths; perhaps we gained unauthorized access to the system configuration files!

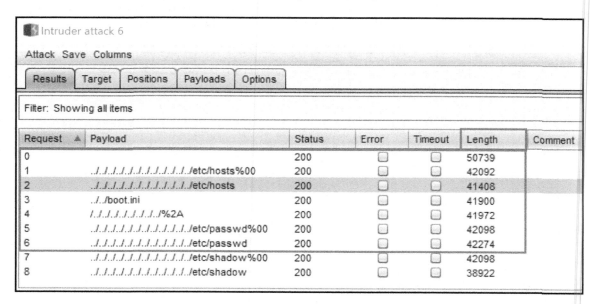

12. Select the Request #2 in the list. From the attack results table, look at the **Response** | **Render** tab and notice the page displays the host file from the system!

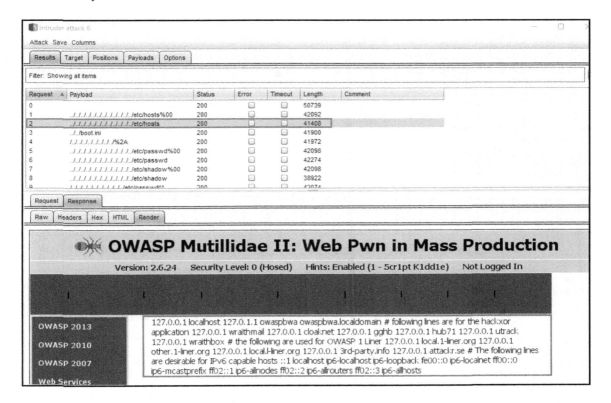

13. Continue scrolling down the list of requests in the attack results table. Look at request #6, and then look at the **Response | Render** tab and notice the page displays the /etc/passwd file from the system!

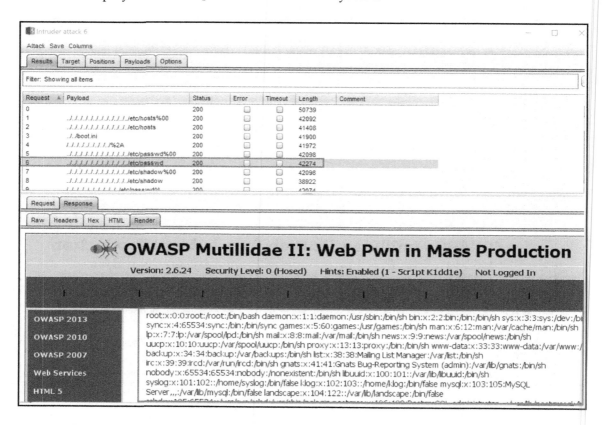

How it works...

Due to poorly protected file permissions and lack of application authorization checks, attackers are able to read privileged local files on a system containing sensitive information.

Testing for Remote File Inclusion (RFI)

Remote File Inclusion (RFI) is an attack attempting to access external URLs and remotely located files. The attack is possible due to parameter manipulation and lack of server-side checks. These oversights allow parameter changes to redirect the user to locations that are not whitelisted or sanitized with proper data validation.

Getting ready

Using OWASP Mutillidae II as our target application, let's determine whether it contains any RFI vulnerabilities.

How to do it...

Ensure Burp and OWASP BWA VM are running and that Burp is configured in the Firefox browser used to view the OWASP BWA applications.

1. From the OWASP BWA Landing page, click the link to the OWASP Mutillidae II application.
2. Open the Firefox browser to the login screen of OWASP Mutillidae II. From the top menu, click **Login**.
3. Find the request you just performed within the **Proxy | HTTP history** table. Look for the call to the `login.php` page:

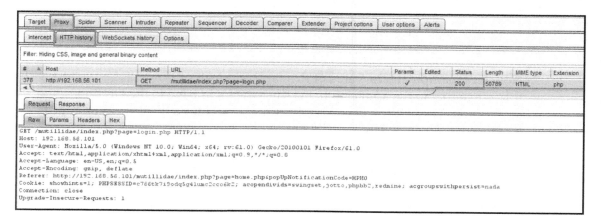

4. Make a note of the `page` parameter that determines the page to load:

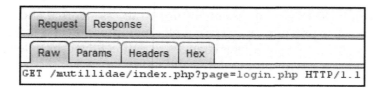

Let's see if we can exploit this parameter by providing a URL that is outside the application. For demonstration purposes, we will use a URL that we control in the OWASP BWA VM. However, in the wild, this URL would be attacker-controlled instead.

5. Switch to the **Proxy | Intercept** tab, and press the **Intercept is on** button.
6. Return to the Firefox browser, and reload the login page. The request is paused and contained within the **Proxy | Intercept** tab:

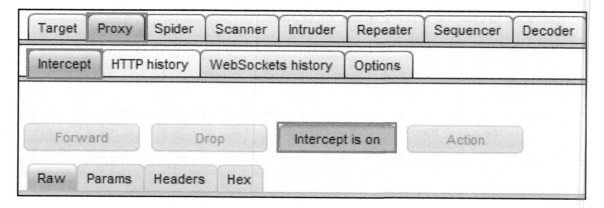

7. Now let's manipulate the value of the `page` parameter from `login.php` to a URL that is external to the application. Let's use the login page to the **GetBoo** application. Your URL will be specific to your machine's IP address, so adjust accordingly. The new URL will be `http://<your_IP_address>/getboo/`
8. Replace the `login.php` value with `http://<your_IP_address>/getboo/` and click the **Forward** button:

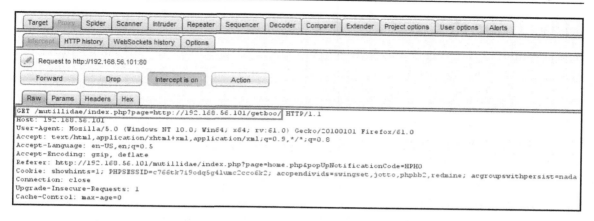

9. Now press the **Intercept is on** again to toggle the intercept button to **OFF** (**Intercept is off**).

10. Return to the Firefox browser, and notice the page loaded is the **GetBoo** index page within the context of the Mutillidae application!

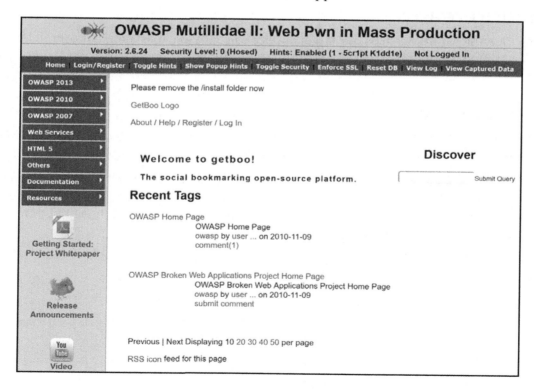

How it works...

The page parameter does not include proper data validation to ensure the values provided to it are whitelisted or contained to a prescribed list of acceptable values. By exploiting this weakness, we are able to dictate values to this parameter, which should not be allowed.

Testing for privilege escalation

Developer code in an application must include authorization checks on assigned roles to ensure an authorized user is not able to elevate their role to a higher privilege. Such privilege escalation attacks occur by modifying the value of the assigned role and replacing the value with another. In the event that the attack is successful, the user gains unauthorized access to resources or functionality normally restricted to administrators or more-powerful accounts.

Getting ready

Using OWASP Mutillidae II as our target application, let's log in as a regular user, John, and determine whether we can escalate our role to admin.

How to do it...

Ensure Burp and OWASP BWA VM are running and that Burp is configured in the Firefox browser used to view the OWASP BWA applications.

1. From the OWASP BWA Landing page, click the link to the OWASP Mutillidae II application.
2. Open the Firefox browser to the login screen of OWASP Mutillidae II. From the top menu, click **Login**.
3. At the login screen, log in with these credentials—username: john and password: monkey.

4. Switch to Burp's **Proxy** | **HTTP history** tab. Find the POST and subsequent GET requests you just made by logging in as john:

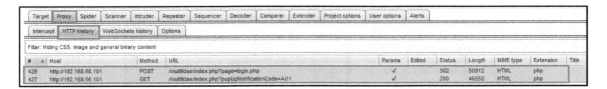

5. Look at the GET request from the listing; notice the cookie name/value pairs shown on the **Cookie:** line.

The name/value pairs of most interest include username=john and uid=3. What if we attempt to manipulate these values to a different role?

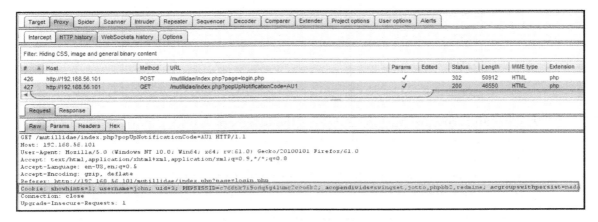

6. Let's attempt to manipulate the parameters username and the uid stored in the cookie to a different role. We will use Burp's **Proxy** | **Intercept** to help us perform this attack.

7. Switch to the **Proxy** | **Intercept** tab, and press the **Intercept is on** button. Return to the Firefox browser and reload the login page.

8. The request is paused within the **Proxy | Intercept** tab. While it is paused, change the value assigned to the username from `john` to `admin`. Also, change the value assigned to the `uid` from 3 to 1:

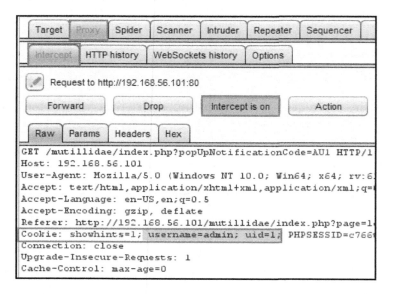

9. Click the **Forward** button, and press the **Intercept is on** again to toggle the intercept button to **OFF (Intercept is off)**.

10. Return to the Firefox browser, and notice we are now logged in as an admin! We were able to escalate our privileges from a regular user to an admin, since the developer did not perform any authorization checks on the assigned role:

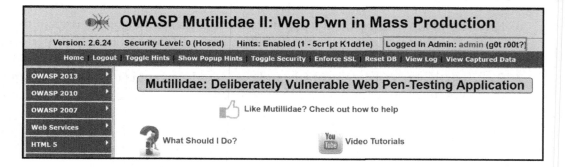

How it works...

There are several application issues associated with the privilege escalation attack shown in this recipe. Any actions related to account provisioning (that is, role assignments) should only be allowed by administrators. Without proper checks in place, users can attempt to escalate their provisioned roles. Another issue exemplified in this recipe is the sequential user ID number (for example, uid=3). Since this number is easily guessable and because most applications start with administrator accounts, changing the digit from 3 to 1 seemed a probable guess for association with the admin account.

Testing for Insecure Direct Object Reference (IDOR)

Allowing unauthorized direct access to files or resources on a system based on user-supplied input is known as **Insecure Direct Object Reference (IDOR)**. This vulnerability allows the bypassing of authorization checks placed on such files or resources. IDOR is a result of unchecked user supplied input to retrieve an object without performing authorization checks in the application code.

Getting ready

Using OWASP Mutillidae II as our target application, let's manipulate the value of the phpfile parameter to determine whether we can make a call to a direct object reference on the system, such as /etc/passwd file.

How to do it...

1. From the Mutillidae menu, select **OWASP 2013 | A4 – Insecure Direct Object References | Source Viewer**:

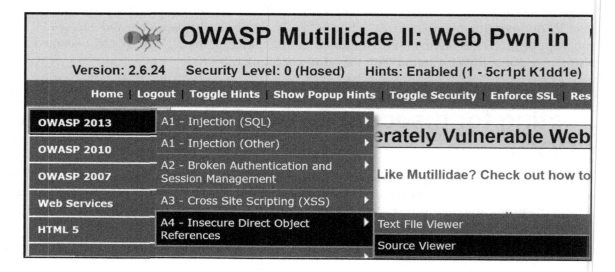

2. From the **Source Viewer** page, using the default file selected in the drop-down box (`upload-file.php`), click the **View File** button to see the contents of the file displayed below the button:

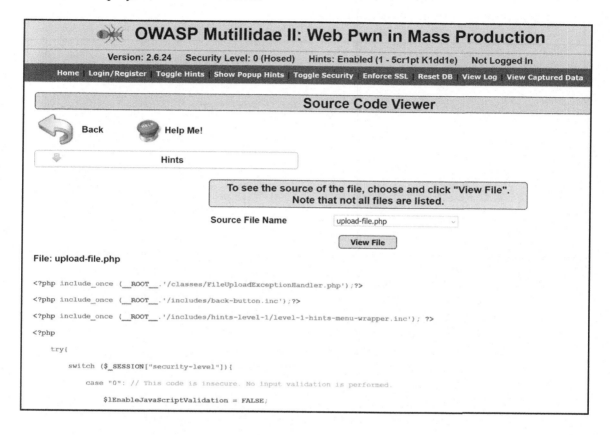

3. Switch to Burp's **Proxy | HTTP history** tab. Find the POST request you just made while viewing the upload-file.php file. Note the phpfile parameter with the value of the file to display. What would happen if we change the value of this parameter to something else?

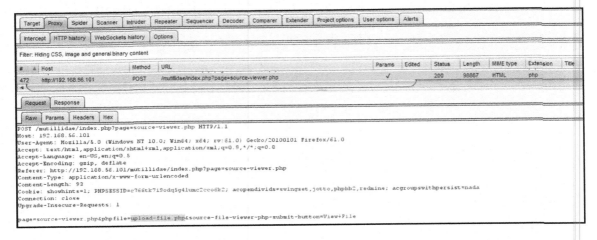

4. Let's perform an IDOR attack by manipulating the value provided to the phpfile parameter to reference a file on the system instead. For example, let's try changing the upload-file.php value to ../../../../etc/passwd via Burp's **Proxy | Intercept** functionality.

5. To perform this attack, follow these steps.
    1. Switch to the **Proxy | Intercept** tab, and press the **Intercept is on** button.
    2. Return to the Firefox browser and reload the login page. The request is paused and contained within the **Proxy | Intercept** tab.

3. As the request is paused, change the value assigned to the `phpfile` parameter to the value `../../../../etc/passwd` instead:

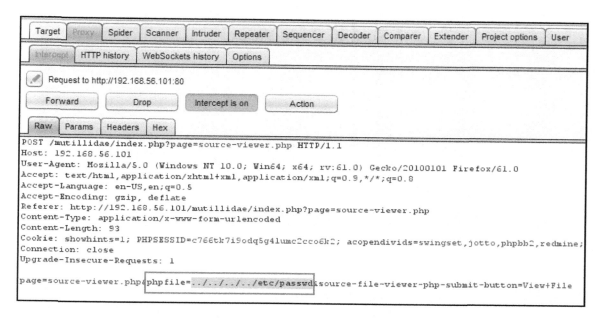

6. Click the **Forward** button. Now press the **Intercept is on** button again to toggle the intercept button to **OFF (Intercept is off)**.

7. Return to the Firefox browser. Notice we can now see the contents of the `/etc/passwd` file!

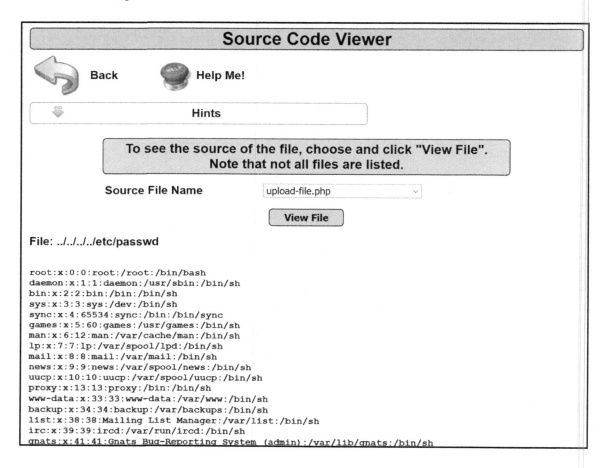

How it works...

Due to lack of proper authorization checks on the `phpfile` parameter within the application code, we are able to view a privileged file on the system. Developers and system administrators provide access controls and checks prior to the revealing of sensitive files and resources. When these access controls are missing, IDOR vulnerabilities may be present.

6
Assessing Session Management Mechanisms

In this chapter, we will cover the following recipes:

- Testing session token strength using Sequencer
- Testing for cookie attributes
- Testing for session fixation
- Testing for exposed session variables
- Testing for Cross-Site Request Forgery

Introduction

This chapter covers techniques used to bypass and assess session management schemes. Session management schemes are used by applications to keep track of user activity, usually by means of session tokens. Web assessments of session management also involve determining the strength of session tokens used and whether those tokens are properly protected. We will learn how to use Burp to perform such tests.

Software tool requirements

To complete the recipes in this chapter, you will need the following:

- OWASP Broken Web Applications (VM)
- OWASP Mutillidae link
- Burp Proxy Community or Professional (https://portswigger.net/burp/)
- A Firefox browser configured to allow Burp to proxy traffic (https://www.mozilla.org/en-US/firefox/new/)

Testing session token strength using Sequencer

To track user activity from page to page within an application, developers create and assign unique session token values to each user. Most session token mechanisms include session IDs, hidden form fields, or cookies. Cookies are placed within the user's browser on the client-side.

These session tokens should be examined by a penetration tester to ensure their uniqueness, randomness, and cryptographic strength, to prevent information leakage.

If a session token value is easily guessable or remains unchanged after login, an attacker could apply (or fixate) a pre-known token value to a user. This is known as a **session fixation attack**. Generally speaking, the purpose of the attack is to harvest sensitive data in the user's account, since the session token is known to the attacker.

Getting ready

We'll check the session tokens used in OWASP Mutillidae II to ensure they are created in a secure and an unpredictable way. An attacker who is able to predict and forge a weak session token can perform session fixation attacks.

How to do it...

Ensure Burp and the OWASP BWA VM are running and that Burp is configured in the Firefox browser used to view OWASP BWA applications.

1. From the **OWASP BWA Landing** page, click the link to the OWASP Mutillidae II application.
2. Open the Firefox browser to access the home page of OWASP Mutillidae II (URL: `http://<your_VM_assigned_IP_address>/mutillidae/`). Make sure you are starting a fresh session of the Mutillidae application and not logged into it already:

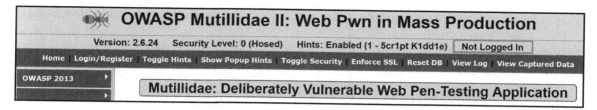

3. Switch to the **Proxy** | **HTTP History** tab and select the request showing your initial browse to the Mutillidae home page.

4. Look for the `GET` request and the associated response containing the `Set-Cookie:` assignments. Whenever you see this assignment, you can ensure you are getting a freshly created cookie for your session. Specifically, we are interested in the `PHPSESSID` cookie value:

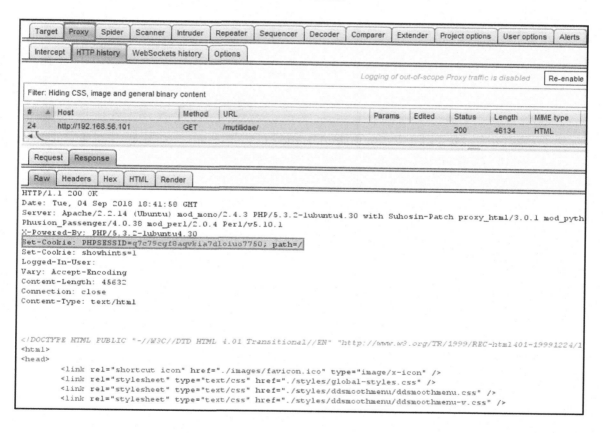

5. Highlight the value of the of the `PHPSESSID` cookie, right-click, and select **Send to Sequencer:**

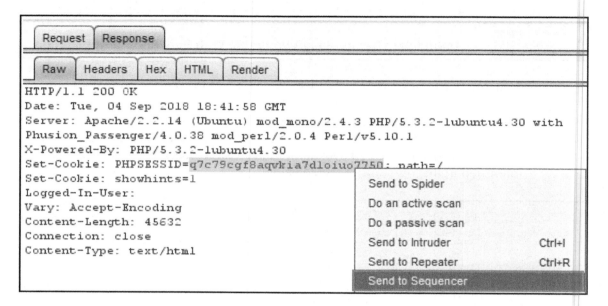

Sequencer is a tool within Burp designed to determine the strength or the quality of the randomness created within a session token.

6. After sending the value of the `PHPSESSID` parameter over to Sequencer, you will see the value loaded in the **Select Live Capture Request** table.

7. Before pressing the **Start live capture** button, scroll down to the **Token Location Within Response** section. In the **Cookie** dropdown list, select `PHPSESSID=<captured session token value>:`

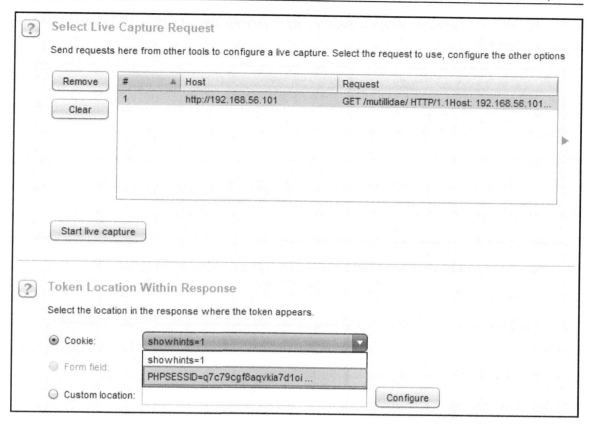

8. Since we have the correct cookie value selected, we can begin the live capture process. Click the **Start live capture** button, and Burp will send multiple requests, extracting the PHPSESSID cookie out of each response. After each capture, Sequencer performs a statistical analysis of the level of randomness in each token.

9. Allow the capture to gather and analyze at least 200 tokens, but feel free to let it run longer if you like:

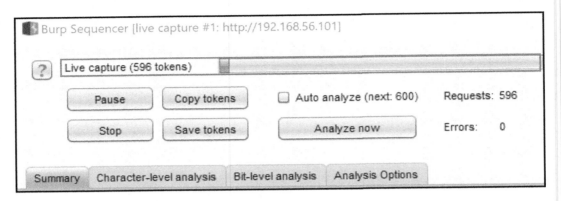

10. Once you have at least 200 samples, click the **Analyze now** button. Whenever you are ready to stop the capturing process, press the **Stop** button and confirm **Yes:**

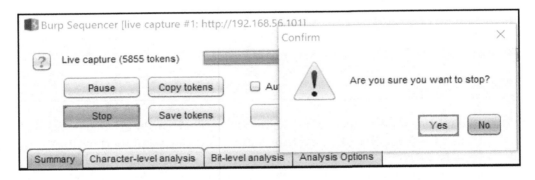

11. After the analysis is complete, the output of Sequencer provides an overall result. In this case, the quality of randomness for the PHPSESSID session token is excellent. The amount of effective entropy is estimated to be 112 bits. From a web pentester perspective, these session tokens are very strong, so there is no vulnerability to report here. However, though there is no vulnerability present, it is good practice to perform such checks on session tokens:

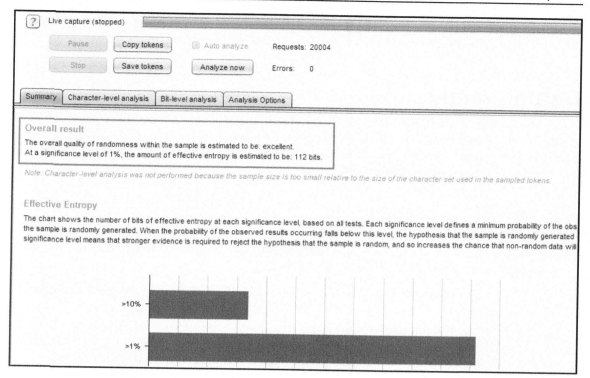

How it works...

To better understand the math and hypothesis behind Sequencer, consult Portswigger's documentation on the topic here: `https://portswigger.net/burp/documentation/desktop/tools/sequencer/tests`.

Testing for cookie attributes

Important user-specific information, such as session tokens, is often stored in cookies within the client browser. Due to their importance, cookies need to be protected from malicious attacks. This protection usually comes in the form of two flags—**secure** and **HttpOnly**.

The secure flag informs the browser to only send the cookie to the web server if the protocol is encrypted (for example, HTTPS, TLS). This flag protects the cookie from eavesdropping over unencrypted channels.

The HttpOnly flag instructs the browser to not allow access or manipulation of the cookie via JavaScript. This flag protects the cookie from cross-site scripting attacks.

Getting ready

Check the cookies used in the OWASP Mutillidae II application, to ensure the presence of protective flags. Since the Mutillidae application runs over an unencrypted channel (for example, HTTP), we can only check for the presence of the HttpOnly flag. Therefore, the secure flag is out of scope for this recipe.

How to do it...

Ensure Burp and OWASP BWA VM are running and that Burp is configured in the Firefox browser used to view OWASP BWA applications.

1. From the **OWASP BWA Landing** page, click the link to the OWASP Mutillidae II application.

2. Open the Firefox Browser, to access the home page of OWASP Mutillidae II (URL: `http://<your_VM_assigned_IP_address>/mutillidae/`). Make sure you are starting a fresh session and you are not logged in to the Mutillidae application:

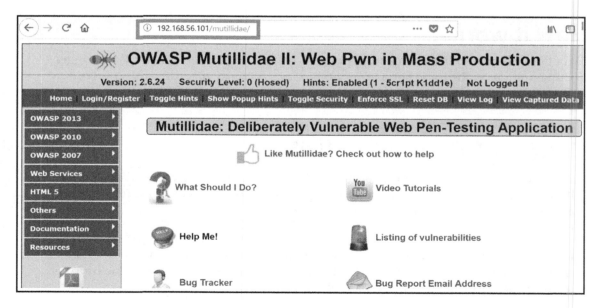

3. Switch to the **Proxy** | **HTTP history** tab, and select the request showing your initial browse to the Mutillidae home page. Look for the GET request and its associated response containing Set-Cookie: assignments. Whenever you see this assignment, you can ensure you are getting a freshly created cookie for your session. Specifically, we are interested in the PHPSESSID cookie value.

4. Examine the end of the Set-Cookie: assignments lines. Notice the absence of the HttpOnly flag for both lines. This means the PHPSESSID and showhints cookie values are not protected from JavaScript manipulation. This is a security finding that you would include in your report:

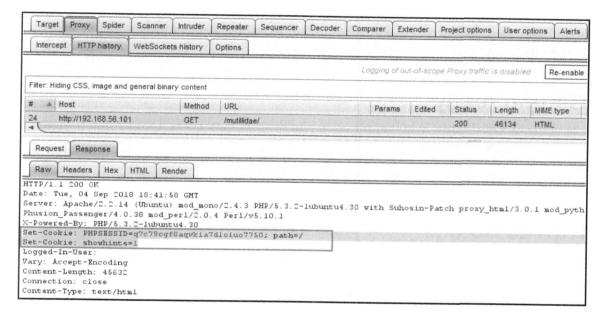

How it works...

If the two cookies had HttpOnly flags set, the flags would appear at the end of the Set-Cookie assignment lines. When present, the flag would immediately follow a semicolon ending the path scope of the cookie, followed by the string HttpOnly. The display is similar for the Secure flag as well:

```
Set-Cookie: PHPSESSID=<session token value>;path=/;Secure;HttpOnly;
```

Testing for session fixation

Session tokens are assigned to users for tracking purposes. This means that when browsing an application as unauthenticated, a user is assigned a unique session ID, which is usually stored in a cookie. Application developers should always create a new session token after the user logs into the website. If this session token does not change, the application could be susceptible to a session fixation attack. It is the responsibility of web penetration testers to determine whether this token changes values from an unauthenticated state to an authenticated state.

Session fixation is present when application developers do not invalidate the unauthenticated session token, allowing the user to use the same one after authentication. This scenario allows an attacker with a stolen session token to masquerade as the user.

Getting ready

Using the OWASP Mutillidae II application and Burp's Proxy HTTP History and Comparer, we will examine unauthenticated PHPSESSID session token value. Then, we will log in to the application and compare the unauthenticated value against the authenticated value to determine the presence of the session fixation vulnerability.

How to do it...

1. Navigate to the login screen (click **Login/Register** from the top menu), but do not log in yet.
2. Switch to Burp's **Proxy HTTP history** tab, and look for the GET request showing when you browsed to the login screen. Make a note of the value assigned to the PHPSESSID parameter placed within a cookie:

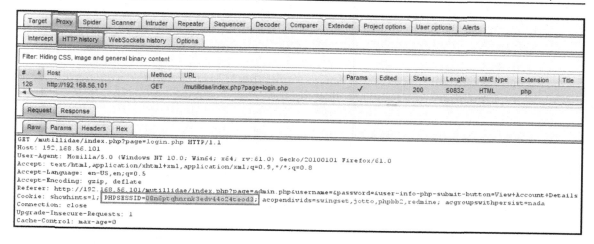

3. Right-click the PHPSESSID parameter and send the request to Comparer:

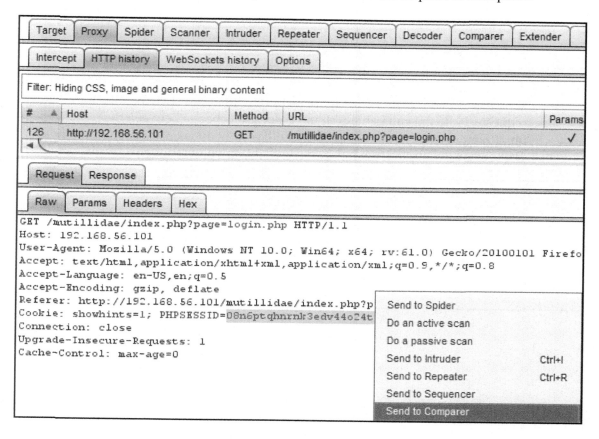

4. Return to the login screen (click **Login/Register** from the top menu), and, this time, log in under the username `ed` and the password `pentest`.

5. After logging in, switch to Burp's **Proxy HTTP history** tab. Look for the `POST` request showing your login (for example, the 302 HTTP status code) as well as the immediate `GET` request following the `POST`. Note the `PHPSESSID` assigned after login. Right-click and send this request to Comparer.

6. Switch to Burp's **Comparer**. The appropriate requests should already be highlighted for you. Click the **Words** button in the bottom right-hand corner:

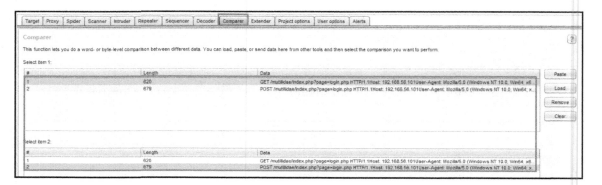

A popup shows a detailed comparison of the differences between the two requests. Note the value of `PHPSESSID` does not change between the unauthenticated session (on the left) and the authenticated session (on the right). This means the application has a session fixation vulnerability:

How it works...

In this recipe, we examined how the PHPSESSID value assigned to an unauthenticated user remained constant even after authentication. This is a security vulnerability allowing for the session fixation attack.

Testing for exposed session variables

Session variables such as tokens, cookies, or hidden form fields are used by application developers to send data between the client and the server. Since these variables are exposed on the client-side, an attacker can manipulate them in an attempt to gain access to unauthorized data or to capture sensitive information.

Burp's Proxy option provides a feature to enhance the visibility of so-called *hidden* form fields. This feature allows web application penetration testers to determine the level of the sensitivity of data held in these variables. Likewise, a pentester can determine whether the manipulation of these values produces a different behavior in the application.

Getting ready

Using the OWASP Mutillidae II application and Burp's Proxy's **Unhide hidden form fields** feature, we'll determine whether manipulation of a hidden form field value results in gaining access to unauthorized data.

How to do it...

1. Switch to Burp's **Proxy** tab, scroll down to the **Response Modification** section, and check the boxes for **Unhide hidden form fields** and **Prominently highlight unhidden fields**:

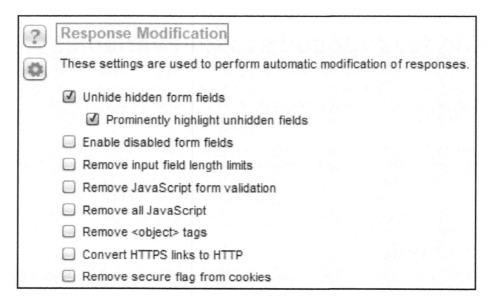

2. Navigate to the **User Info** page. OWASP 2013 | **A1 – Injection (SQL)** | **SQLi – Extract Data** | **User Info (SQL)**:

3. Note the hidden form fields now prominently displayed on the page:

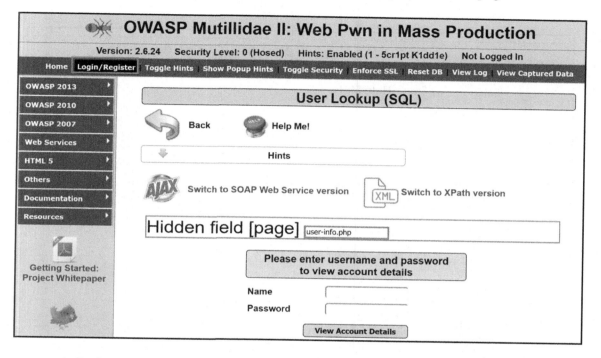

4. Let's try to manipulate the value shown, user-info.php, by changing it to admin.php and see how the application reacts. Modify the user-info.php to admin.php within the **Hidden field [page]** textbox:

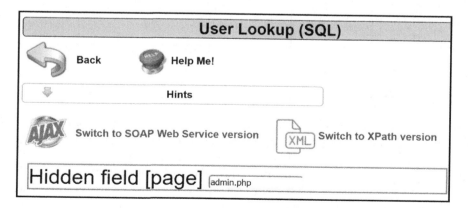

5. Hit the *Enter* key after making the change. You should now see a new page loaded showing **PHP Server Configuration** information:

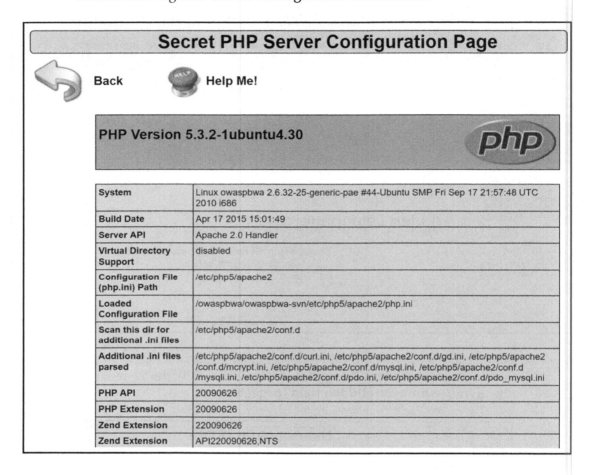

How it works...

As seen in this recipe, there isn't anything hidden about hidden form fields. As penetration testers, we should examine and manipulate these values, to determine whether sensitive information is, inadvertently, exposed or whether we can change the behavior of the application from what is expected, based on our role and authentication status. In the case of this recipe, we were not even logged into the application. We manipulated the hidden form field labeled **page** to access a page containing fingerprinting information. Access to such information should be protected from unauthenticated users.

Testing for Cross-Site Request Forgery

Cross-Site Request Forgery (CSRF) is an attack that rides on an authenticated user's session to allow an attacker to force the user to execute unwanted actions on the attacker's behalf. The initial lure for this attack can be a phishing email or a malicious link executing through a cross-site scripting vulnerability found on the victim's website. CSRF exploitation may lead to a data breach or even a full compromise of the web application.

Getting ready

Using the OWASP Mutillidae II application registration form, determine whether a CSRF attack is possible within the same browser (a different tab) while an authenticated user is logged into the application.

How to do it...

To level set this recipe, let's first baseline the current number of records in the account table and perform SQL Injection to see this:

1. Navigate to the **User Info** page: **OWASP 2013 | A1 – Injection (SQL) | SQLi – Extract Data | User Info (SQL)**.

2. At the username prompt, type in a SQL Injection payload to dump the entire account table contents. The payload is `'` `or 1=1--` <space> (tick or 1 equals 1 dash dash space). Then press the **View Account Details** button.

3. Remember to include the space after the two dashes, since this is a MySQL database; otherwise, the payload will not work:

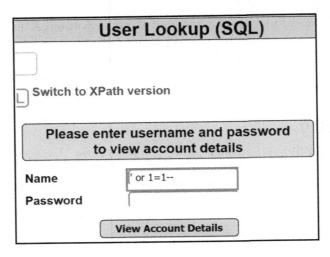

4. When performed correctly, a message displays that there are 24 records found in the database for users. The data shown following the message reveals the usernames, passwords, and signature strings of all 24 accounts. Only two account details are shown here as a sample:

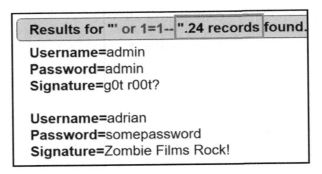

We confirmed 24 records currently exist in the accounts table of the database.

5. Now, return to the login screen (click **Login/Register** from the top menu) and select the link **Please register here**.

6. After clicking the **Please register here** link, you are presented with a registration form.

7. Fill out the form to create a tester account. Type in the **Username** as *tester*, the **Password** as *tester*, and the **Signature** as This is a tester account:

Username	tester	
Password	••••••	Password Generator
Confirm Password	••••••	
Signature	This is a tester account	

8. After clicking the **Create Account** button, you should receive a green banner confirming the account was created:

> **Account created for tester. 1 rows inserted.**

9. Return to the **User Info** page: OWASP 2013| **A1 – Injection (SQL)** | **SQLi – Extract Data** | **User Info (SQL)**.

10. Perform the SQL Injection attack again and verify that you can now see 25 rows in the account table, instead of the previous count of 24:

> **Results for "' or 1=1-- ".25 records found.**

11. Switch to Burp's Proxy **HTTP history** tab and view the POST request that created the account for the tester.

12. Studying this POST request shows the POST action (register.php) and the body data required to perform the action, in this case, username, password, confirm_password, and my_signature. Also notice there is no CSRF-token used. CSRF-tokens are placed within web forms to protect against the very attack we are about to perform. Let's proceed.

13. Right-click the POST request and click on **Send to Repeater:**

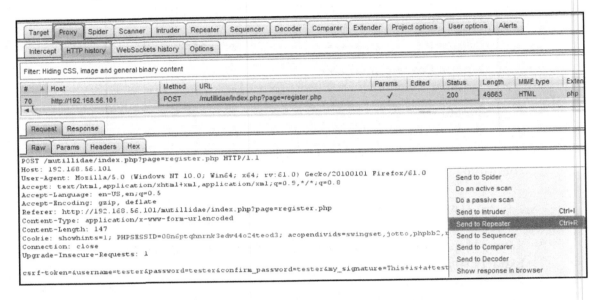

14. If you're using Burp Professional, right-click select **Engagement tools | Generate CSRF PoC:**

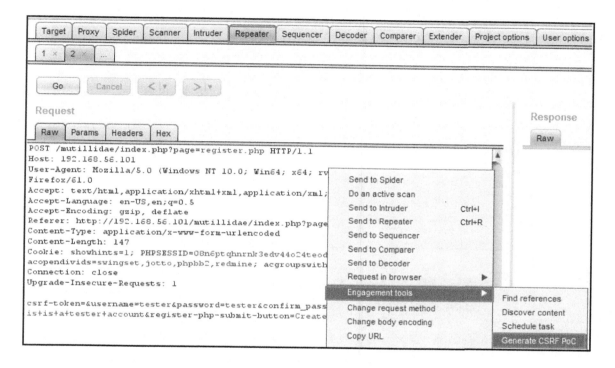

15. Upon clicking this feature, a pop-up box generates the same form used on the registration page but without any CSRF token protection:

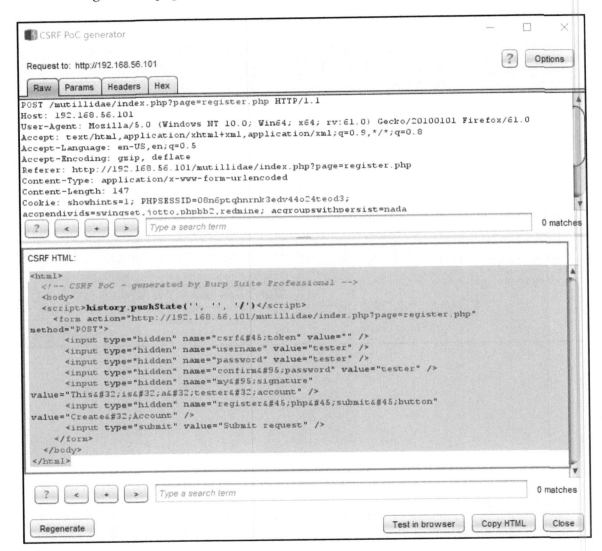

16. If you are using Burp Community, you can easily recreate the **CSRF PoC** form by viewing the source code of the registration page:

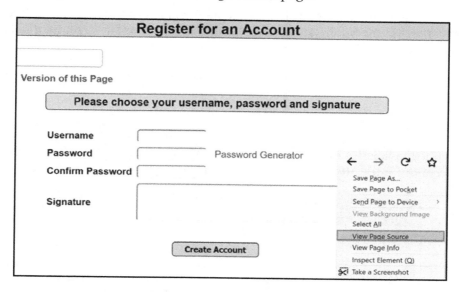

17. While viewing the page source, scroll down to the `<form>` tag section. For brevity, the form is recreated next. Insert `attacker` as a value for the username, password, and the signature. Copy the following HTML code and save it in a file entitled `csrf.html`:

```
<html>
  <body>
  <script>history.pushState('', '', '/')</script>
    <form
action="http://192.168.56.101/mutillidae/index.php?page=register.ph
p" method="POST">
      <input type="hidden" name="csrf-token" value="" />
      <input type="hidden" name="username" value="attacker" />
      <input type="hidden" name="password" value="attacker" />
      <input type="hidden" name="confirm_password" value="attacker"
/>      <input type="hidden" name="my_signature" value="attacker
account" />
      <input type="hidden" name="register-php-submit-button"
value="Create Account" />
      <input type="submit" value="Submit request" />
    </form>
  </body>
</html>
```

18. Now, return to the login screen (click **Login/Register** from the top menu), and log in to the application, using the username `ed` and the password `pentest`.

19. Open the location on your machine where you saved the `csrf.html` file. Drag the file into the browser where ed is authenticated. After you drag the file to this browser, `csrf.html` will appear as a separate tab in the same browser:

20. For demonstration purposes, there is a **Submit request** button. However, in the wild, a JavaScript function would automatically execute the action of creating an account for the attacker. Click the **Submit request** button:

You should receive a confirmation that the attacker account is created:

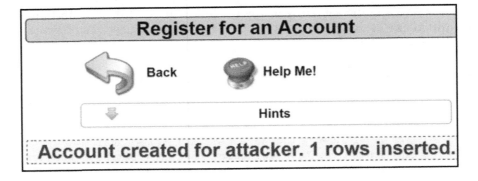

21. Switch to Burp's **Proxy | HTTP history** tab and find the maliciously executed POST used to create the account for the attacker, while riding on the authenticated session of ed's:

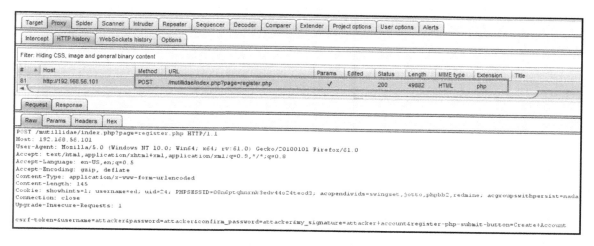

22. Return to the **User Info** page: **OWASP 2013 | A1 – Injection (SQL) | SQLi – Extract Data | User Info (SQL),** and perform the SQL Injection attack again. You will now see 26 rows in the account table instead of the previous count of 25:

> **Results for "' or 1=1-- ".26 records found.**

How it works...

CSRF attacks require an authenticated user session to surreptitiously perform actions within the application on behalf of the attacker. In this case, an attacker rides on ed's session to re-run the registration form, to create an account for the attacker. If ed had been an admin, this could have allowed the account role to be elevated as well.

Assessing Business Logic

In this chapter, we will cover the following recipes:

- Testing business logic data validation
- Unrestricted file upload – bypassing weak validation
- Performing process-timing attacks
- Testing for the circumvention of workflows
- Uploading malicious files – polyglots

Introduction

This chapter covers the basics of **business logic testing**, including an explanation of some of the more common tests performed in this area. Web penetration testing involves key assessments of business logic to determine how well the design of an application performs integrity checks, especially within sequential application function steps, and we will be learning how to use Burp to perform such tests.

Software tool requirements

To complete the recipes in this chapter, you will need the following:

- OWASP Broken Web Applications (VM)
- OWASP Mutillidae link
- Burp Proxy Community or Professional (https://portswigger.net/burp/)

Testing business logic data validation

Business logic data validation errors occur due to a lack of server-side checks, especially in a sequence of events such as shopping cart checkouts. If design flaws, such as thread issues, are present, those flaws may allow an attacker to modify or change their shopping cart contents or prices, prior to purchasing them, to lower the price paid.

Getting ready

Using the **OWASP WebGoat** application and Burp, we will exploit a business logic design flaw, to purchase many large ticket items for a very cheap price.

How to do it...

1. Ensure the **owaspbwa** VM is running. Select the **OWASP WebGoat** application from the initial landing page of the VM. The landing page will be configured to an IP address specific to your machine:

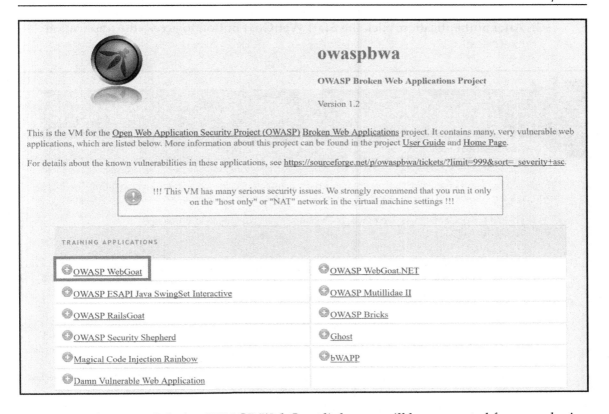

2. After you click the **OWASP WebGoat** link, you will be prompted for some login credentials. Use these credentials: User Name: guest Password: guest.

3. After authentication, click the **Start WebGoat** button to access the application exercises:

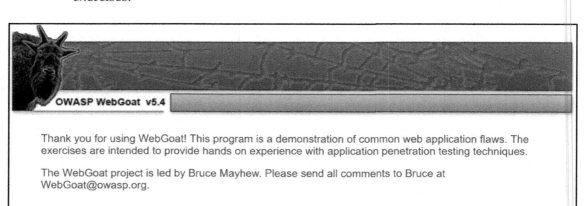

OWASP WebGoat v5.4

Thank you for using WebGoat! This program is a demonstration of common web application flaws. The exercises are intended to provide hands on experience with application penetration testing techniques.

The WebGoat project is led by Bruce Mayhew. Please send all comments to Bruce at WebGoat@owasp.org.

WebGoat Authors
Bruce Mayhew
Jeff Williams

WebGoat Design Team	**V5.4 Lesson Contributers**
David Anderson	Sherif Koussa
Laurence Casey (Graphics)	Yiannis Pavlosoglou
Rogan Dawes	
Bruce Mayhew	

Special Thanks for V5.4	**Documentation Contributers**
Brian Ciomei (Multitude of bug fixes)	Erwin Geirnaert
To all who have sent comments	Aung Khant
	Sherif Koussa

Start WebGoat

4. Click **Concurrency | Shopping Cart Concurrency Flaw** from the left-hand menu:

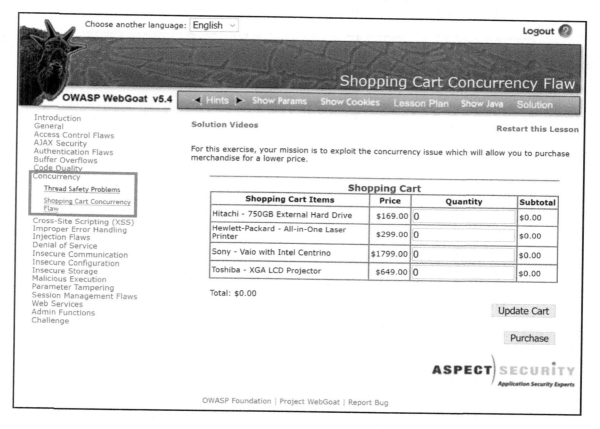

The exercise explains there is a thread issue in the design of the shopping cart that will allow us to purchase items at a lower price. Let's exploit the design flaw!

5. Add 1 to the `Quantity` box for the `Sony - Vaio with Intel Centrino` item. Click the **Update Cart** button:

<table>
<tr><td colspan="4" align="center">**Shopping Cart**</td></tr>
<tr><td>**Shopping Cart Items**</td><td>**Price**</td><td>**Quantity**</td><td>**Subtotal**</td></tr>
<tr><td>Hitachi - 750GB External Hard Drive</td><td>$169.00</td><td>0</td><td>$0.00</td></tr>
<tr><td>Hewlett-Packard - All-in-One Laser Printer</td><td>$299.00</td><td>0</td><td>$0.00</td></tr>
<tr><td>Sony - Vaio with Intel Centrino</td><td>$1799.00</td><td>1</td><td>$0.00</td></tr>
<tr><td>Toshiba - XGA LCD Projector</td><td>$649.00</td><td>0</td><td>$0.00</td></tr>
</table>

Total: $0.00

Update Cart

Purchase

6. Switch to Burp **Proxy | HTTP history** tab. Find the cart request, right-click, and click **Send to Repeater**:

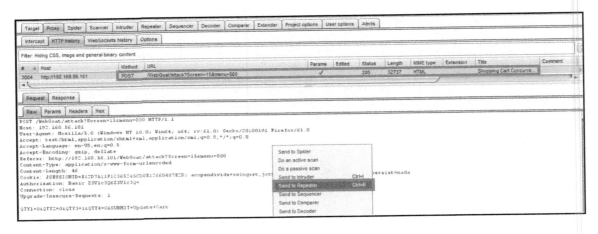

7. Inside Burp's **Repeater** tab, change the QTY3 parameter from 1 to 10:

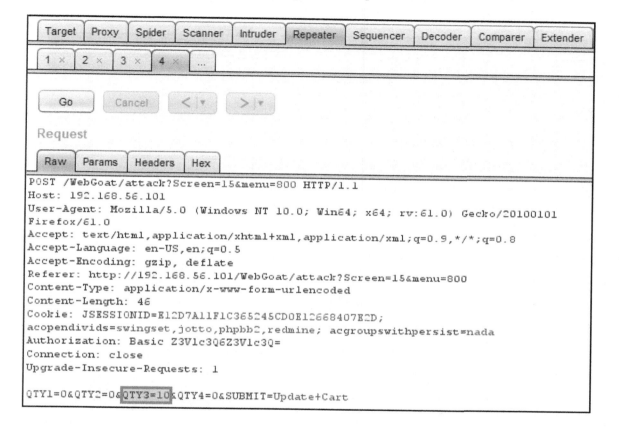

8. Stay in Burp **Repeater**, and in the request pane, right-click and select **Request in browser | In current browser session**:

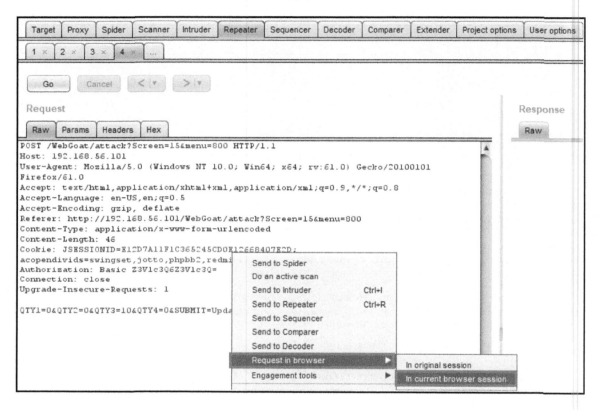

9. A pop-up displays the modified request. Click the **Copy** button:

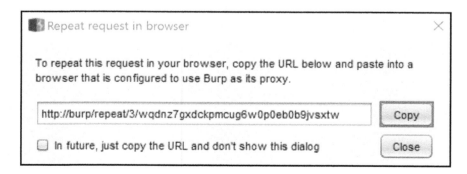

10. Using the same Firefox browser containing the shopping cart, open a new tab and paste in the URL that you copied into the clipboard in the previous step:

11. Press the *Enter* key to see the request resubmitted with a modified quantity of 10:

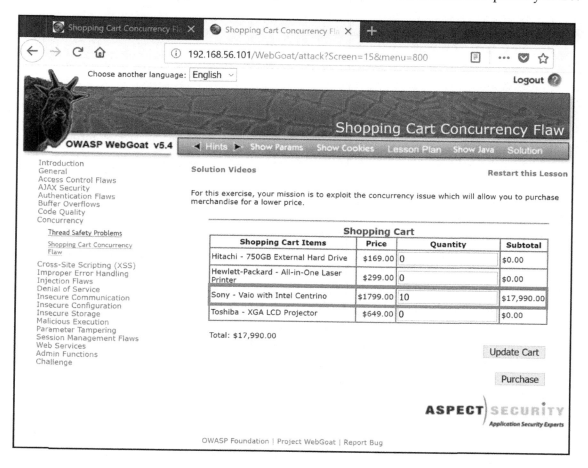

12. Switch to the original tab containing your shopping cart (the cart with the original quantity of 1). Click the **Purchase** button:

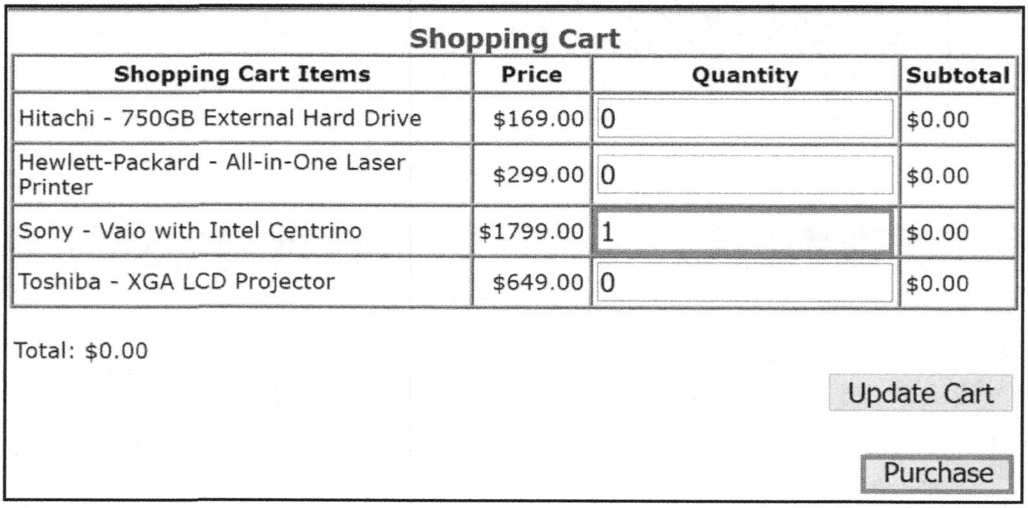

Shopping Cart			
Shopping Cart Items	**Price**	**Quantity**	**Subtotal**
Hitachi - 750GB External Hard Drive	$169.00	0	$0.00
Hewlett-Packard - All-in-One Laser Printer	$299.00	0	$0.00
Sony - Vaio with Intel Centrino	$1799.00	1	$0.00
Toshiba - XGA LCD Projector	$649.00	0	$0.00

Total: $0.00

Update Cart

Purchase

13. At the next screen, before clicking the **Confirm** button, switch to the second tab, and update the cart again, but this time with our new quantity of 10, and click on **Update Cart**:

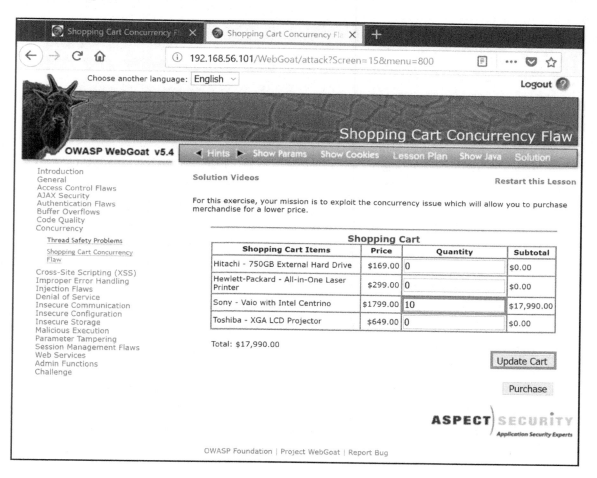

14. Return to the first tab, and click the **Confirm** button:

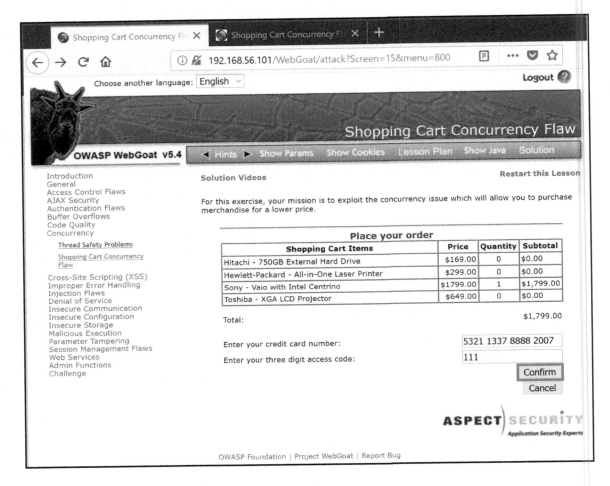

Notice we were able to purchase 10 Sony Vaio laptops for the price of one!

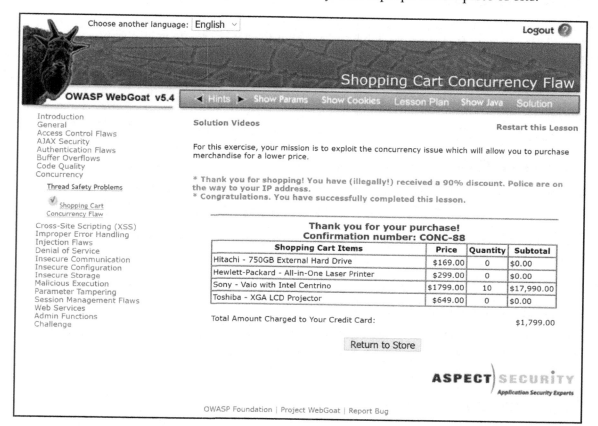

How it works...

Thread-safety issues can produce unintended results. For many languages, the developer's knowledge of how to declare variables and methods as thread-safe is imperative. Threads that are not isolated, such as the cart contents shown in this recipe, can result in users gaining unintended discounts on products.

Unrestricted file upload – bypassing weak validation

Many applications allow for files to be uploaded for various reasons. Business logic on the server-side must include checking for acceptable files; this is known as **whitelisting**. If such checks are weak or only address one aspect of file attributes (for example, file extensions only), attackers can exploit these weaknesses and upload unexpected file types that may be executable on the server.

Getting ready

Using the **Damn Vulnerable Web Application (DVWA)**application and Burp, we will exploit a business logic design flaw in the file upload page.

How to do it...

1. Ensure the owaspbwa VM is running. Select **DVWA** from the initial landing page of the VM. The landing page will be configured to an IP address specific to your machine.

2. At the login page, use these credentials: Username: user; Password: user.

3. Select the **DVWA Security** option from the menu on the left. Change the default setting of **low** to **medium** and then click **Submit**:

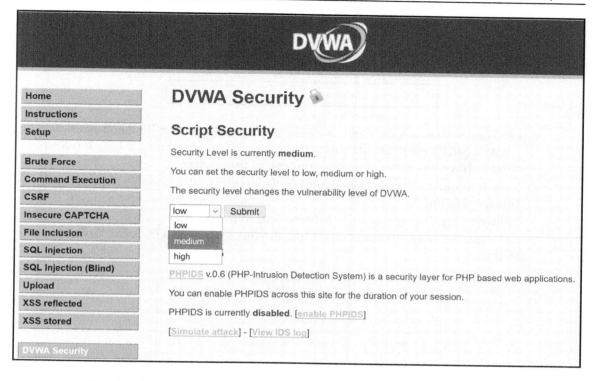

4. Select the **Upload** page from the menu on the left:

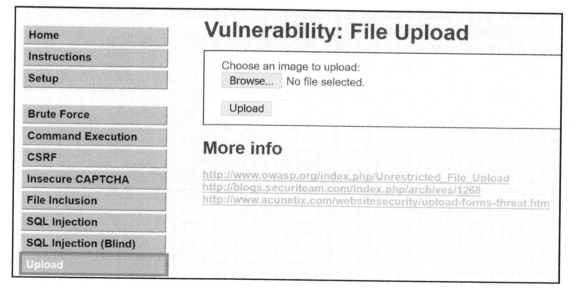

5. Note the page instructs users to only upload images. If we try another type of file other than a JPG image, we receive an error message in the upper left-hand corner:

> Your image was not uploaded.

6. On your local machine, create a file of any type, other than JPG. For example, create a Microsoft Excel file called `malicious_spreadsheet.xlsx`. It does not need to have any content for the purpose of this recipe.

7. Switch to Burp's **Proxy** | **Intercept** tab. Turn Interceptor on with the button **Intercept is on**.

8. Return to Firefox, and use the **Browse** button to find the `malicious_spreadsheet.xlsx` file on your system and click the **Upload** button:

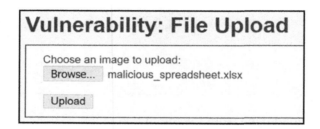

9. With the request paused in Burp's **Proxy** | **Interceptor**, change the **Content-type** from `application/vnd.openxmlformats-officedocument.spreadsheet.sheet` to `image/jpeg` instead.

   - Here is the original:

```
-----------------------------180903101018069
Content-Disposition: form-data; name="MAX_FILE_SIZE"

100000
-----------------------------180903101018069
Content-Disposition: form-data; name="uploaded"; filename="malicious_spreadsheet.xlsx"
Content-Type: application/vnd.openxmlformats-officedocument.spreadsheetml.sheet
```

- Here is the modified version:

```
------------------------------180903101018069
Content-Disposition: form-data; name="MAX_FILE_SIZE"

100000
------------------------------180903101018069
Content-Disposition: form-data; name="uploaded"; filename="malicious_spreadsheet.xlsx"
Content-Type: image/jpeg
```

10. Click the **Forward** button. Now turn Interceptor off by clicking the toggle button to **Intercept is off**.

11. Note the file uploaded successfully! We were able to bypass the weak data validation checks and upload a file other than an image:

How it works...

Due to weak server-side checks, we are able to easily circumvent the image-only restriction and upload a file type of our choice. The application code only checks for content types matching image/jpeg, which is easily modified with an intercepting proxy such as Burp. Developers need to simultaneously whitelist both content-type as well as file extensions in the application code to prevent this type of exploit from occurring.

Performing process-timing attacks

By monitoring the time an application takes to complete a task, it is possible for attackers to gather or infer information about how an application is coded. For example, a login process using valid credentials receives a response quicker than the same login process given invalid credentials. This delay in response time leaks information related to system processes. An attacker could use a response time to perform account enumeration and determine valid usernames based upon the time of the response.

Getting ready

For this recipe, you will need the `common_pass.txt` wordlist from `wfuzz`:

- https://github.com/xmendez/wfuzz
    - **Path:** `wordlists | other | common_pass.txt`

Using OWASP Mutillidae II, we will determine whether the application provides information leakage based on the response time from forced logins.

How to do it...

Ensure Burp is running, and also ensure that the owaspbwa VM is running and that Burp is configured in the Firefox browser used to view owaspbwa applications.

1. From the owaspbwa landing page, click the link to OWASP Mutillidae II application.
2. Open Firefox browser to the home of OWASP Mutillidae II (URL: `http://<your_VM_assigned_IP_address>/mutillidae/`).
3. Go to the login page and log in using the username `ed` and the password `pentest`.
4. Switch to Burp's **Proxy | HTTP history** tab, find the login you just performed, right-click, and select **Send to Intruder**:

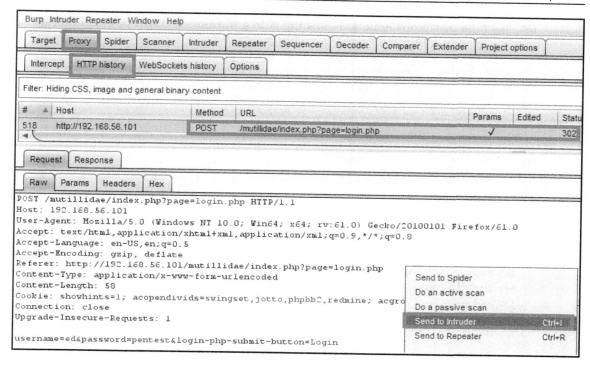

5. Go to the **Intruder** | **Positions** tab, and clear all the payload markers, using the **Clear §** button on the right-hand side:

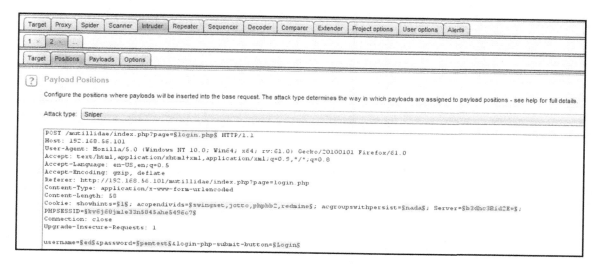

6. Select the password field and click the **Add §** button to wrap a payload marker around that field:

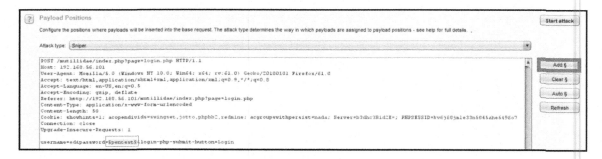

7. Also, remove the PHPSESSID token. Delete the value present in this token (the content following the equals sign) and leave it blank. This step is very important, because if you happen to leave this token in the requests, you will be unable to see the difference in the timings, since the application will think you are already logged in:

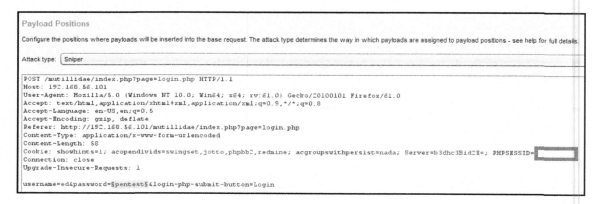

8. Go to the **Intruder** | **Payloads** tab. Within the **Payload Options [Simple list]**, we will add some invalid values by using a `wordlist` from `wfuzz` containing common passwords: `wfuzz` | `wordlists` | `other` | `common_pass.txt`:

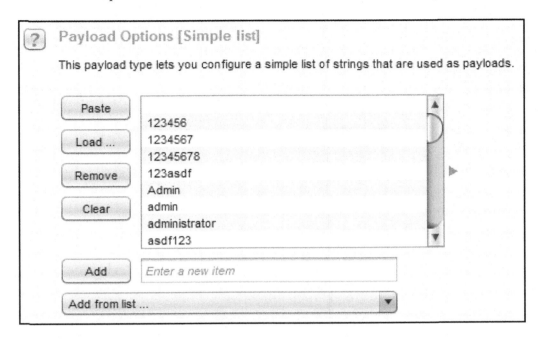

9. Scroll to the bottom and uncheck the checkbox for `Payload Encoding`:

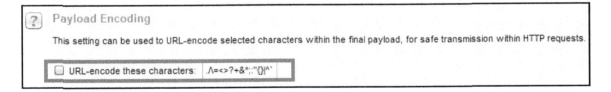

10. Click the **Start attack** button. An attack results table appears. Let the attacks complete. From the attack results table, select **Columns** and check **Response received**. Check **Response completed** to add these columns to the attack results table:

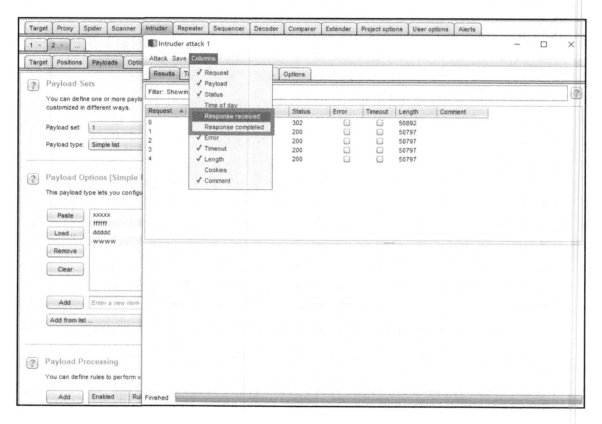

11. Analyze the results provided. Though not obvious on every response, note the delay when an invalid password is used such as `administrator`. The `Response received` timing is `156`, but the `Response completed` timing is `166`. However, the valid password of `pentest` (only `302`) receives an immediate response: `50` (received), and `50` (completed):

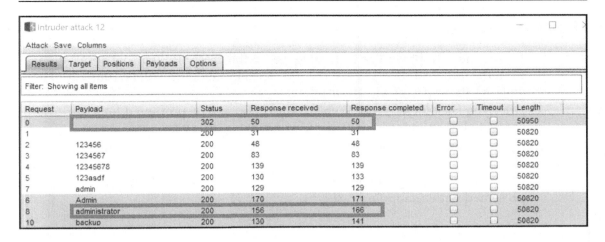

How it works...

Information leakage can occur when processing error messages or invalid coding paths takes longer than valid code paths. Developers must ensure the business logic does not give away such clues to attackers.

Testing for the circumvention of work flows

Shopping cart to payment gateway interactions must be tested by web app penetration testers to ensure the workflow cannot be performed out of sequence. A payment should never be made unless a verification of the cart contents is checked on the server-side first. In the event this check is missing, an attacker can change the price, quantity, or both, prior to the actual purchase.

Getting ready

Using the OWASP WebGoat application and Burp, we will exploit a business logic design flaw in which there is no server-side validation prior to a purchase.

How to do it...

1. Ensure the owaspbwa VM is running. Select the OWASP WebGoat application from the initial landing page of the VM. The landing page will be configured to an IP address specific to your machine.

2. After you click the OWASP WebGoat link, you will be prompted for login credentials. Use these credentials: User Name: `guest`; password: `guest`.

3. After authentication, click the **Start WebGoat** button to access the application exercises.

4. Click **AJAX Security** | **Insecure Client Storage** from the left-hand menu. You are presented with a shopping cart:

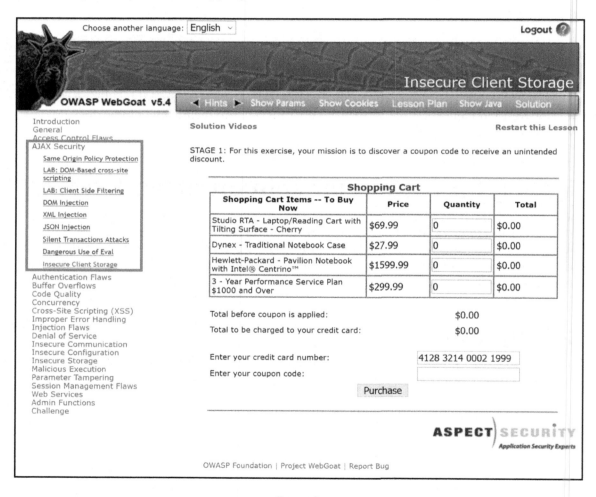

5. Switch to Burp's **Proxy** | **HTTP history** tab, Click the **Filter** button, and ensure your **Filter by MIME type** section includes **Script**. If **Script** is not checked, be sure to check it now:

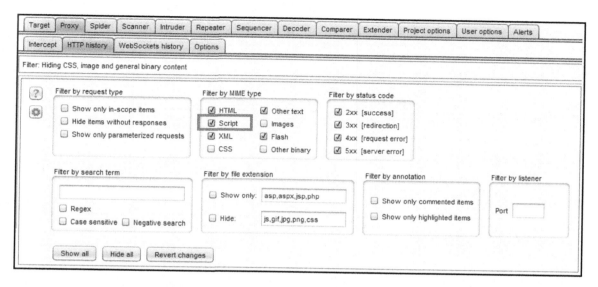

6. Return to the Firefox browser with WebGoat and specify a quantity of 2 for the `Hewlett-Packard - Pavilion Notebook with Intel Centrino` item:

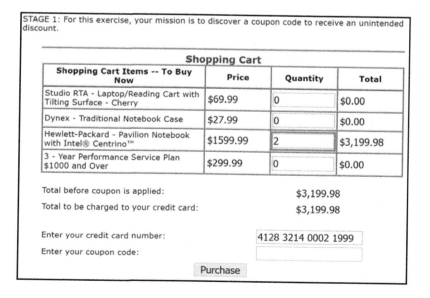

7. Switch back to Burp's **Proxy** | **HTTP history** tab and notice the JavaScript (*.js) files associated with the change you made to the quantity. Note a script called clientSideValiation.js. Make sure the status code is 200 and not 304 (not modified). Only the *200* status code will show you the source code of the script:

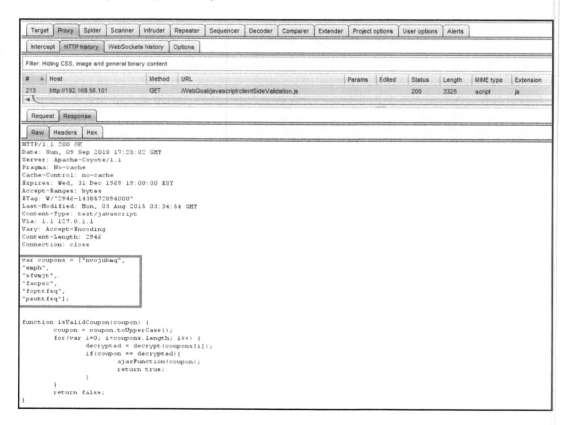

203	http://192.168.56.101	GET	/WebGoat/attack?Screen=119&menu=400	✓	200	34155	HTML		Insecure Client Storage
208	http://192.168.56.101	GET	/WebGoat/javascript/javascript.js		304	229	script	js	
209	http://192.168.56.101	GET	/WebGoat/javascript/menu_system.js		304	230	script	js	
210	http://192.168.56.101	GET	/WebGoat/javascript/toggle.js		304	230	script	js	
211	http://192.168.56.101	GET	/WebGoat/javascript/makeWindow.js		304	229	script	js	
212	http://192.168.56.101	GET	/WebGoat/javascript/lessonNav.js		304	230	script	js	
213	http://192.168.56.101	GET	/WebGoat/javascript/clientSideValidation.js		200	3325	script	js	

8. Select the clientSideValidation.js file and view its source code in the **Response** tab.

9. Note that coupon codes are hard-coded within the JavaScript file. However, used literally as they are, they will not work:

| Target | Proxy | Spider | Scanner | Intruder | Repeater | Sequencer | Decoder | Comparer | Extender | Project options | User options | Alerts |

| Intercept | HTTP history | WebSockets history | Options |

Filter: Hiding CSS, image and general binary content

#	▲ Host	Method	URL	Params	Edited	Status	Length	MIME type	Extension
213	http://192.168.56.101	GET	/WebGoat/javascript/clientSideValidation.js			200	3325	script	js

| Request | Response |

| Raw | Headers | Hex |

```
HTTP/1.1 200 OK
Date: Sun, 09 Sep 2018 17:28:02 GMT
Server: Apache-Coyote/1.1
Pragma: No-cache
Cache-Control: no-cache
Expires: Wed, 31 Dec 1969 19:00:00 EST
Accept-Ranges: bytes
ETag: W/"2946-1438572894000"
Last-Modified: Mon, 03 Aug 2015 03:34:54 GMT
Content-Type: text/javascript
Via: 1.1 127.0.1.1
Vary: Accept-Encoding
Content-Length: 2946
Connection: close

var coupons = ["nvojubmq",
"emph",
"sfwmjt",
"faopsc",
"fopttfsq",
"pxuttfsq"];


function isValidCoupon(coupon) {
        coupon = coupon.toUpperCase();
        for(var i=0; i<coupons.length; i++) {
                decrypted = decrypt(coupons[i]);
                if(coupon == decrypted){
                        ajaxFunction(coupon);
                        return true;
                }
        }
        return false;
}
```

10. Keep looking at the source code and notice there is a `decrypt` function found in the JavaScript file. We can test one of the coupon codes by sending it through this function. Let's try this test back in the Firefox browser:

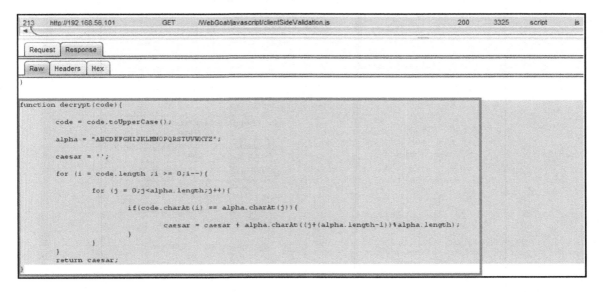

11. In the browser, bring up the developer tools (*F12*) and go to the **Console** tab. Paste into the console (look for the >> prompt) the following command:

```
decrypt('emph');
```

12. You may use this command to call the `decrypt` function on any of the coupon codes declared within the array:

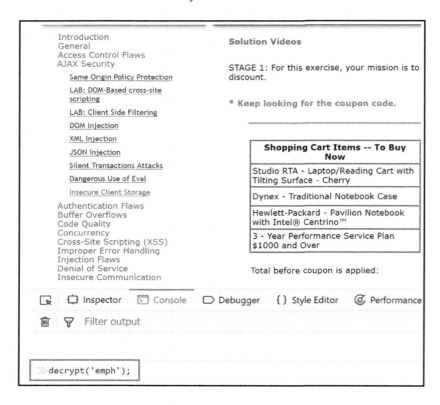

13. After pressing *Enter,* you will see the coupon code is decrypted to the word GOLD:

14. Place the word GOLD within the **Enter your coupon code** box. Notice the amount is now much less. Next, click the **Purchase** button:

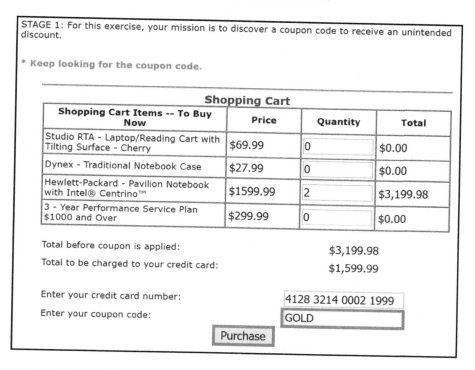

15. We receive confirmation regarding stage 1 completion. Let's now try to get the purchase for free:

16. Switch to Burp's **Proxy | Intercept** tab and turn Interceptor on with the button **Intercept is on**.

17. Return to Firefox and press the **Purchase** button. While the request is paused, modify the $1,599.99 amount to $0.00. Look for the GRANDTOT parameter to help you find the grand total to change:

18. Click the **Forward** button. Now turn Interceptor off by clicking the toggle button to **Intercept is off**.

19. You should receive a success message. Note the total charged is now $0.00:

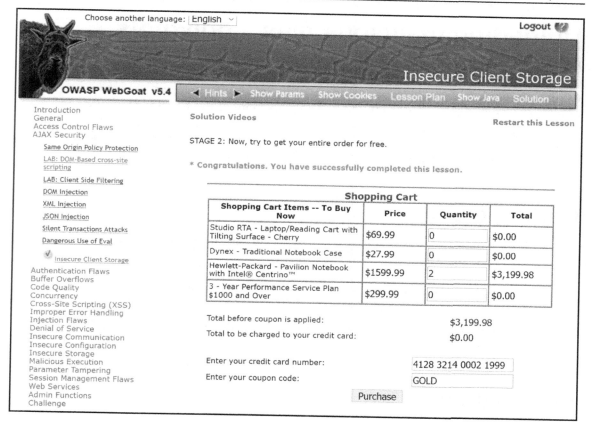

How it works...

Due to a lack of server-side checking for both the coupon code as well as the grand total amount prior to charging the credit card, we are able to circumvent the prices assigned and set our own prices instead.

Uploading malicious files – polyglots

Polyglot is a term defined as something that uses several languages. If we carry this concept into hacking, it means the creation of a **cross-site scripting** (**XSS**) attack vector by using different languages as execution points. For example, attackers can construct valid images and embed JavaScript with them. The placement of the JavaScript payload is usually in the comments section of an image. Once the image is loaded in a browser, the XSS content may execute, depending upon the strictness of the content-type declared by the web server and the interpretation of the content-type by the browser.

Getting ready

- Download a JPG file containing a cross-site scripting vulnerability from the PortSwigger blog page: `https://portswigger.net/blog/bypassing-csp-using-polyglot-jpegs`
    - Here is a direct link to the polyglot image: `http://portswigger-labs.net/polyglot/jpeg/xss.jpg`
- Using the OWASP WebGoat file upload functionality, we will plant an image into the application that contains an XSS payload.

How to do it...

1. Ensure the owaspbwa VM is running. Select the OWASP WebGoat application from the initial landing page of the VM. The landing page will be configured to an IP address specific to your machine.
2. After you click the OWASP WebGoat link, you will be prompted for login credentials. Use these credentials: username: `guest`; password: `guest`.
3. After authentication, click the **Start WebGoat** button to access the application exercises.

4. Click **Malicious Execution | Malicious File Execution** from the left-hand menu. You are presented with a file upload functionality page. The instructions state that only images are allowed for upload:

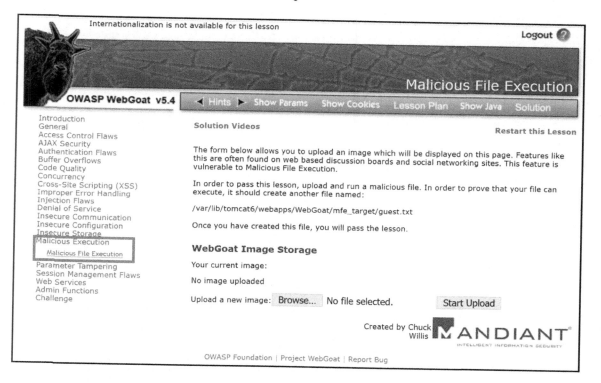

5. Browse to the location where you saved the `xss.jpg` image that you downloaded from the PortSwigger blog page mentioned at the beginning of this recipe.

6. The following screenshot how the image looks. As you can see, it is difficult to detect any XSS vulnerability contained within the image. It is hidden from plain view.

7. Click the **Browse** button to select the `xss.jpg` file:

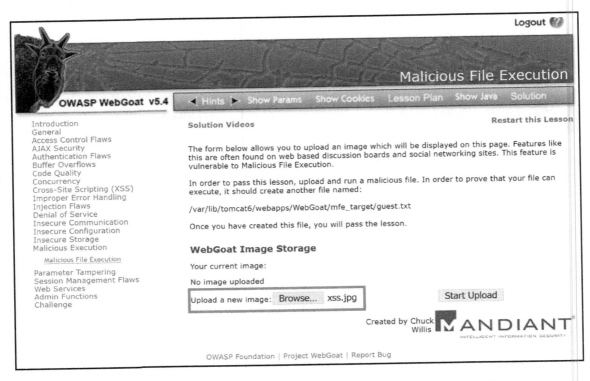

8. Switch to Burp's **Proxy | Options**. Make sure you are capturing **Client responses** and have the following settings enabled. This will allow us to capture HTTP responses modified or intercepted:

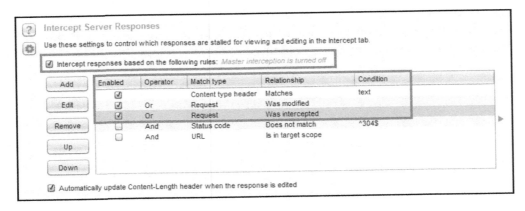

9. Switch to Burp's **Proxy | Intercept** tab. Turn Interceptor on with the button **Intercept is on**.

10. Return to the Firefox browser, and click the **Start Upload** button. The message should be paused within Burp's Interceptor.

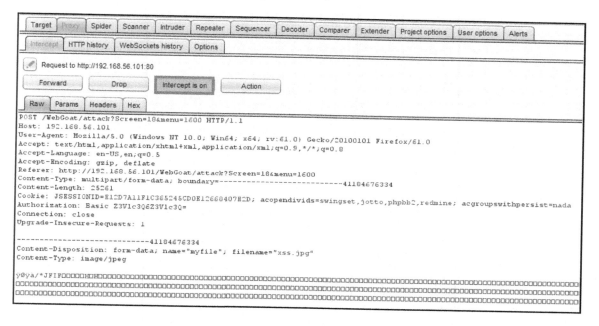

11. Within the **Intercept** window while the request is paused, type `Burp rocks` into the search box at the bottom. You should see a match in the middle of the image. This is our polyglot payload. It is an image, but it contains a hidden XSS script within the comments of the image:

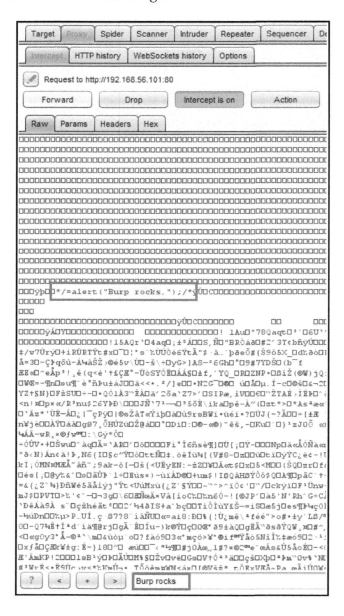

12. Click the **Forward** button. Now turn Interceptor off by clicking the toggle button to **Intercept is off**.

13. Using Notepad or your favorite text editor, create a new file called `poly.jsp`, and write the following code within the file:

```
<HTML>

<% java.io.File file = new
java.io.File("/var/lib/tomcat6/webapps/WebGoat/mfe_target/guest.txt");

  file.createNewFile();%>

</HTML>
```

14. Return to the **Malicious File Execution** page, and browse to the `poly.jsp` file you created, and then click the **Start Upload** button. The `poly.jsp` is a Java Server Pages file that is executable on this web server. Following the instructions, we must create a `guest.txt` file in the path provided. This code creates that file in JSP scriptlet tag code:

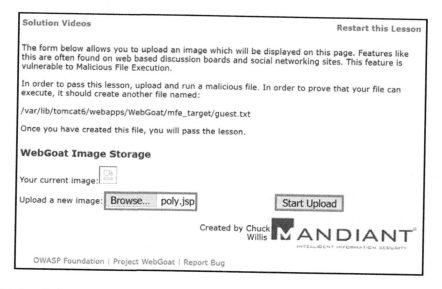

15. Right-click the unrecognized image, and select **Copy Image Location**.

16. Open a new tab within the same Firefox browser as WebGoat, and paste the image location in the new tab. Press *Enter* to execute the script, and give the script a few seconds to run in the background before moving to the next step.

17. Flip back to the first tab, *F5*, to refresh the page, and you should receive the successfully completed message. If your script is running slowly, try uploading the `poly.jsp` on the upload page again. The success message should appear:

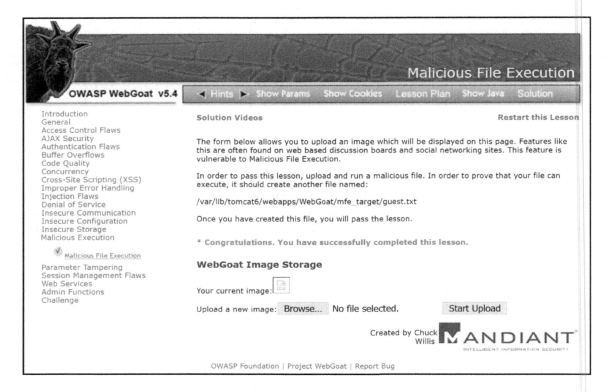

How it works...

Due to unrestricted file upload vulnerability, we can upload a malicious file such as a polyglot without detection from the web server. Many sites allow images to be uploaded, so developers must ensure such images do not carry XSS payloads within them. Protection in this area can be in the form of magic number checks or special proxy servers screening all uploads.

There's more...

To read more about polyglots, please refer to the Portswigger blog: `https://portswigger.net/blog/bypassing-csp-using-polyglot-jpegs`.

8
Evaluating Input Validation Checks

In this chapter, we will cover the following recipes:

- Testing for reflected cross-site scripting
- Testing for stored cross-site scripting
- Testing for HTTP verb tampering
- Testing for HTTP Parameter Pollution
- Testing for SQL injection
- Testing for command injection

Introduction

Failure to validate any input received from the client before using it in the application code is one of the most common security vulnerabilities found in web applications. This flaw is the source for major security issues, such as SQL injection and **cross-site scripting** (**XSS**). Web-penetration testers must evaluate and determine whether any input is reflected back or executed upon by the application. We'll learn how to use Burp to perform such tests.

Software tool requirements

In order to complete the recipes in this chapter, you will need the following:

- OWASP Broken Web Applications (VM)
- OWASP Mutillidae link
- Burp Proxy Community or Professional (`https://portswigger.net/burp/`)

Testing for reflected cross-site scripting

Reflected cross-site scripting occurs when malicious JavaScript is injected into an input field, parameter, or header and, after returning from the web server, is executed within the browser. Reflected XSS occurs when the execution of the JavaScript reflects in the browser only and is not a permanent part of the web page. Penetration testers need to test all client values sent to the web server to determine whether XSS is possible.

Getting ready

Using OWASP Mutillidae II, let's determine whether the application protects against reflected **cross-site scripting (XSS)**.

How to do it...

1. From the OWASP Mutilliae II menu, select **Login** by navigating to **OWASP 2013 | A3 - Cross Site Scripting (XSS) | Reflected (First Order) | Pen Test Tool Lookup**:

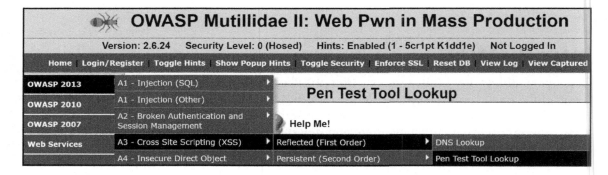

2. Select a tool from the drop-down listing and click the **Lookup Tool** button. Any value from the drop-down list will work for this recipe:

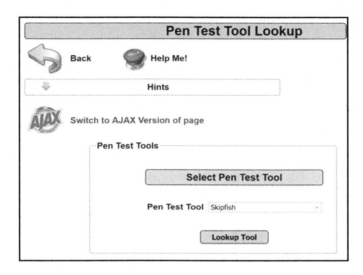

3. Switch to Burp **Proxy** | **HTTP history** and find the HTTP message you just created by selecting the lookup tool. Note that in the request is a parameter called ToolID. In the following example, the value is 16:

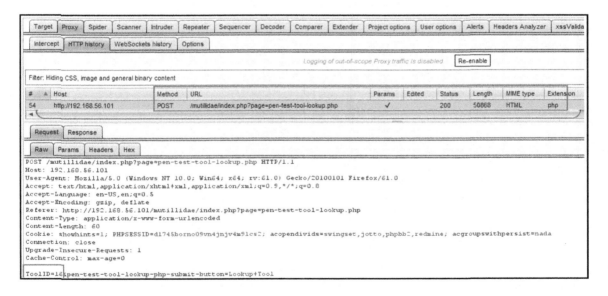

4. Flip over to the **Response** tab and note the JSON returned from the request. You can find the JavaScript function in the response more easily by typing `PenTest` in the search box at the bottom. Note that the `tool_id` is reflected in a response parameter called `toolIDRequested`. This may be an attack vector for XSS:

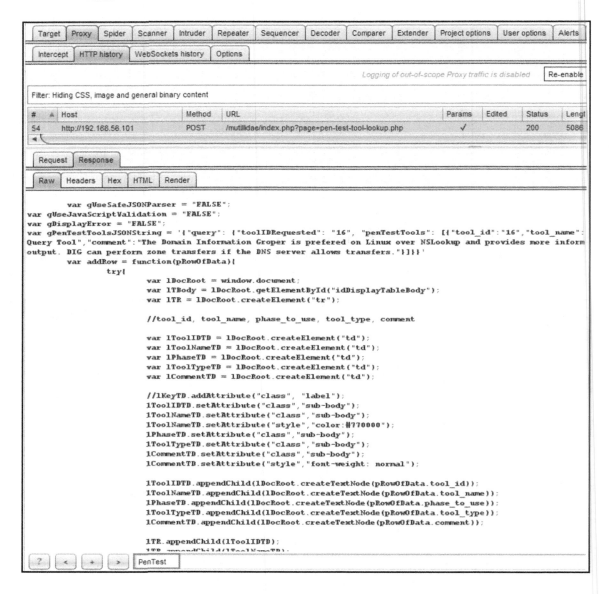

5. Send the request over to **Repeater**. Add an XSS payload within the `ToolID` parameter immediately following the number. Use a simple payload such as `<script>alert(1);</script>`:

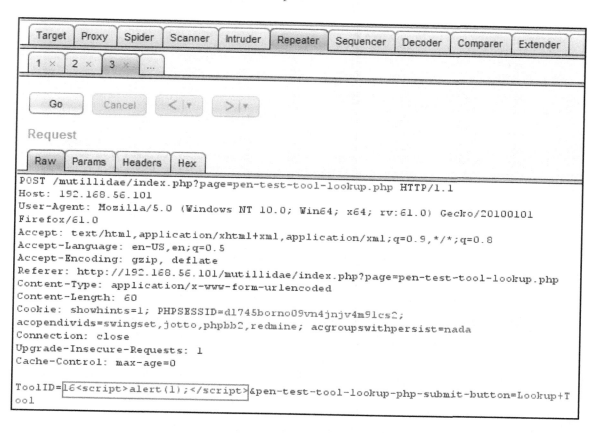

6. Click **Go** and examine the returned JSON response, searching for `PenTest`. Notice our payload is returned exactly as inputted. It looks like the developer is not sanitizing any of the input data before using it. Let's exploit the flaw:

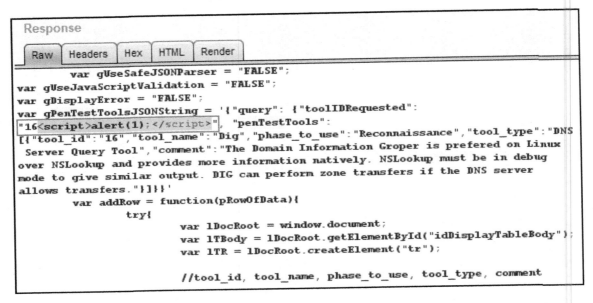

7. Since we are working with JSON instead of HTML, we will need to adjust the payload to match the structure of the JSON returned. We will fool the JSON into thinking the payload is legitimate. We will modify the original `<script>alert(1);</script>` payload to `"}} )%3balert(1)%3b//` instead.

8. Switch to the Burp **Proxy** | **Intercept** tab. Turn Interceptor on with the button **Intercept is on**.

9. Return to Firefox, select another tool from the drop-down list, and click the **Lookup Tool** button.

10. While **Proxy | Interceptor** has the request paused, insert the new payload of `"}})%3balert(1)%3b//` immediately after the `Tool ID` number:

```
POST /mutillidae/index.php?page=pen-test-tool-lookup.php HTTP/1.1
Host: 192.168.56.101
User-Agent: Mozilla/5.0 (Windows NT 10.0; Win64; x64; rv:61.0) Gecko/20100101 Firefox/61.0
Accept: text/html,application/xhtml+xml,application/xml;q=0.9,*/*;q=0.8
Accept-Language: en-US,en;q=0.5
Accept-Encoding: gzip, deflate
Referer: http://192.168.56.101/mutillidae/index.php?page=pen-test-tool-lookup.php
Content-Type: application/x-www-form-urlencoded
Content-Length: 60
Cookie: showhints=1; PHPSESSID=d1745borno09vn4jnjv4m9lcs2; acopendivids=swingset,jotto,phpbb2,redmine; acgroupswithpersist=nada
Connection: close
Upgrade-Insecure-Requests: 1

ToolID=12"}} )%3balert(1)%3b//&pen-test-tool-lookup-php-submit-button=Lookup+Tool
```

11. Click the **Forward** button. Turn Interceptor off by toggling to **Intercept is off**.
12. Return to the Firefox browser and see the pop-up alert box displayed. You've successfully shown a **proof of concept (PoC)** for the reflected XSS vulnerability:

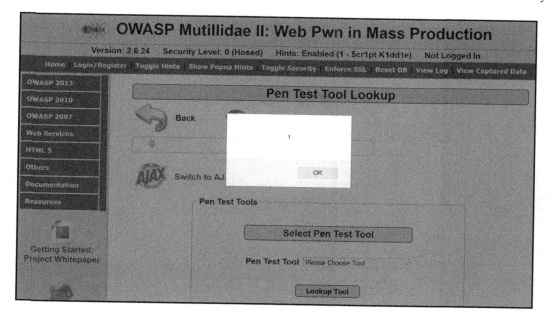

How it works...

Due to inadequate input cleansing prior to using data received from the client. In this case, the penetration testing tools identifier is reflected in the response as it is received from the client, allowing an attack vector for an XSS attack.

Testing for stored cross-site scripting

Stored cross-site scripting occurs when malicious JavaScript is injected into an input field, parameter, or header and, after returning from the web server, is executed within the browser and becomes a permanent part of the page. Stored XSS occurs when the malicious JavaScript is stored in the database and is used later to populate the display of a web page. Penetration testers need to test all client values sent to the web server to determine whether XSS is possible.

Getting ready

Using OWASP Mutillidae II, let's determine whether the application protects against stored cross-site scripting.

How to do it...

1. From the OWASP Mutilliae II menu, select **Login** by navigating to **OWASP 2013 | A3 - Cross Site Scripting (XSS) | Persistent (First Order) | Add to your blog**:

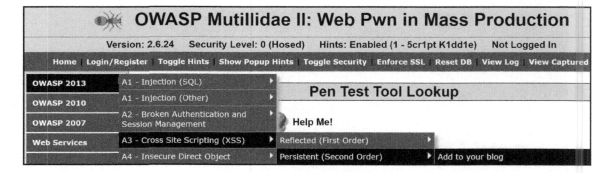

2. Place some verbiage into the text area. Before clicking the **Save Blog Entry** button, let's try a payload with the entry:

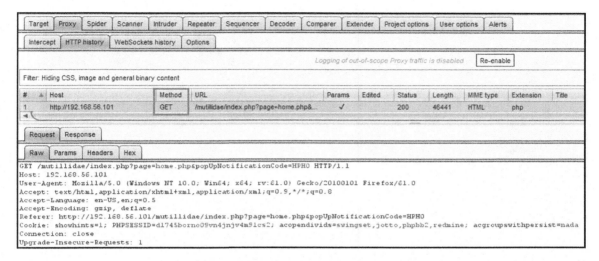

3. Switch to the Burp **Proxy | Intercept** tab. Turn Interceptor on with the button **Intercept is on**.

4. While **Proxy | Interceptor** has the request paused, insert the new payload of `<script>alert(1);</script>` immediately following the verbiage you added to the blog:

5. Click the **Forward** button. Turn Interceptor off by toggling to **Intercept is off**.

6. Return to the Firefox browser and see the pop-up alert box displayed:

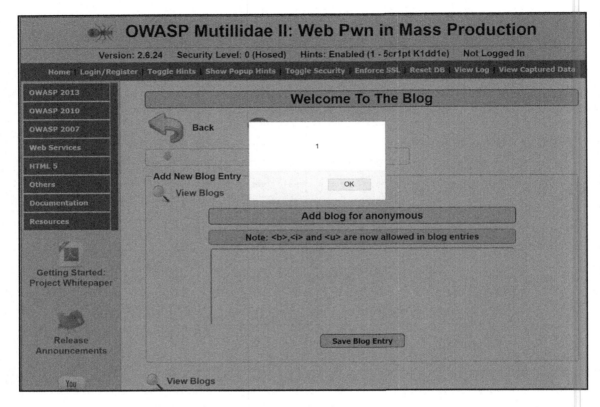

7. Click the **OK** button to close the pop-ups. Reload the page and you will see the alert pop-up again. This is because your malicious script has become a permanent part of the page. You've successfully shown a **proof of concept (PoC)** for the stored XSS vulnerability!

How it works...

Stored or persistent XSS occurs because the application not only neglects to sanitize the input but also stores the input within the database. Therefore, when a page is reloaded and populated with database data, the malicious script is executed along with that data.

Testing for HTTP verb tampering

HTTP requests can include methods beyond GET and POST. As a penetration tester, it is important to determine which other HTTP verbs (that is, methods) the web server allows. Support for other verbs may disclose sensitive information (for example, TRACE) or allow for a dangerous invocation of application code (for example, DELETE). Let's see how Burp can help test for HTTP verb tampering.

Getting ready

Using OWASP Mutillidae II, let's determine whether the application allows HTTP verbs beyond GET and POST.

How to do it...

1. Navigate to the homepage of OWASP Mutillidae II.
2. Switch to Burp **Proxy** | **HTTP history** and look for the HTTP request you just created while browsing to the homepage of Mutillidae. Note the method used is GET. Right-click and send the request to **Intruder**:

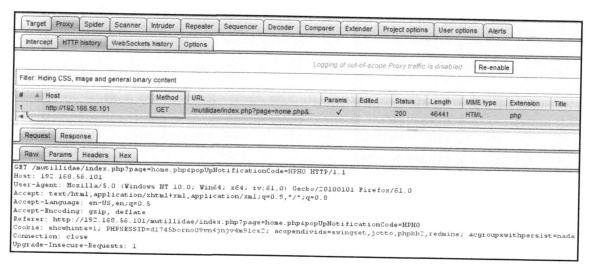

3. In the **Intruder** | **Positions** tab, clear all suggested payload markers. Highlight the GET verb, and click the **Add $** button to place payload markers around the verb:

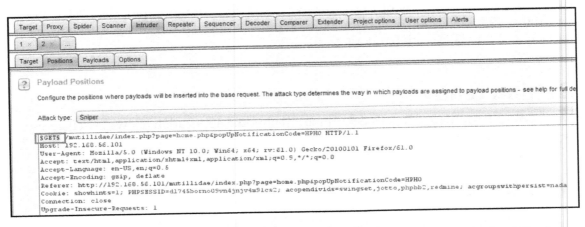

4. In the **Intruder** | **Payloads** tab, add the following values to the **Payload Options [Simple list]** text box:
   - OPTIONS
   - HEAD
   - POST
   - PUT
   - DELETE
   - TRACE
   - TRACK
   - CONNECT
   - PROPFIND
   - PROPPATCH
   - MKCOL
   - COPY

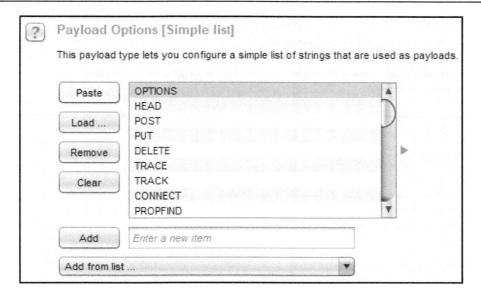

5. Uncheck the **Payload Encoding** box at the bottom of the **Payloads** page and then click the **Start attack** button.

6. When the attack results table appears, and the attack is complete, note all of the verbs returning a status code of **200**. This is worrisome as most web servers should not be supporting so many verbs. In particular, the support for **TRACE** and **TRACK** would be included in the findings and final report as vulnerabilities:

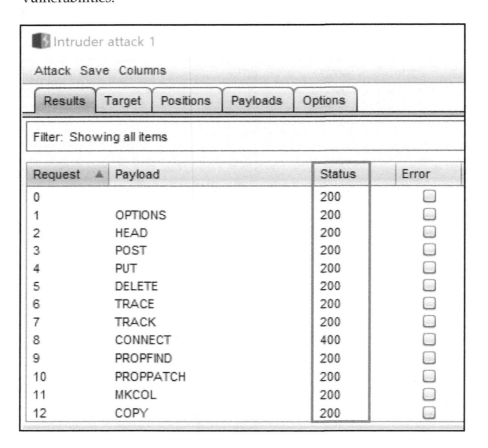

How it works...

Testing for HTTP verb tampering includes sending requests against the application using different HTTP methods and analyzing the response received. Testers need to determine whether a status code of **200** is returned for any of the verbs tested, indicating the web server allows requests of this verb type.

Testing for HTTP Parameter Pollution

HTTP Parameter Pollution (HPP) is an attack in which multiple HTTP parameters are sent to the web server with the same name. The intention is to determine whether the application responds in an unanticipated manner, allowing exploitation. For example, in a GET request, additional parameters can be added to the query string—in this fashion: "`&name=value`"—where name is a duplicate parameter name already known by the application code. Likewise, HPP attacks can be performed on POST requests by duplicating a parameter name in the POST body data.

Getting ready

Using OWASP Mutillidae II, let's determine whether the application allows HPP attacks.

How to do it...

1. From the OWASP Mutilliae II menu, select **Login** by navigating to **OWASP 2013 | A1 - Injection (Other) | HTTP Parameter Pollution | Poll Question**:

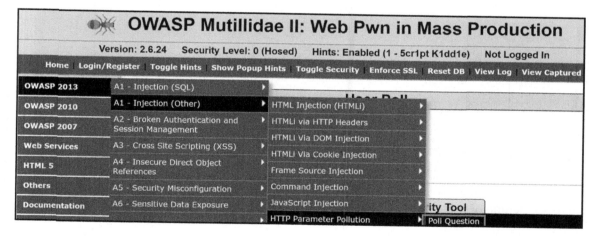

2. Select a tool from one of the radio buttons, add your initials, and click the **Submit Vote** button:

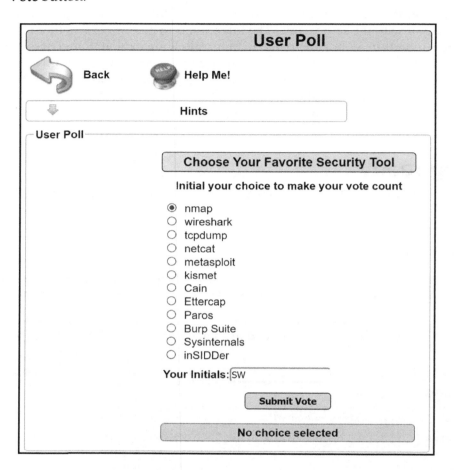

3. Switch to the Burp **Proxy | HTTP history** tab, and find the request you just performed from the **User Poll** page. Note the parameter named `choice`. The value of this parameter is Nmap. Right-click and send this request to **Repeater**:

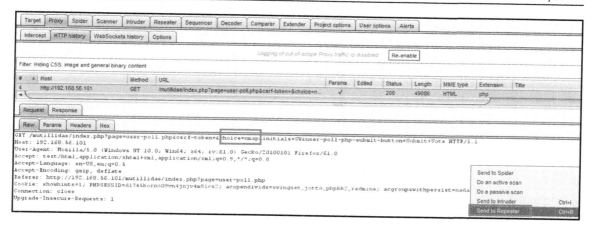

4. Switch to the Burp **Repeater** and add another parameter with the same name to the query string. Let's pick another tool from the **User Poll** list and append it to the query string, for example, "`&choice=tcpdump`". Click **Go** to send the request:

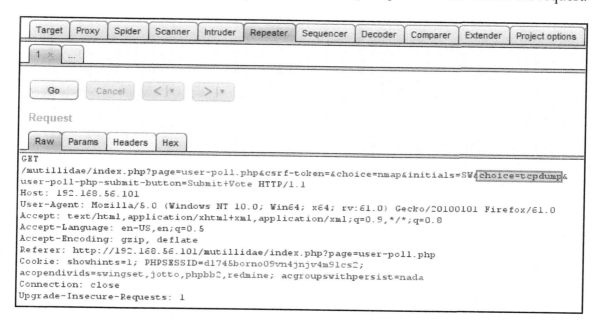

5. Examine the response. Which choice did the application code accept? This is easy to find by searching for the `Your choice was` string. Clearly, the duplicate choice parameter value is the one the application code accepted to count in the **User Poll** vote:

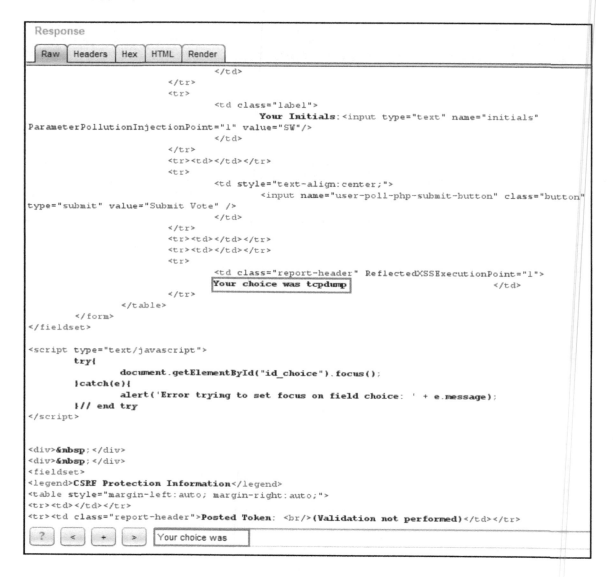

How it works...

The application code fails to check against multiple parameters with the same name when passed into a function. The result is that the application usually acts upon the last parameter match provided. This can result in odd behavior and unexpected results.

Testing for SQL injection

A SQL injection attack involves an attacker providing input to the database, which is received and used without any validation or sanitization. The result is divulging sensitive data, modifying data, or even bypassing authentication mechanisms.

Getting ready

Using the OWASP Mutillidae II **Login** page, let's determine whether the application is vulnerable to **SQL injection (SQLi)** attacks.

How to do it...

1. From the OWASP Mutilliae II menu, select **Login** by navigating to **OWASP 2013 | A1-Injection (SQL) | SQLi – Bypass Authentication | Login**:

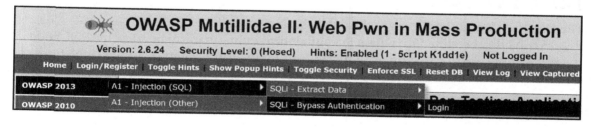

2. At the **Login** screen, place invalid credentials into the username and password text boxes. For example, username is tester and password is tester. Before clicking the **Login** button, let's turn on **Proxy | Interceptor**.
3. Switch to the Burp **Proxy | Intercept** tab. Turn the Interceptor on by toggling to **Intercept is on**.

4. While **Proxy | Interceptor** has the request paused, insert the new payload of '
or 1=1--<space> within the username parameter and click the **Login** button:

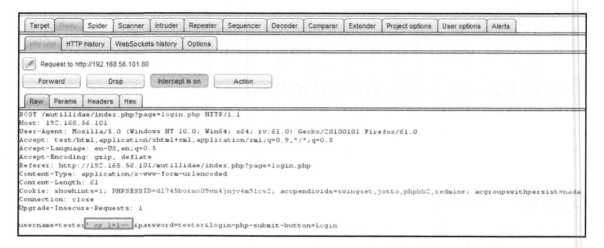

5. Click the **Forward** button. Turn Interceptor off by toggling to **Intercept is off**.
6. Return to the Firefox browser and note you are now logged in as admin!

How it works...

The tester account did not exist in the database; however, the ' or 1=1--
<space> payload resulted in bypass the authentication mechanism because the SQL code
constructed the query based on unsanitized user input. The account of admin is the first
account created in the database, so the database defaulted to that account.

There's more...

We used a SQLi wordlist from wfuzz within Burp **Intruder** to test many different payloads within the same **username** field. Examine the response for each attack in the results table to determine whether the payload successfully performed a SQL injection.

The construction of SQL injection payloads requires some knowledge of the backend database and the particular syntax required.

Testing for command injection

Command injection involves an attacker attempting to invoke a system command, normally performed at a terminal session, within an HTTP request instead. Many web applications allow system commands through the UI for troubleshooting purposes. A web-penetration tester must test whether the web page allows further commands on the system that should normally be restricted.

Getting ready

For this recipe, you will need the SecLists Payload for Unix commands:

- **SecLists-master** | **Fuzzing** | FUZZDB_UnixAttacks.txt
    - Download from GitHub: https://github.com/danielmiessler/ SecLists

Using the OWASP Mutillidae II DNS Lookup page, let's determine whether the application is vulnerable to command injection attacks.

How to do it...

1. From the OWASP Mutilliae II menu, select **DNS Lookup** by navigating to **OWASP 2013 | A1-Injection (Other) | Command Injection | DNS Lookup**:

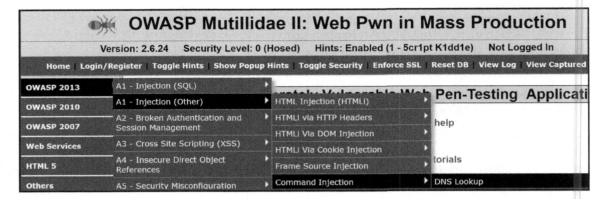

2. On the **DNS Lookup** page, type the IP address 127.0.0.1 in the text box and click the **Lookup DNS** button:

3. Switch to the Burp **Proxy** | **HTTP history** tab and look for the request you just performed. Right-click on **Send to Intruder**:

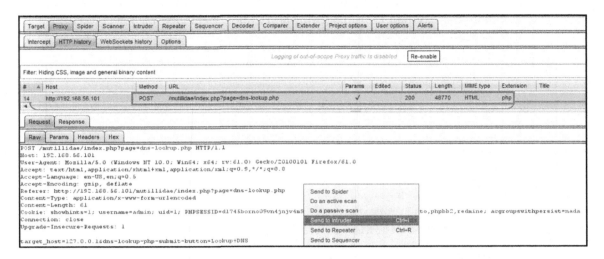

4. In the **Intruder** | **Positions** tab, clear all suggested payload markers with the **Clear $** button. In the `target_host` parameter, place a pipe symbol (|) immediately following the `127.0.0.1` IP address. After the pipe symbol, place an X. Highlight the X and click the **Add $** button to wrap the X with payload markers:

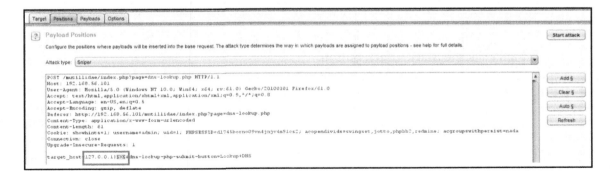

5. In the **Intruder** | **Payloads** tab, click the **Load** button. Browse to the location where you downloaded the **SecLists-master** wordlists from GitHub. Navigate to the location of the FUZZDB_UnixAttacks.txt wordlist and use the following to populate the **Payload Options [Simple list]** box: **SecLists-master** | **Fuzzing** | FUZZDB_UnixAttacks.txt

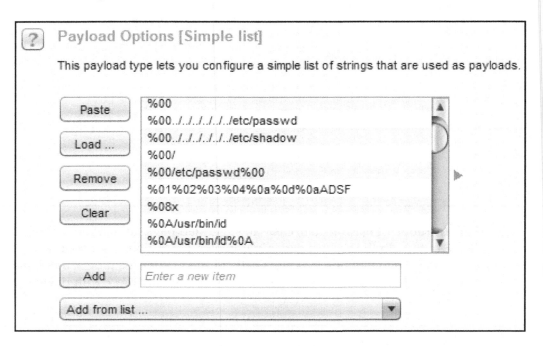

6. Uncheck the **Payload Encoding** box at the bottom of the **Payloads** tab page and then click the **Start Attack** button.
7. Allow the attack to continue until you reach payload 50. Notice the responses through the **Render** tab around payload 45 or so. We are able to perform commands, such as id, on the operating system, which displays the results of the commands on the web page:

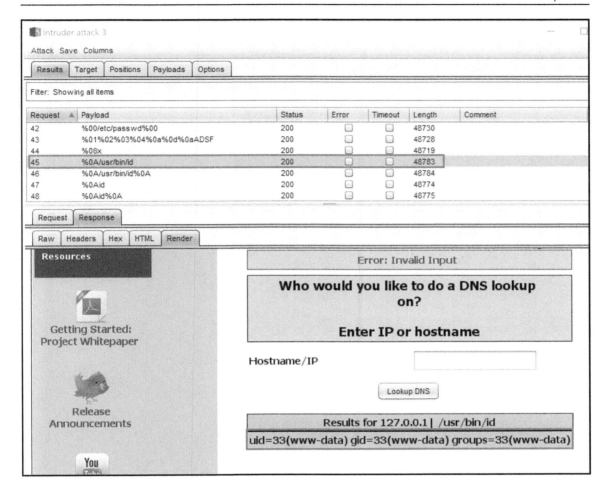

How it works...

Failure to define and validate user input against an acceptable list of system commands can lead to command injection vulnerabilities. In this case, the application code does not confine system commands available through the UI, allowing visibility and execution of commands on the operating system that should be restricted.

Attacking the Client

9

In this chapter, we will cover the following recipes:

- Testing for Clickjacking
- Testing for DOM-based cross-site scripting
- Testing for JavaScript execution
- Testing for HTML injection
- Testing for client-side resource manipulation

Introduction

Code available on the client that is executed in the browser requires testing to determine any presence of sensitive information or the allowance of user input without server-side validation. Learn how to perform these tests using Burp.

Software tool requirements

To complete the recipes in this chapter, you will need the following:

- **OWASP Broken Web Applications (VM)**
- **OWASP Mutillidae link**
- **Burp Proxy Community** or **Professional** (https://portswigger.net/burp/)

Testing for Clickjacking

Clickjacking is also known as the **UI redress attack**. This attack is a deceptive technique that tricks a user into interacting with a transparent iframe and, potentially, send unauthorized commands or sensitive information to an attacker-controlled website. Let's see how to use the Burp Clickbandit to test whether a site is vulnerable to Clickjacking.

Getting ready

Using the OWASP Mutillidae II application and the Burp Clickbandit, let's determine whether the application protects against Clickjacking attacks.

How to do it...

1. Navigate to the **Home** page of the OWASP Mutillidae II.
2. Switch to **Burp,** and from the top-level menu, select **Burp Clickbandit**:

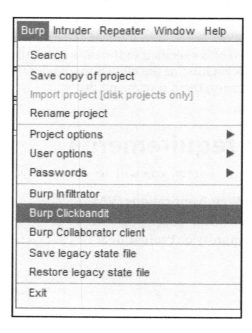

3. A pop-up box explains the tool. Click the button entitled **Copy Clickbandit to clipboard**:

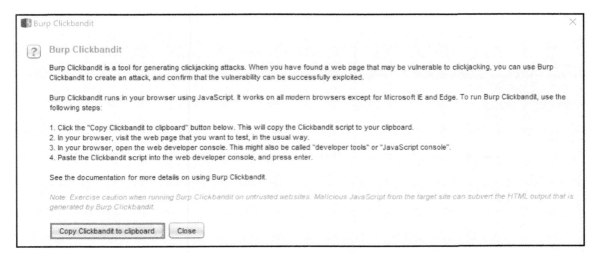

4. Return to the Firefox browser, and press *F12* to bring up the developer tools. From the developer tools menu, select **Console,** and look for the prompt at the bottom:

5. At the **Console** prompt (for example, >>), paste into the prompt the Clickbandit script you copied to your clipboard:

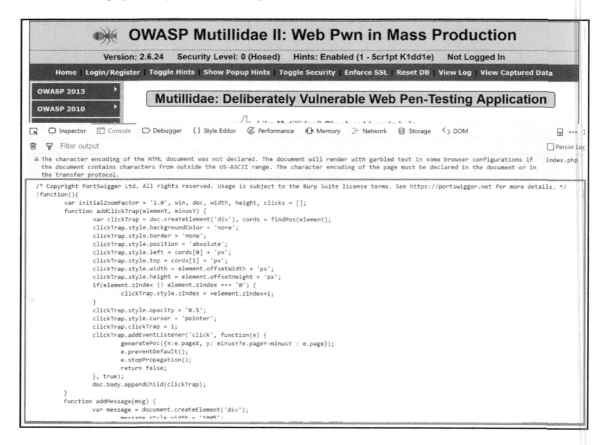

6. After pasting in the script into the prompt, press the *Enter* key. You should see the Burp Clickbandit **Record mode**. Click the **Start** button to begin:

7. Start clicking around on the application after it appears. Click available links at the top Mutillidae menu, click available links on the side menu, or browse to pages within Mutillidae. Once you've clicked around, press the **Finish** button on the Burp Clickbandit menu.

8. You should notice big red blocks appear transparently on top of the Mutillidae web pages. Each red block indicates a place where a malicious iframe can appear. Feel free to click each red block to see the next red block appear, and so on:

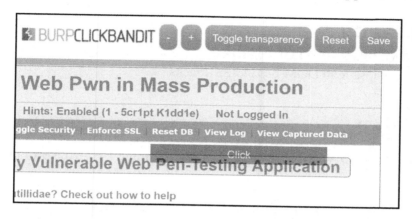

9. Once you wish to stop and save your results, click the **Save** button. This will save the Clickjacking PoC in an HTML file for you to place inside your penetration test report.

How it works...

Since the Mutillidae application does not make use of the X-FRAME-OPTIONS header set to DENY, it is possible to inject a malicious iframe in to the Mutillidae web pages. The Clickbandit increases the level of opaqueness of the iframe for visibility and creates a **proof of concept (PoC)** to illustrate how the vulnerability can be exploited.

Testing for DOM-based cross-site scripting

The **Document Object Model (DOM)** is a tree-like structural representation of all HTML web pages captured in a browser. Developers use the DOM to store information inside the browser for convenience. As a web penetration tester, it is important to determine the presence of DOM-based **cross-site scripting (XSS)** vulnerabilities.

Getting ready

Using OWASP Mutillidae II HTML5 web storage exercise, let's determine whether the application is susceptible to DOM-based XSS attacks.

How to do it...

1. Navigate to **OWASP 2013 | HTML5 Web Storage | HTML5 Storage**:

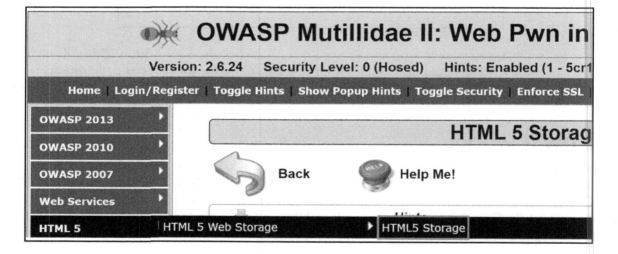

2. Note the name/value pairs stored in the DOM using **HTML5 Web Storage** locations. Web storage includes **Session** and **Local** variables. Developers use these storage locations to conveniently store information inside a user's browser:

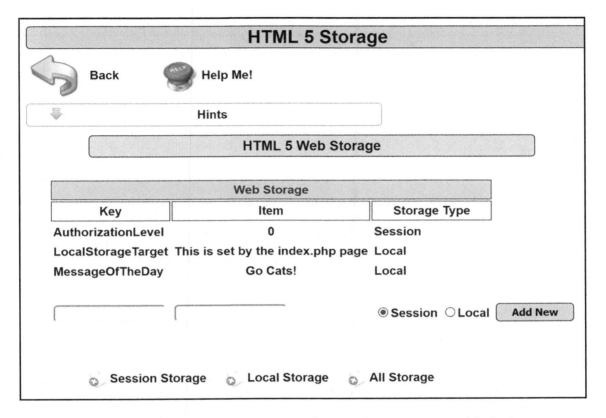

3. Switch to the Burp Proxy **Intercept** tab. Turn Interceptor on with the button **Intercept is on**.
4. Reload the **HTML 5 Web Storage** page in Firefox browser by pressing *F5* or clicking the reload button.

5. Switch to the Burp Proxy **HTTP history** tab. Find the paused request created by the reload you just performed. Note that the `User-Agent` string is highlighted, as shown in the following screenshot:

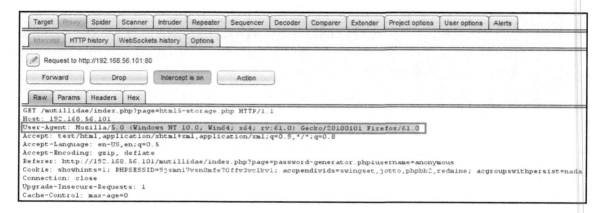

6. Replace the preceding highlighted `User-Agent` with the following script:

```
<script>try{var m = "";var l = window.localStorage; var s =
window.sessionStorage;for(i=0;i<l.length;i++){var lKey = l.key(i);m
+= lKey + "=" + l.getItem(lKey) +
";\n";};for(i=0;i<s.length;i++){var lKey = s.key(i);m += lKey + "="
+ s.getItem(lKey) +
";\n";};alert(m);}catch(e){alert(e.message);}</script>
```

7. Click the **Forward** button. Now, turn Interceptor off by clicking the toggle button to **Intercept is off**.

8. Note the alert popup showing the contents of the DOM storage:

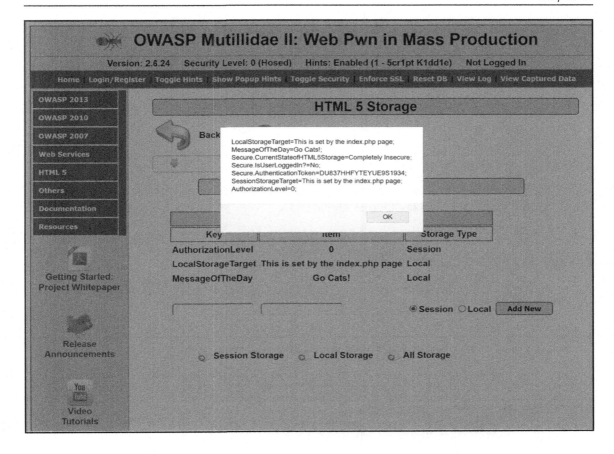

How it works...

The injected script illustrates how the presence of a cross-site scripting vulnerability combined with sensitive information stored in the DOM can allow an attacker to steal sensitive data.

Testing for JavaScript execution

JavaScript injection is a subtype of cross-site scripting attacks specific to the arbitrary injection of JavaScript. Vulnerabilities in this area can affect sensitive information held in the browser, such as user session cookies, or it can lead to the modification of page content, allowing script execution from attacker-controlled sites.

Getting ready

Using the OWASP Mutillidae II **Password Generator** exercise, let's determine whether the application is susceptible to JavaScript XSS attacks.

How to do it...

1. Navigate to **OWASP 2013** | **A1 – Injection (Other)** | **JavaScript Injection** | **Password Generator**:

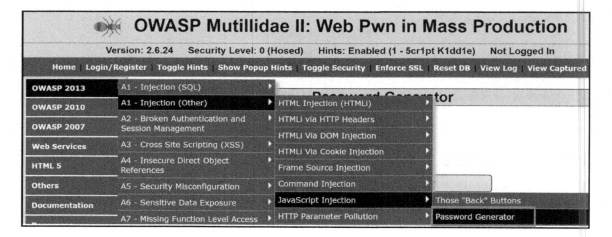

2. Note after clicking the **Generate Password** button, a password is shown. Also, note the username value provided in the URL is reflected back *as is* on the web page:
   `http://192.168.56.101/mutillidae/index.php?page=password-genera`
   `tor.php&username=anonymous`. This means a potential XSS vulnerability may exist on the page:

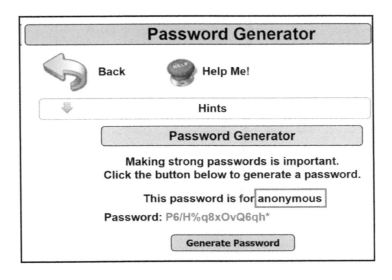

3. Switch to the Burp Proxy **HTTP history** tab and find the HTTP message associated with the **Password Generator** page. Flip to the **Response** tab in the message editor, and perform a search on the string `catch`. Note that the JavaScript returned has a catch block where error messages display to the user. We will use this position for the placement of a carefully crafted JavaScript injection attack:

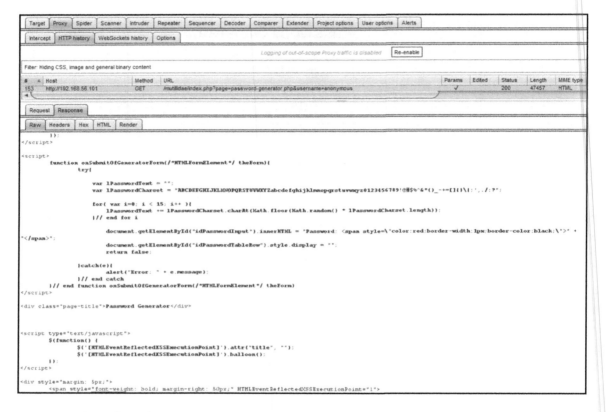

4. Switch to the Burp Proxy **Intercept** tab. Turn Interceptor on with the button **Intercept is on**.
5. Reload the **Password Generator** page in Firefox browser by pressing *F5* or clicking the reload button.
6. Switch to the Burp Proxy **Interceptor** tab. While the request is paused, note the `username` parameter value highlighted as follows:

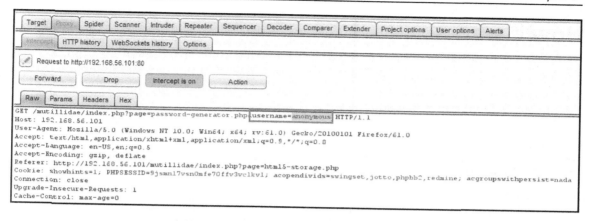

7. Replace the preceding highlighted value of anonymous with the following carefully crafted JavaScript injection script:

```
canary";}catch(e){}alert(1);try{a="
```

8. Click the **Forward** button. Now, turn Interceptor off by clicking the toggle button to **Intercept is off**.

9. Note the alert popup. You've successfully demonstrated the presence of a JavaScript injection XSS vulnerability!

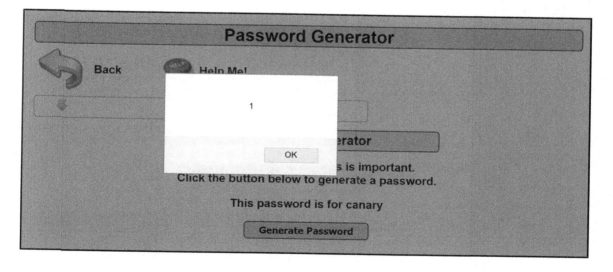

How it works...

The JavaScript snippet injected into the web page matched the structure of the original catch statement. By creating a fake name of *canary* and ending the statement with a semicolon, a specially crafted *new* catch block was created, which contained the malicious JavaScript payload.

Testing for HTML injection

HTML injection is the insertion of arbitrary HTML code into a vulnerable web page. Vulnerabilities in this area may lead to the disclosure of sensitive information or the modification of page content for the purposes of socially engineering the user.

Getting ready

Using the OWASP Mutillidae II **Capture Data Page**, let's determine whether the application is susceptible to HTML injection attacks.

How to do it...

1. Navigate to **OWASP 2013 | A1 – Injection (Other) | HTMLi Via Cookie Injection | Capture Data Page**:

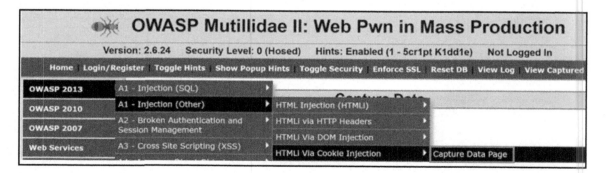

2. Note how the page looks before the attack:

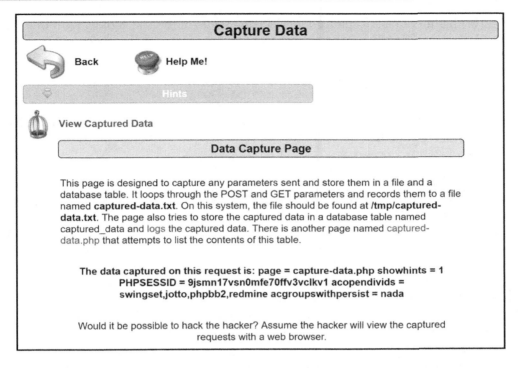

Capture Data

Back   Help Me!

Hints

View Captured Data

Data Capture Page

This page is designed to capture any parameters sent and store them in a file and a database table. It loops through the POST and GET parameters and records them to a file named **captured-data.txt**. On this system, the file should be found at **/tmp/captured-data.txt**. The page also tries to store the captured data in a database table named captured_data and logs the captured data. There is another page named captured-data.php that attempts to list the contents of this table.

The data captured on this request is: page = capture-data.php showhints = 1
PHPSESSID = 9jsmn17vsn0mfe70ffv3vclkv1 acopendivids =
swingset,jotto,phpbb2,redmine acgroupswithpersist = nada

Would it be possible to hack the hacker? Assume the hacker will view the captured
requests with a web browser.

3. Switch to the Burp Proxy **Intercept** tab, and turn Interceptor on with the button **Intercept is on**.

4. While the request is paused, make note of the last cookie, `acgroupswitchpersist=nada`:

5. While the request is paused, replace the value of the last cookie, with this HTML injection script:

```
<h1>Sorry, please login again</h1><br/>Username<input
type="text"><br/>Password<input type="text"><br/><input
type="submit" value="Submit"><h1> </h1>
```

6. Click the **Forward** button. Now turn Interceptor off by clicking the toggle button to **Intercept is off**.
7. Note how the HTML is now included inside the page!

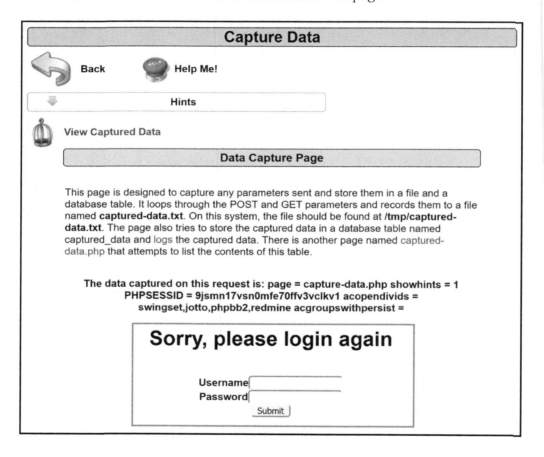

How it works...

Due to the lack of input validation and output encoding, an HTML injection vulnerability can exist. The result of exploiting this vulnerability is the insertion of arbitrary HTML code, which can lead to XSS attacks or social engineering schemes such as the one seen in the preceding recipe.

Testing for client-side resource manipulation

If an application performs actions based on client-side URL information or pathing to a resource (that is, AJAX call, external JavaScript, iframe source), the result can lead to a client-side resource manipulation vulnerability. This vulnerability relates to attacker-controlled URLs in, for example, the JavaScript location attribute, the location header found in an HTTP response, or a POST body parameter, which controls redirection. The impact of this vulnerability could lead to a cross-site scripting attack.

Getting ready

Using the OWASP Mutillidae II application, determine whether it is possible to manipulate any URL parameters that are exposed on the client side and whether the manipulation of those values causes the application to behave differently.

How to do it...

1. Navigate to **OWASP 2013** | **A10 – Unvalidated Redirects and Forwards** | **Credits**:

2. Click the **ISSA Kentuckiana** link available on the **Credits** page:

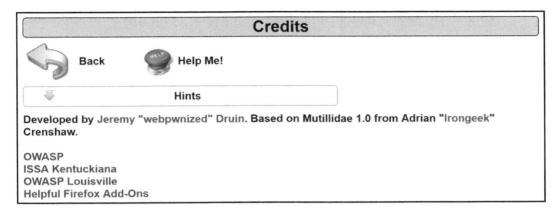

3. Switch to the Burp Proxy **HTTP history** tab, and find your request to the **Credits** page. Note that there are two query string parameters: page and forwardurl. What would happen if we manipulated the URL where the user is sent?

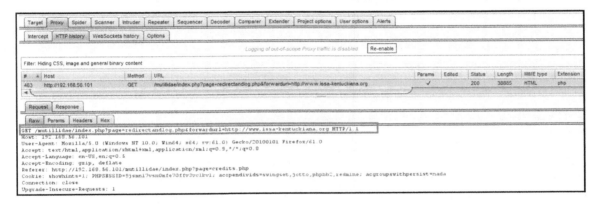

4. Switch to the Burp Proxy **Intercept** tab. Turn Interceptor on with the button **Intercept is on**.

5. While the request is paused, note the current value of the `fowardurl` parameter:

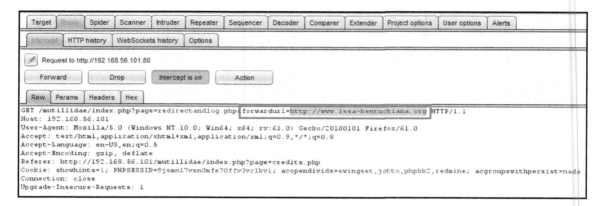

6. Replace the value of the `forwardurl` parameter to be `https://www.owasp.org` instead of the original choice of `http://www.issa-kentuckiana.org`:

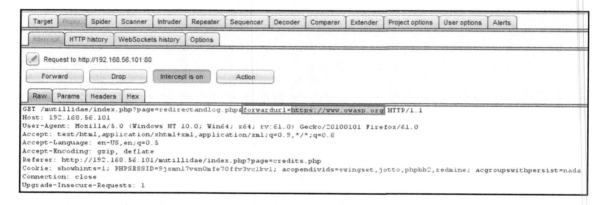

7. Click the **Forward** button. Now turn Interceptor off by clicking the toggle button to **Intercept is off**.

8. Note how we were redirected to a site other than the one originally clicked!

How it works...

Application code decisions, such as where to redirect a user, should never rely on client-side available values. Such values can be tampered with and modified, to redirect users to attacker-controlled websites or to execute attacker-controlled scripts.

Working with Burp Macros and Extensions

10

In this chapter, we will cover the following recipes:

- Creating session-handling macros
- Getting caught in the cookie jar
- Adding great pentester plugins
- Creating new issues via Manual-Scan Issue Extension
- Working with Active Scan++ Extension

Introduction

This chapter covers two separate topics that can also be blended together: macros and extensions. Burp macros enable penetration testers to automate events, such as logins or parameter reads, to overcome potential error situations. Extensions, also known as plugins, extend the core functionality found in Burp.

Software tool requirements

In order to complete the recipes in this chapter, you will need the following:

- OWASP Broken Web Applications (VM)
- OWASP Mutillidae
  (`http://<Your_VM_Assigned_IP_Address>/mutillidae`)
- GetBoo (`http://<Your_VM_Assigned_IP_Address>/getboo`)
- Burp Proxy Community or Professional (`https://portswigger.net/burp/`)

Creating session-handling macros

In Burp, the **Project** options tab allows testers to set up session-handling rules. A session-handling rule allows a tester to specify a set of actions Burp will take in relation to session tokens or CSRF tokens while making HTTP Requests. There is a default session-handling rule in scope for Spider and Scanner. However, in this recipe, we will create a new session-handling rule and use a macro to help us create an authenticated session from an unauthenticated one while using Repeater.

Getting ready

Using the OWASP Mutilliae II application, we will create a new Burp Session-Handling rule, with an associated macro, to create an authenticated session from an unauthenticated one while using Repeater.

How to do it...

1. Navigate to the Login page in Mutillidae. Log into the application as username `ed` with password `pentest`.

2. Immediately log out of the application by clicking the **Logout** button and make sure the application confirms you are logged out.

3. Switch to the Burp Proxy **HTTP history** tab. Look for the logout request you just made along with the subsequent, unauthenticated GET request. Select the unauthenticated request, which is the second GET. Right-click and send that request to Repeater, as follows:

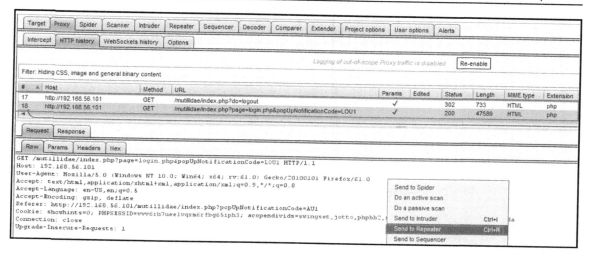

4. Switch to Burp Repeater, then click the **Go** button. On the **Render** tab of the response, ensure you receive the **Not Logged In** message. We will use this scenario to build a session-handling rule to address the unauthenticated session and make it an authenticated one, as follows:

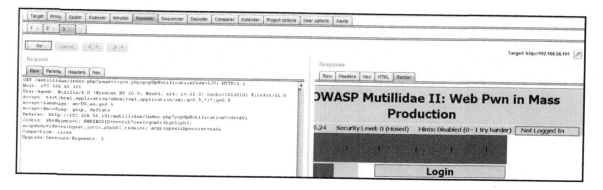

5. Switch to the Burp **Project options** tab, then the **Sessions** tab, and click the **Add** button under the **Session Handling Rules** section, as follows:

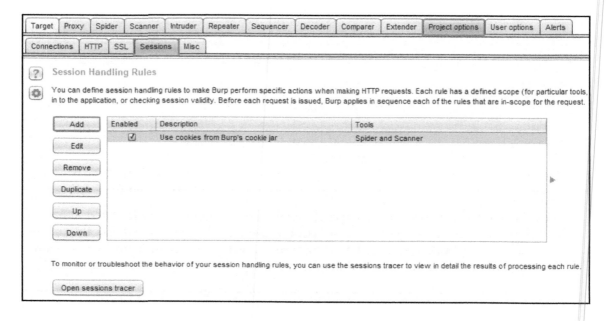

6. After clicking the **Add** button, a pop-up box appears. Give your new rule a name, such as `LogInSessionRule`, and, under **Rule Actions**, select **Run a macro**, as follows:

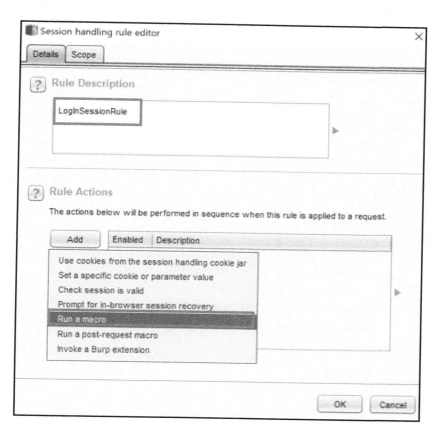

7. Another pop-up box appears, which is the **Session handling action editor**. In the first section, under **Select macro**, click the **Add** button, as follows:

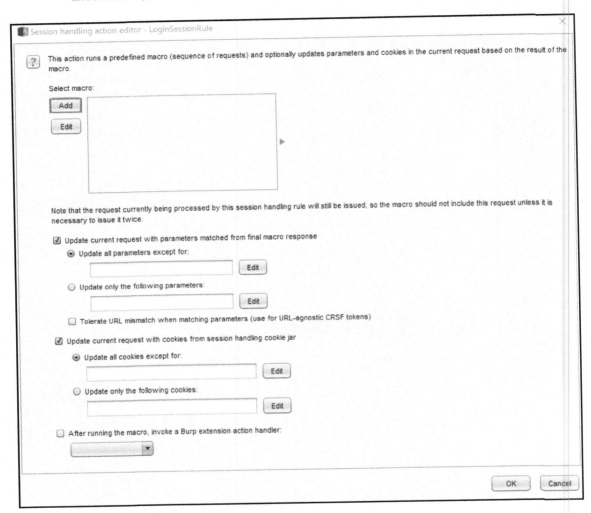

8. After clicking the **Add** button, the macro editor appears along with another pop-up of the **Macro Recorder**, as follows:

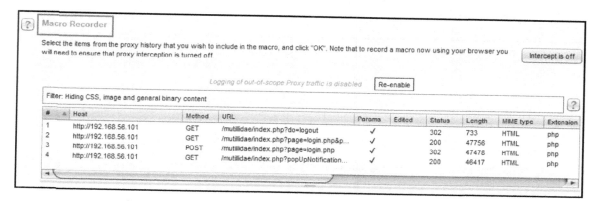

Note: A bug exists in 1.7.35 that disables Macro Recorder. Therefore, after clicking the **Add** button, if the recorder does not appear, upgrade the Burp version to 1.7.36 or higher.

9. Inside the **Macro Recorder**, look for the POST request where you logged in as Ed as well as the following GET request. Highlight both of those requests within the **Macro Recorder** window and click **OK**, as follows:

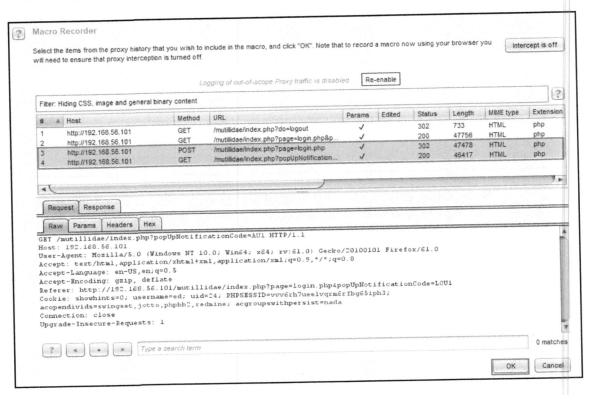

10. Those two highlighted requests in the previous dialog box now appear inside the **Macro Editor** window. Give the macro a description, such as `LogInMacro`, as follows:

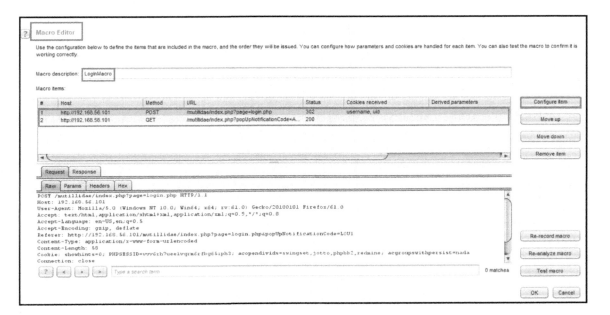

11. Click the **Configure item** button to validate that the **username** and **password** values are correct. Click **OK** when done, as follows:

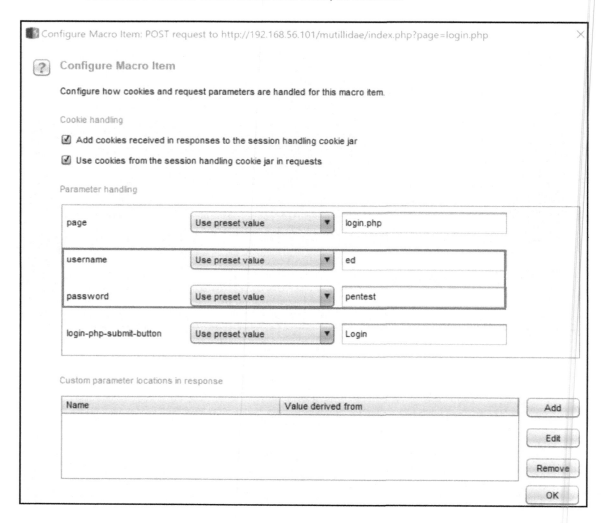

12. Click **OK** to close the Macro Editor. You should see the newly-created macro in the **Session handling action editor**. Click **OK** to close this dialog window, as follows:

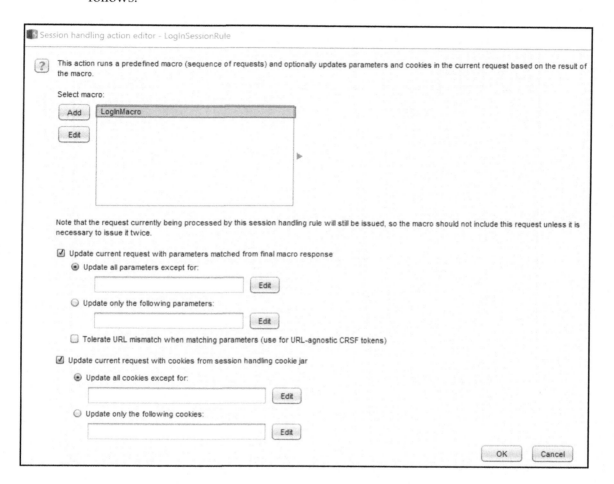

13. After closing the **Session handling action editor**, you are returned to the **Session handling rule editor** where you now see the **Rule Actions** section populated with the name of your macro. Click the **Scope** tab of this window to define which tool will use this rule:

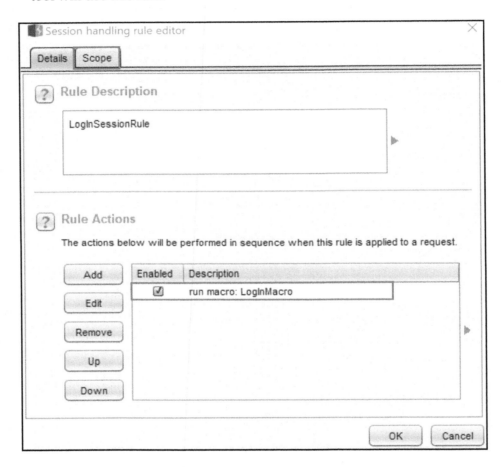

14. On the **Scope** tab of the **Session handling rule editor**, uncheck the other boxes, leaving only the **Repeater** checked. Under **URL Scope**, click the **Include all URLs** radio button. Click **OK** to close this editor, as follows:

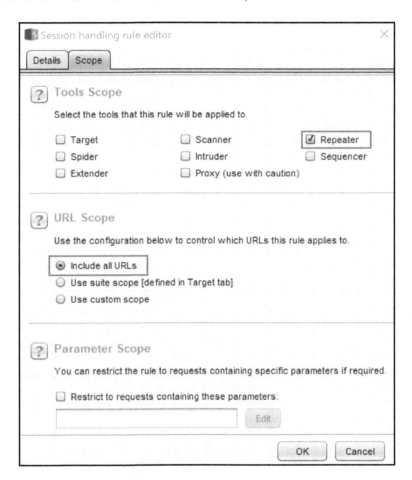

15. You should now see the new session-handling rule listed in the **Session Handling Rules** window, as follows:

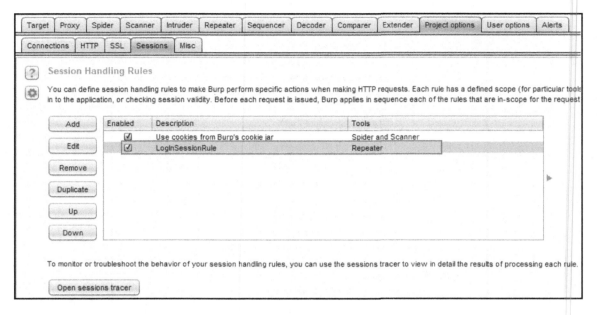

16. Return to the **Repeater** tab where you, previously, were not logged in to the application. Click the **Go** button to reveal that you are now logged in as Ed! This means your session-handling rule and associated macro worked:

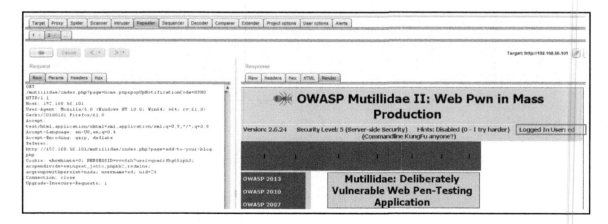

How it works...

In this recipe, we saw how an unauthenticated session can be changed to an authenticated one by replaying the login process. The creation of macros allows manual steps to be scripted and assigned to various tools within the Burp suite.

Burp allows testers to configure session-handling rules to address various conditions that the suite of tools may encounter. The rules provide additional actions to be taken when those conditions are met. In this recipe, we addressed an unauthenticated session by creating a new session-handling rule, which called a macro. We confined the scope for this rule to Repeater only for demonstration purposes.

Getting caught in the cookie jar

While targeting an application, Burp captures all of the cookies it encounters while proxying and spidering HTTP traffic against a target site. Burp stores these cookies in a cache called the **cookie jar**. This cookie jar is used within the default session-handling rule and can be shared among the suite of Burp tools, such as Proxy, Intruder, and Spider. Inside the cookie jar, there is a historical table of requests. The table details each cookie domain and path. It is possible to edit or remove cookies from the cookie jar.

Getting ready

We will open the Burp Cookie Jar and look inside. Then, using the OWASP GetBoo application, we'll identify new cookies added to the Burp Cookie Jar.

How to do it...

1. Shut down and restart Burp so it is clean of any history. Switch to the Burp **Project options** tab, then the **Sessions** tab. In the **Cookie Jar** section, click the **Open cookie jar** button, as follows:

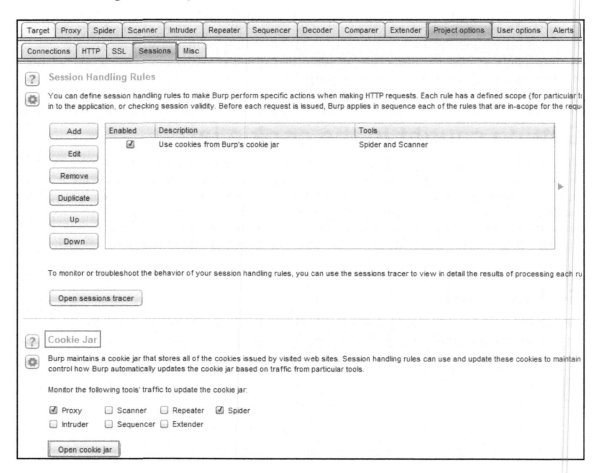

2. A new pop-up box appears. Since we have no proxied traffic yet, the cookie jar is empty. Let's target an application and get some cookies captured, as follows:

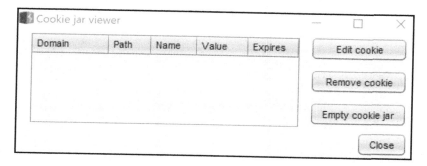

3. From the OWASP Landing page, click the link to access the GetBoo application, as follows:

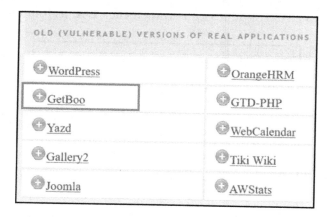

4. Click the **Login** button. At the login screen, type both the username and password as demo, and then click the **Log In** button.

5. Return to the Burp Cookie Jar. You now have three cookies available. Each cookie has a **Domain**, **Path**, **Name**, and **Value** identified, as follows:

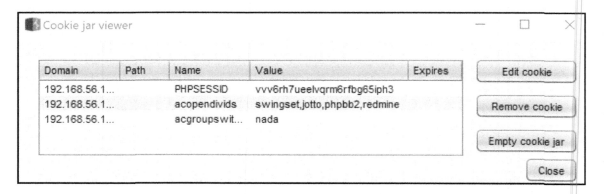

6. Select the last cookie in the list and click the **Edit cookie** button. Modify the value from nada to thisIsMyCookie and then click **OK**, as follows:

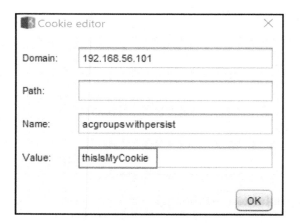

7. The value is now changed, as follows:

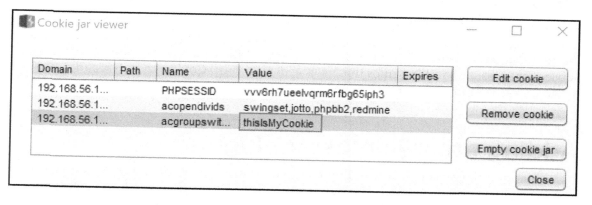

8. The default scope for the Burp Cookie Jar is Proxy and Spider. However, you may expand the scope to include other tools. Click the checkbox for **Repeater**, as follows:

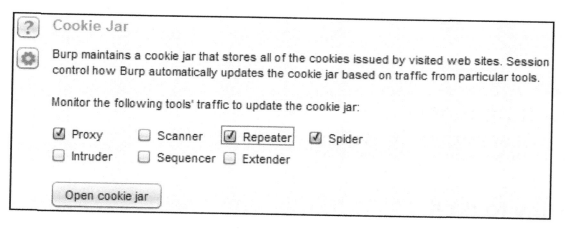

Now, if you create a new session-handling rule and use the default Burp Cookie Jar, you will see the new value for that cookie used in the requests.

How it works...

The Burp Cookie Jar is used by session-handling rules for cookie-handling when automating requests against a target application. In this recipe, we looked into the Cookie Jar, understood its contents, and even modified one of the values of a captured cookie. Any subsequent session-handling rules that use the default Burp Cookie Jar will see the modified value in the request.

Adding great pentester plugins

As web-application testers, you will find handy tools to add to your repertoire to make your assessments more efficient. The Burp community offers many wonderful extensions. In this recipe, we will add a couple of them and explain how they can make your assessments better. Retire.js and Software Vulnerability Scanner are the two plugins, these two plugins are used with the passive scanner.

 Note: Both of these plugins require the Burp Professional version.

Getting ready

Using the OWASP Mutilliae II application, we will add two handy extensions that will help us find more vulnerabilities in our target.

How to do it...

1. Switch to the Burp **Extender** tab. Go to the **BApp Store** and find two plugins—`Retire.js` and `Software Vulnerability Scanner`. Click the **Install** button for each plugin, as follows:

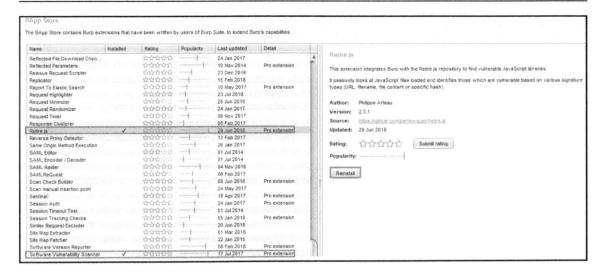

2. After installing the two plugins, go to the **Extender** tab, then **Extensions**, and then the **Burp Extensions** section. Make sure both plugins are enabled with check marks inside the check boxes. Also, notice the **Software Vulnerability Scanner** has a new tab, as follows:

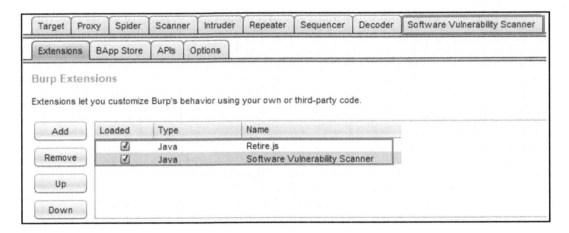

3. Return to the Firefox browser and browse to the Mutillidae homepage. Perform a lightweight, less-invasive passive scan by right-clicking and selecting **Passively scan this branch**, as follows:

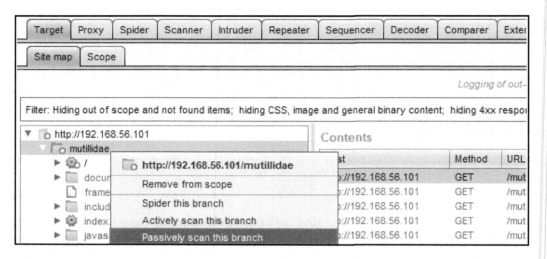

4. Note the additional findings created from the two plugins. The `Vulners` plugin, which is the Software Vulnerability Scanner, found numerous CVE issues, and `Retire.js` identified five instances of a vulnerable version of jQuery, as follows:

Issues

▶ ! File path traversal [2]
! XPath injection
! [Vulners] Vulnerable Software detected
▼ ⚠ Vulnerable version of the library 'jquery' found [5]
⚠ /mutillidae/javascript/ddsmoothmenu/jquery.min.js
⚠ /mutillidae/javascript/ddsmoothmenu/jquery.min.js
⚠ /mutillidae/javascript/jQuery/jquery.js
⚠ /mutillidae/javascript/jQuery/jquery.js
⚠ /mutillidae/javascript/jQuery/jquery.js
⚠ Password field with autocomplete enabled
▶ ! Client-side HTTP parameter pollution (reflected) [2]
▶ i Input returned in response (reflected) [9]
▶ i Cross-domain Referer leakage [3]

| Advisory | Request | Response |

❗ [Vulners] Vulnerable Software detected

Issue:	[Vulners] Vulnerable Software detected
Severity:	**High**
Confidence:	**Firm**
Host:	**http://192.168.56.101**
Path:	**/mutillidae/**

Note: This issue was generated by a Burp extension.

Issue detail

The following vulnerabilities for software OpenSSL, headers - 0.9.8k found:

● <u>OPENSSL:CVE-2014-0224</u> - 6.8 - Vulnerability in OpenSSL
   (CVE-2014-0224)
   An attacker can force the use of weak keying material in
   OpenSSL SSL/TLS clients and servers. This can be exploited by a
   Man-in-the-middle (MITM) attack where the attacker can decrypt
   and modify traffic from the attacked client and server. Reported
   by KIKU...

How it works...

Burp functionality can be extended through a PortSwigger API to create custom extensions, also known as plugins. In this recipe, we installed two plugins that assist with identifying older versions of software contained in the application with known vulnerabilities.

Creating new issues via the Manual-Scan Issues Extension

Though Burp provides a listing of many security vulnerabilities commonly found in web applications, occasionally you will identify an issue and need to create a custom scan finding. This can be done using the Manual-Scan Issues Extension.

 Note: This plugin requires the Burp Professional edition.

Getting ready

Using the OWASP Mutillidae II application, we will add the Manual Scan Issues Extension, create steps revealing a finding, then use the extension to create a custom issue.

How to do it...

1. Switch to the Burp **Extender** tab. Go to the **BApp Store** and find the plugin labeled `Manual Scan Issues`. Click the **Install** button:

2. Return to the Firefox browser and browse to the Mutillidae homepage.
3. Switch to the Burp **Proxy** | **HTTP history** tab and find the request you just made browsing to the homepage. Click the **Response** tab. Note the overly verbose Server header indicating the web server type and version along with the operating system and programming language used. This information can be used by an attacker to fingerprint the technology stack and identify vulnerabilities that can be exploited:

4. Since this is a finding, we need to create a new issue manually to capture it for our report. While viewing the **Request**, right-click and select **Add Issue**, as follows:

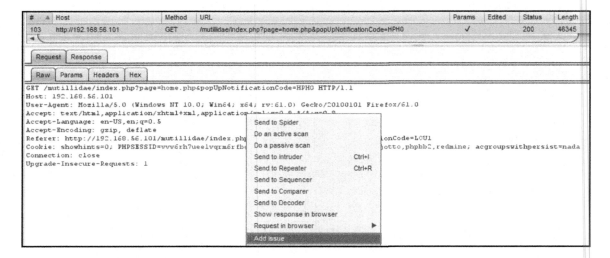

5. A pop-up dialog box appears. Within the **General** tab, we can create a new issue name of Information Leakage in Server Response. Obviously, you may add more verbiage around the issue detail, background, and remediation areas, as follows:

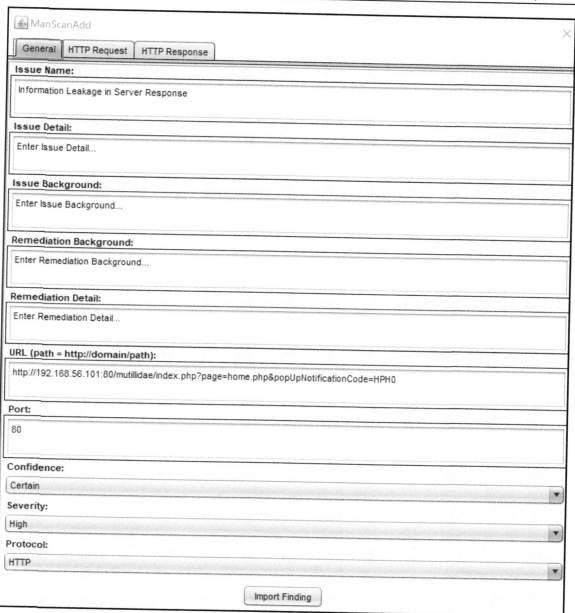

6. If we flip to the **HTTP Request** tab, we can copy and paste into the text area the contents of the **Request** tab found within the message editor, as follows:

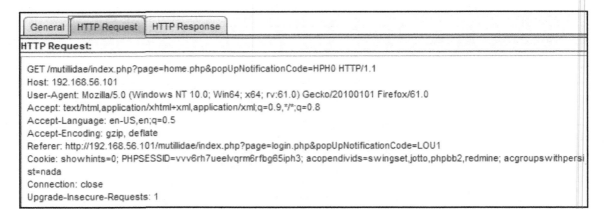

7. If we flip to the **HTTP Response** tab, we can copy and paste into the text area the contents of the **Response** tab found within the message editor.
8. Once completed, flip back to the **General** tab and click the **Import Finding** button. You should see the newly-created scan issue added to the **Issues** window, as follows:

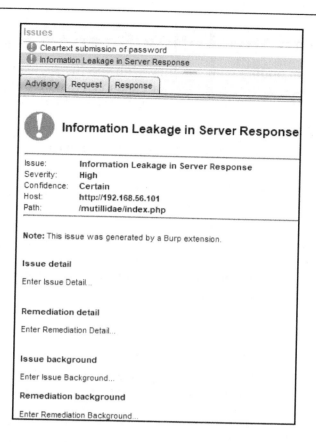

How it works...

In cases where an issue is not available within the Burp core issue list, a tester can create their own issue using the Manual-Scan Issue Extension. In this recipe, we created an issue for Information Leakage in Server Responses.

See also

For a listing of all issue definitions identified by Burp, go to `https://portswigger.net/kb/issues`.

Working with the Active Scan++ Extension

Some extensions assist in finding vulnerabilities with specific payloads, such as XML, or help to find hidden issues, such as cache poisoning and DNS rebinding. In this recipe, we will add an active scanner extension called **Active Scan++**, which assists with identifying these more specialized vulnerabilities.

 Note: This plugin requires the Burp Professional edition.

Getting ready

Using the OWASP Mutillidae II application, we will add the Active Scan++ extension, and then run an active scan against the target.

How to do it...

1. Switch to the Burp **Extender** | **BApp Store** and select the `Active Scan++` extension. Click the **Install** button to install the extension, as follows:

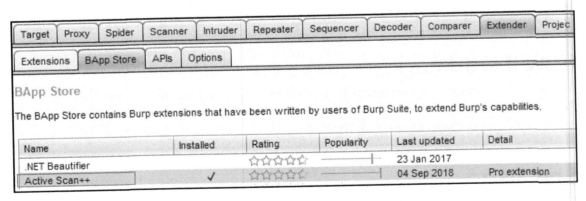

2. Return to the Firefox browser and browse to the Mutillidae homepage.

3. Switch to the Burp **Target** tab, then the **Site map** tab, right-click on the
   `mutillidae` folder, and select **Actively scan this branch**, as follows:

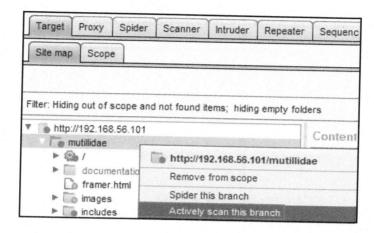

4. When the **Active scanning wizard** appears, you may leave the default settings
   and click the **Next** button, as follows:

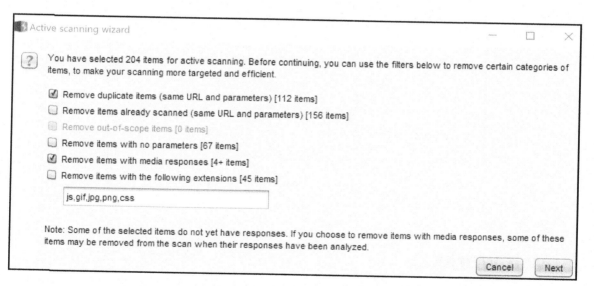

Follow the prompts and click **OK** to begin the scanning process.

5. After the active scanner completes, browse to the **Issues** window. Make note of any additional issues found by the newly-added extension. You can always tell which ones the extension found by looking for the **This issue was generated by the Burp extension: Active Scan++** message, as follows:

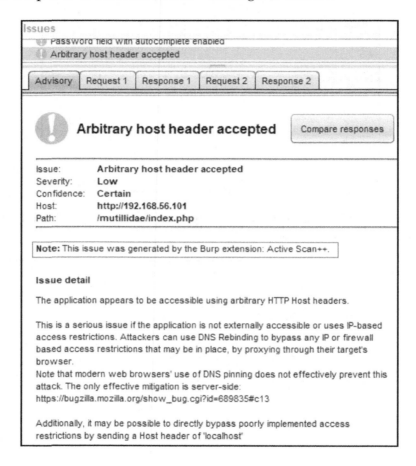

How it works...

Burp functionality can be extended beyond core findings with the use of extensions. In this recipe, we installed a plugin that extends the Active Scanner functionality to assist with identifying additional issues such as Arbitrary Header Injection, as seen in this recipe.

Implementing Advanced Topic Attacks

11

In this chapter, we will cover the following recipes:

- Performing **XML External Entity (XXE)** attacks
- Working with **JSON Web Token (JWT)**
- Using Burp Collaborator to determine **Server-Side Request Forgery (SSRF)**
- Testing **Cross-Origin Resource Sharing (CORS)**
- Performing Java deserialization attacks

Introduction

This chapter covers intermediate to advanced topics such as working with JWT, XXE, and Java deserialization attacks, and how to use Burp to assist with such assessments. With some advanced attacks, Burp plugins provide tremendous help in easing the task required by the tester.

Software tool requirements

In order to complete the recipes in this chapter, you will need the following:

- OWASP **Broken Web Applications (BWA)**
- OWASP Mutillidae link
- Burp Proxy Community or Professional (https://portswigger.net/burp/)

Performing XXE attacks

XXE is a vulnerability that targets applications parsing XML. Attackers can manipulate the XML input with arbitrary commands and send those commands as external entity references within the XML structure. The XML is then executed by a weakly-configured parser, giving the attacker the requested resource.

Getting ready

Using the OWASP Mutillidae II XML validator page, determine whether the application is susceptible to XXE attacks.

How to do it...

1. Navigate to the **XML External Entity Injection** page, that is, through **Others** | **XML External Entity Injection** | **XML Validator**:

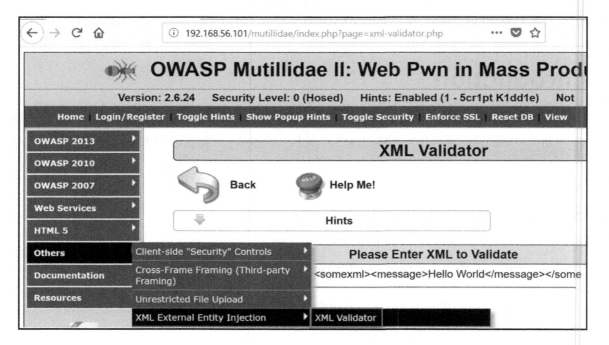

2. While on the **XML Validator** page, perform the example XML that is provided on the page. Click on the **Validate XML** button:

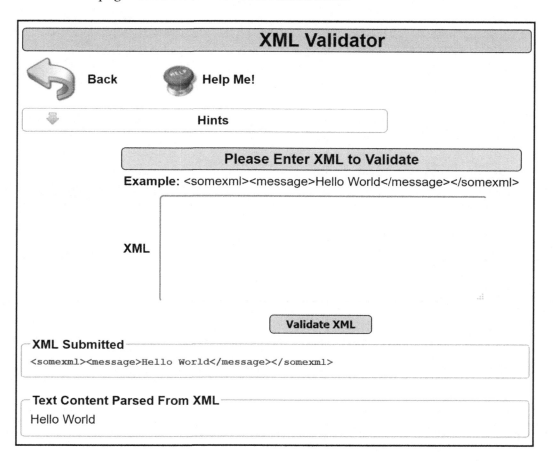

3. Switch to Burp **Proxy| HTTP history** tab and look for the request you just submitted to validate the XML. Right-click and send the request to the repeater:

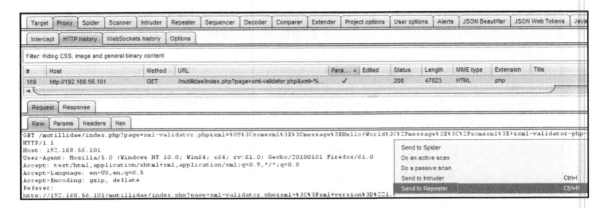

4. Note the value provided in the `xml` parameter:

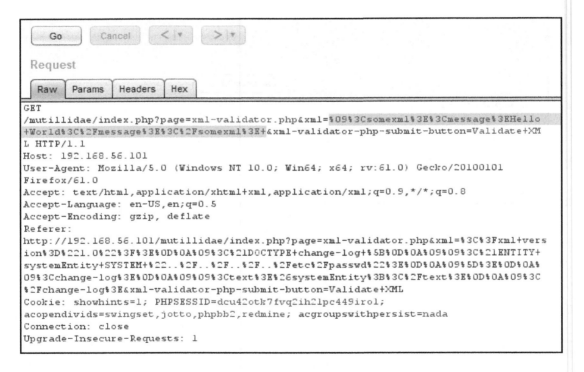

5. Use Burp Proxy Interceptor to replace this XML parameter value with the following payload. This new payload will make a request to a file on the operating system that should be restricted from view, namely, the `/etc/passwd` file:

```xml
<?xml version="1.0"?>
    <!DOCTYPE change-log[
        <!ENTITY systemEntity SYSTEM "../../../../etc/passwd">
    ]>
    <change-log>
        <text>&systemEntity;</text>
    </change-log>
```

Since there are odd characters and spaces in the new XML message, let's type this payload into the **Decoder** section and URL-encode it before we paste it into the `xml` parameter.

6. Switch to the **Decoder** section, type or paste the new payload into the text area. Click the **Encode as...** button and select the **URL** option from the drop-down listing. Then, copy the URL-encoded payload using *Ctrl + C*. Make sure you copy all of the payload by scrolling to the right:

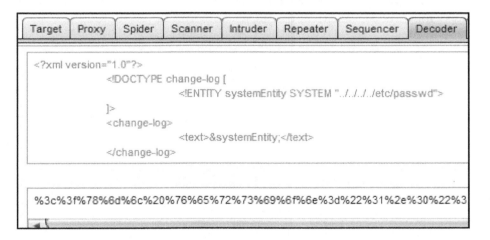

7. Switch to the Burp **Proxy Intercept** tab. Turn the interceptor on with the **Intercept is on** button.

8. Return to the Firefox browser and reload the page. As the request is paused, replace the current value of the xml parameter with the new URL-encoded payload:

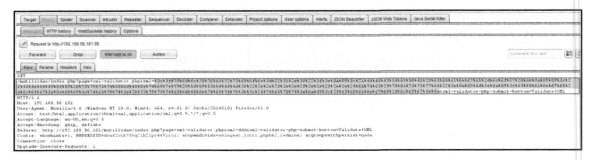

9. Click the **Forward** button. Turn interceptor off by toggling the button to **Intercept is off**.

10. Note that the returned XML now shows the contents of the /etc/passwd file! The XML parser granted us access to the /etc/passwd file on the operating system:

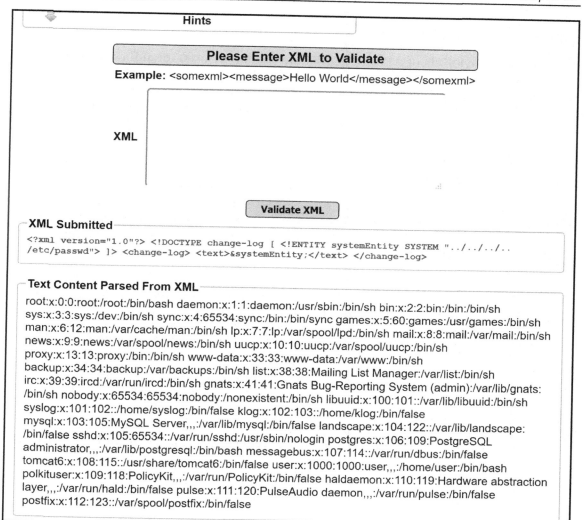

How it works...

In this recipe, the insecure XML parser receives the request within the XML for the /etc/passwd file residing on the server. Since there is no validation performed on the XML request due to a weakly-configured parser, the resource is freely provided to the attacker.

Working with JWT

As more sites provide client API access, JWT are commonly used for authentication. These tokens hold identity and claims information tied to the resources the user is granted access to on the target site. Web-penetration testers need to read these tokens and determine their strength. Fortunately, there are some handy plugins that make working with JWT tokens inside of Burp much easier. We will learn about these plugins in this recipe.

Getting ready

In this recipe, we need to generate JWT tokens. Therefore, we will use the **OneLogin** software to assist with this task. In order to complete this recipe, browse to the OneLogin website: `https://www.onelogin.com/`. Click the **Developers** link at the top and then click the **GET A DEVELOPER ACCOUNT** link (`https://www.onelogin.com/developer-signup`).

After you sign up, you will be asked to verify your account and create a password. Please perform these account setup tasks prior to starting this recipe.

Using the OneLogin SSO account, we will use two Burp extensions to examine the JWT tokens assigned as authentication by the site.

How to do it...

1. Switch to Burp **BApp Store** and install two plugins—**JSON Beautifier** and **JSON Web Tokens**:

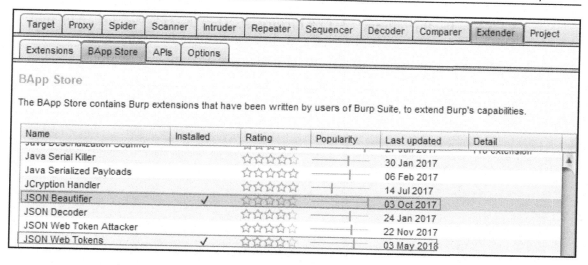

2. In the Firefox browser, go to your OneLogin page. The URL will be specific to the developer account you created. Log in to the account using the credentials you established when you set up the account before beginning this recipe:

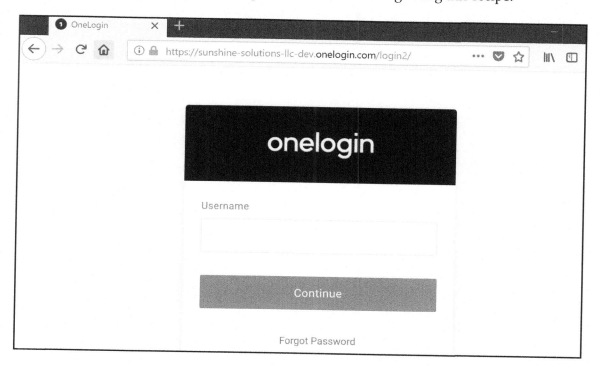

3. Switch to the Burp **Proxy | HTTP history** tab. Find the POST request with the URL `/access/auth`. Right-click and click the **Send to Repeater** option.

4. Your host value will be specific to the OneLogin account you set up:

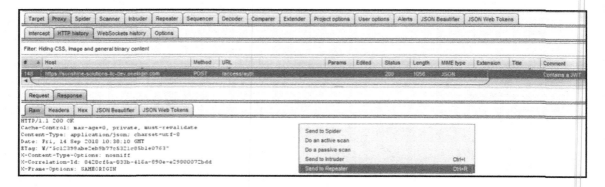

5. Switch to the **Repeater** tab and notice that you have two additional tabs relating to the two extensions you installed:

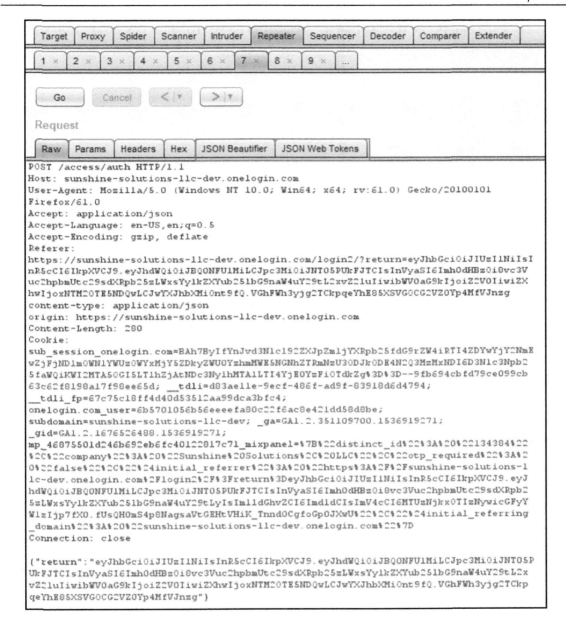

POST /access/auth HTTP/1.1
Host: sunshine-solutions-llc-dev.onelogin.com
User-Agent: Mozilla/5.0 (Windows NT 10.0; Win64; x64; rv:61.0) Gecko/20100101
Firefox/61.0
Accept: application/json
Accept-Language: en-US,en;q=0.5
Accept-Encoding: gzip, deflate
Referer:
https://sunshine-solutions-llc-dev.onelogin.com/login2/?return=eyJhbGciOiJIUzI1NiIsI
nR5cCI6IkpXVCJ9.eyJhdWQiOiJBQQNFU1MiLCJpc3Mi0iJNT05PUkFJTCIsInVyaSI6ImhOdHBz0i8vc3V
uc2hpbmUtc29sdXRpb25zLWxsYy1kZXYub251bG9naW4uY29tL2xvZ2luIiwibWV0aG9kIjoiZ2V0IiwiZX
hwIjoxNTM2OTE5NDQwLCJwYXJhbXMiOnt9fQ.VGhFWh3yjg2TCkpqeYhE85XSVGOCG2VZOYp4MfVJnzg
content-type: application/json
origin: https://sunshine-solutions-llc-dev.onelogin.com
Content-Length: 280
Cookie:
sub_session_onelogin.com=BAh7ByIfYnJvd3Nlc192ZXJpZmljYXRpb25fdG9rZW4iRTI4ZDYwYjY2NmE
wZjFjNDlmOWNlYWUz0WYxMjY5ZDkyZWU0YzhmMWE5NGNhZTRmNzU3ODJkR0DE4N2Q3MzMxNDI6D3Nlc3Npb2
5faWQiKWI2MTA50GI5LT1hZjAtNDc3NylhMTA1LTI4YjY0Yz1FiOTdkZg%3D%3D--9fb694cbfd79ce099cb
63c62f8198a17f98ee65d; __tdli=d83aelle-9ecf-486f-ad9f-83918d6d4794;
__tdli_fp=67c75c18ff4d40d53512aa99dca3bfc4;
onelogin.com_user=6b5701056b56eeeefa80c22f6ac8e421dd58d8be;
subdomain=sunshine-solutions-llc-dev; _ga=GA1.2.351109700.1536919271;
_gid=GA1.2.1676526488.1536919271;
mp_46875501d246b692eb6fc40122817c71_mixpanel=%7B%22distinct_id%22%3A%20%22134384%22
%2C%22company%22%3A%20%22Sunshine%20Solutions%2C%20LLC%22%2C%22otp_required%22%3A%2
0%22false%22%2C%22%24initial_referrer%22%3A%20%22https%3A%2F%2Fsunshine-solutions-l
lc-dev.onelogin.com%2Flogin2%2F%3Freturn%3DeyJhbGciOiJIUzI1NiIsInR5cCI6IkpXVCJ9.eyJ
hdWQiOiJBQQNFU1MiLCJpc3Mi0iJNT05PUkFJTCIsInVyaSI6ImhOdHBz0i8vc3Vuc2hpbmUtc29sdXRpb2
5zLWxsYy1kZXYub251bG9naW4uY29tLyIsIm1ldGhvZCI6ImdldCIsImV4cCI6MTUzNjkx0TIzNywicGFyY
W1zIjp7fX0.fUsQH0mS4p8NagsaVtGEHtVHiK_Tnnd0CgfoGpOJXwU%22%2C%22%24initial_referring
_domain%22%3A%20%22sunshine-solutions-llc-dev.onelogin.com%22%7D
Connection: close

{"return":"eyJhbGciOiJIUzI1NiIsInR5cCI6IkpXVCJ9.eyJhdWQiOiJBQQNFU1MiLCJpc3Mi0iJNT05P
UkFJTCIsInVyaSI6ImhOdHBz0i8vc3Vuc2hpbmUtc29sdXRpb25zLWxsYy1kZXYub251bG9naW4uY29tL2x
vZ2luIiwibWV0aG9kIjoiZ2V0IiwiZXhwIjoxNTM2OTE5NDQwLCJwYXJhbXMiOnt9fQ.VGhFWh3yjg2TCkp
qeYhE85XSVGOCG2VZOYp4MfVJnzg"}

6. Click the **JSON Beautifier** tab to view the JSON structure in a more readable manner:

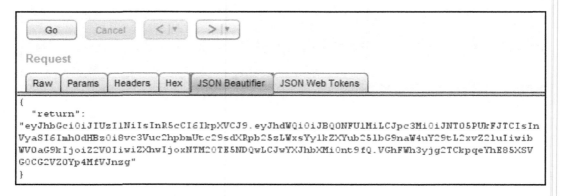

7. Click the **JSON Web Tokens** tab to reveal a debugger very similar to the one available at `https://jwt.io`. This plugin allows you to read the claims content and manipulate the encryption algorithm for various brute-force tests. For example, in the following screenshot, notice how you can change the algorithm to **nOnE** in order to attempt to create a new JWT token to place into the request:

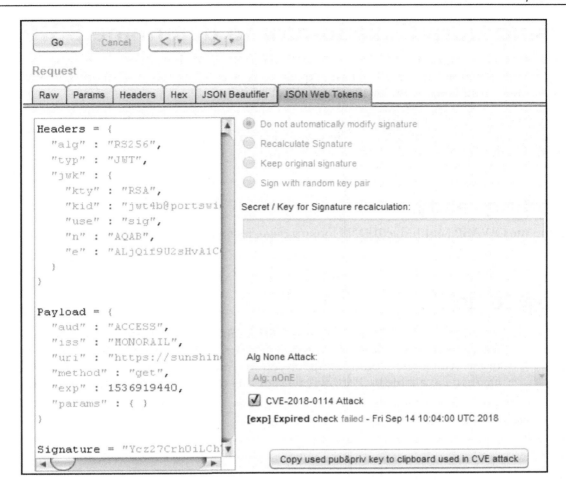

How it works...

Two extensions, JSON Beautifier and JSON Web Tokens, help testers to work with JWT tokens in an easier way by providing debugger tools conveniently available with the Burp UI.

Using Burp Collaborator to determine SSRF

SSRF is a vulnerability that allows an attacker to force applications to make unauthorized requests on the attacker's behalf. These requests can be as simple as DNS queries or as maniacal as commands from an attacker-controlled server.

In this recipe, we will use Burp Collaborator to check open ports available for SSRF requests, and then use Intruder to determine whether the application will perform DNS queries to the public Burp Collaborator server through an SSRF vulnerability.

Getting ready

Using the OWASP Mutillidae II DNS lookup page, let's determine whether the application has an SSRF vulnerability.

How to do it...

1. Switch to the Burp **Project options** | **Misc** tab. Note the **Burp Collaborator Server** section. You have options available for using a private Burp Collaborator server, which you would set up, or you may use the publicly internet-accessible one made available by PortSwigger. For this recipe, we will use the public one:

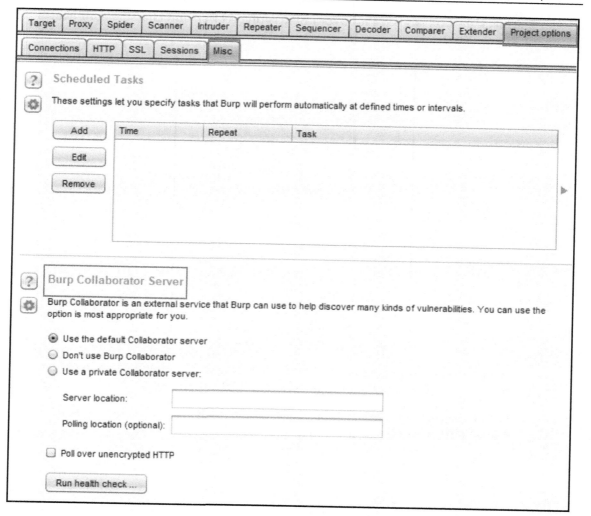

2. Check the box labeled **Poll over unencrypted HTTP** and click the **Run health check...** button:

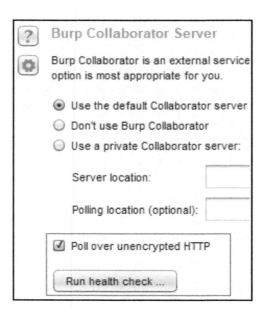

3. A pop-up box appears to test various protocols to see whether they will connect to the public Burp Collaborator server available on the internet.

4. Check the messages for each protocol to see which are successful. Click the **Close** button when you are done:

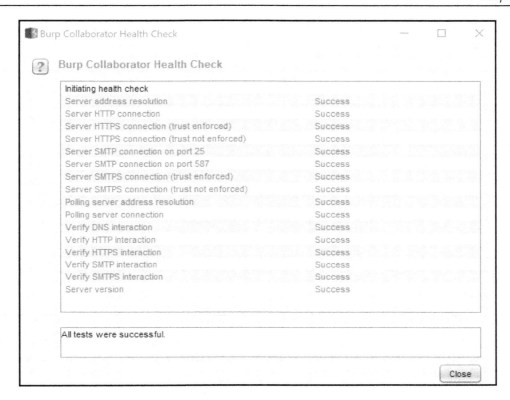

Burp Collaborator Health Check	— □ ×

Burp Collaborator Health Check

Initiating health check	
Server address resolution	Success
Server HTTP connection	Success
Server HTTPS connection (trust enforced)	Success
Server HTTPS connection (trust not enforced)	Success
Server SMTP connection on port 25	Success
Server SMTP connection on port 587	Success
Server SMTPS connection (trust enforced)	Success
Server SMTPS connection (trust not enforced)	Success
Polling server address resolution	Success
Polling server connection	Success
Verify DNS interaction	Success
Verify HTTP interaction	Success
Verify HTTPS interaction	Success
Verify SMTP interaction	Success
Verify SMTPS interaction	Success
Server version	Success

All tests were successful.

Close

5. From the top-level menu, select **Burp** | **Burp Collaborator client**:

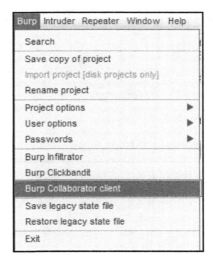

Burp	Intruder	Repeater	Window	Help

Search
Save copy of project
Import project [disk projects only]
Rename project
Project options ▶
User options ▶
Passwords ▶
Burp Infiltrator
Burp Clickbandit
Burp Collaborator client
Save legacy state file
Restore legacy state file
Exit

6. A pop-up box appears. In the section labeled **Generate Collaborator payloads**, change the **1** to **10**:

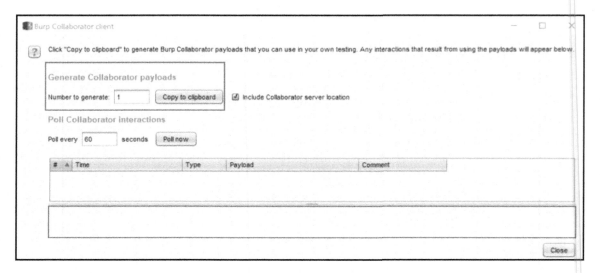

7. Click the **Copy to clipboard** button. Leave all other defaults as they are. Do not close the Collaborator client window. If you close the window, you will lose the client session:

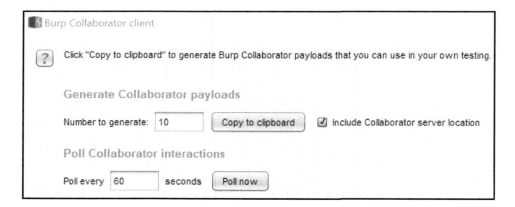

8. Return to the Firefox browser and navigate to **OWASP 2013** | **A1 – Injection (Other)** | **HTML Injection (HTMLi)** | **DNS Lookup**:

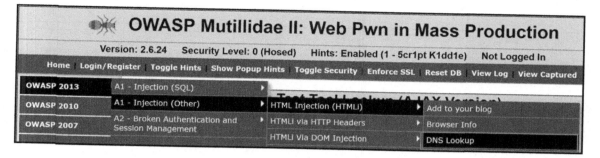

9. On the **DNS Lookup** page, type an IP address and click the **Lookup DNS** button:

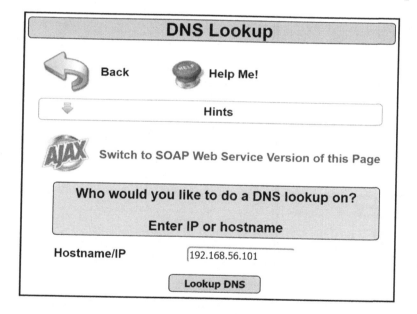

10. Switch to the Burp **Proxy | HTTP history** tab and find the request you just created on the **DNS Lookup** page. Right-click and select the **Send to Intruder** option:

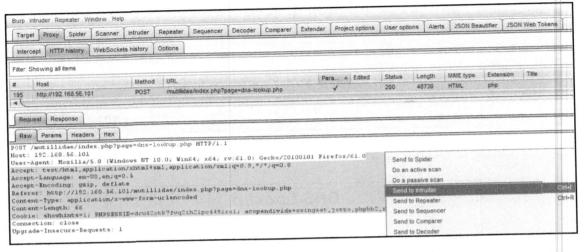

11. Switch to the Burp **Intruder | Positions** tab. Clear all suggested payload markers and highlight the IP address, click the **Add §** button to place payload markers around the IP address value of the `target_host` parameter:

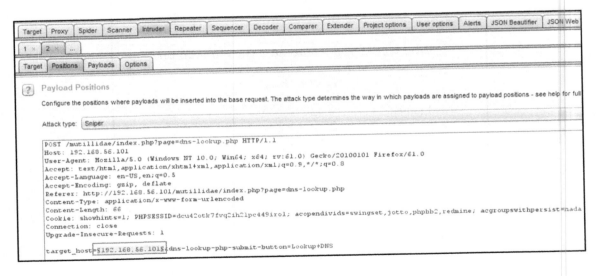

12. Switch to the Burp **Intruder | Payloads** tab and paste the 10 payloads you copied to the clipboard from the Burp Collaborator client into the **Payload Options [Simple list]** textbox using the **Paste** button:

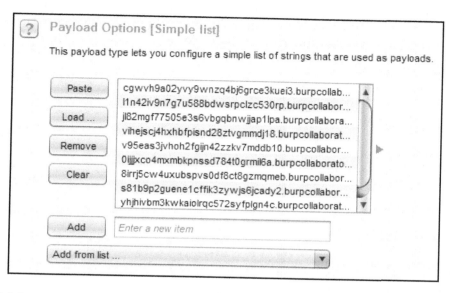

Make sure you uncheck the **Payload Encoding** checkbox.

13. Click the **Start attack** button. The attack results table will pop up as your payloads are processing. Allow the attacks to complete. Note the `burpcollaborator.net` URL is placed in the payload marker position of the `target_host` parameter:

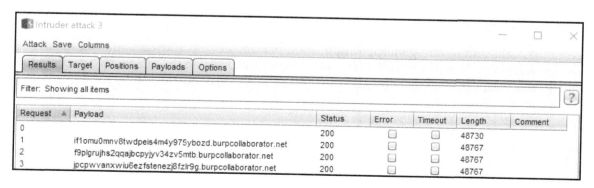

14. Return to the Burp Collaborator client and click the **Poll now** button to see whether any SSRF attacks were successful over any of the protocols. If any requests leaked outside of the network, those requests will appear in this table along with the specific protocol used. If any requests are shown in this table, you will need to report the SSRF vulnerability as a finding. As you can see from the results shown here, numerous DNS queries were made by the application on behalf of the attacker-provided payloads:

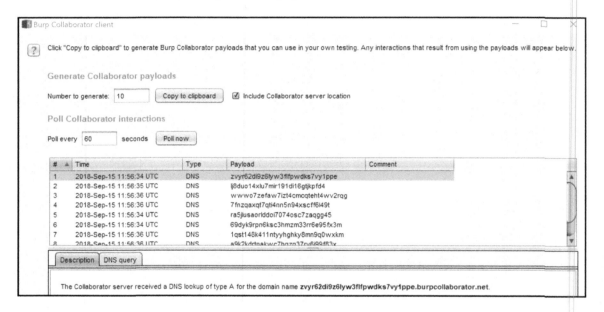

How it works...

Network leaks and overly-generous application parameters can allow an attacker to have an application make unauthorized calls via various protocols on the attacker's behalf. In the case of this recipe, the application allows DNS queries to leak outside of the local machine and connect to the internet.

See also

For more information on SSRF attacks, see this PortSwigger blog entry at `https://portswigger.net/blog/cracking-the-lens-targeting-https-hidden-attack-surface`.

Testing CORS

An application that implements HTML5 CORS means the application will share browser information with another domain that resides at a different origin. By design, browser protections prevent external scripts from accessing information in the browser. This protection is known as **Same-Origin Policy (SOP)**. However, CORS is a means of bypassing SOP, permissively. If an application wants to share browser information with a completely different domain, it may do so with properly-configured CORS headers.

Web-penetration testers must ensure applications that handle AJAX calls (for example, HTML5) do not have misconfigured CORS headers. Let's see how Burp can help us identify such misconfigurations.

Getting ready

Using the OWASP Mutillidae II AJAX version of the **Pen Test Tool Lookup** page, determine whether the application contains misconfigured CORS headers.

How to do it...

1. Navigate to **HTML5 | Asynchronous JavaScript and XML | Pen Test Tool Lookup (AJAX)**:

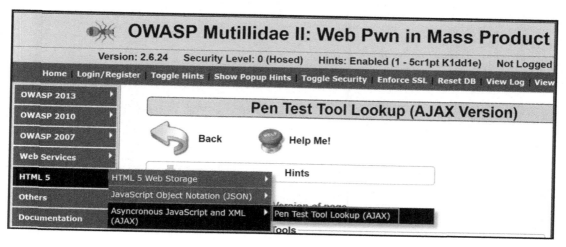

2. Select a tool from the listing and click the **Lookup Tool** button:

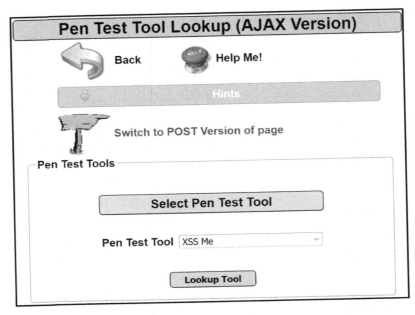

3. Switch to the Burp **Proxy** | **HTTP history** tab and find the request you just made from the AJAX Version **Pen Test Tool Lookup** page. Flip to the **Response** tab:

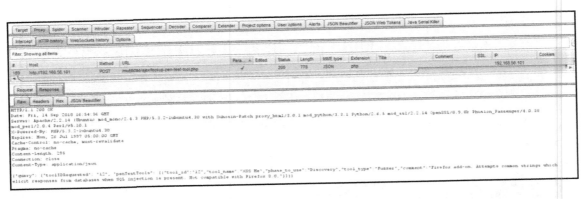

4. Let's examine the headers more closely by selecting the **Headers** tab of the same **Response** tab. Though this is an AJAX request, the call is local to the application instead of being made to a cross-origin domain. Thus, no CORS headers are present since it is not required. However, if a call to an external domain were made (for example, Google APIs), then CORS headers would be required:

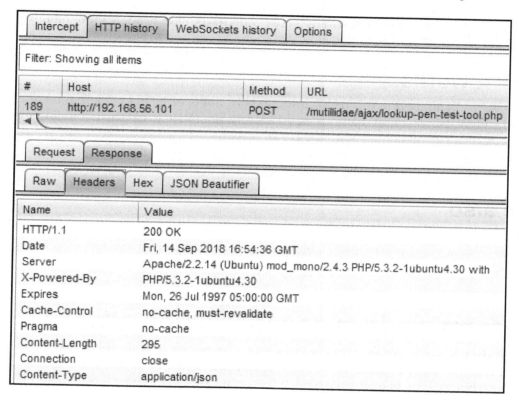

5. In an AJAX request, there is a call out to an external URL (for example, a cross-domain). In order to permit the external domain to receive DOM information from the user's browser session, CORS headers must be present, including `Access-Control-Allow-Origin: <name of cross domain>`.

6. In the event the CORS header does not specify the name of the external domain and, instead, uses a wild card (`*`), this is a vulnerability. Web pentesters should include this in their report as a misconfigured CORS headers vulnerability.

How it works...

Since the AJAX call used in this recipe originated from the same place, there is no need for CORS headers. However, in many cases, AJAX calls are made to external domains and require explicit permission through the HTTP response `Access-Control-Allow-Origin` header.

See also

For more information on misconfigured CORS headers, see this PortSwigger blog entry at `https://portswigger.net/blog/exploiting-cors-misconfigurations-for-bitcoins-and-bounties`.

Performing Java deserialization attacks

Serialization is a mechanism provided in various languages that allows the saving of an object's state in binary format. It is used for speed and obfuscation. The turning of an object back from binary into an object is deserialization. In cases where user input is used within an object and that object is later serialized, it creates an attack vector for arbitrary code-injection and possible remote code-execution. We will look at a Burp extension that will assist web-penetration testers in assessing applications for Java Deserialization vulnerabilities.

Getting Ready

Using OWASP Mutillidae II and a hand-crafted serialized code snippet, we will demonstrate how to use the **Java Serial Killer Burp** extension to assist in performing Java deserialization attacks.

How to do it...

1. Switch to Burp **BApp Store** and install the **Java Serial Killer** plugin:

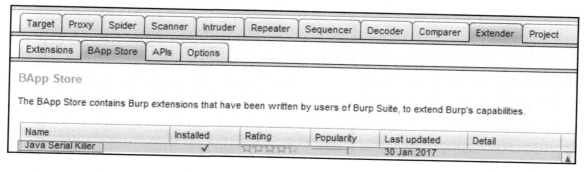

In order to create a scenario using a serialized object, we will take a standard request and add a serialized object to it for the purposes of demonstrating how you can use the extension to add attacker-controlled commands to serialized objects.

2. Note the new tab added to your Burp UI menu at the top dedicated to the newly-installed plugin.

3. Navigate to the Mutillidae homepage.

4. Switch to the Burp **Proxy**| **HTTP history** tab and look for the request you just created by browsing to the Mutillidae homepage:

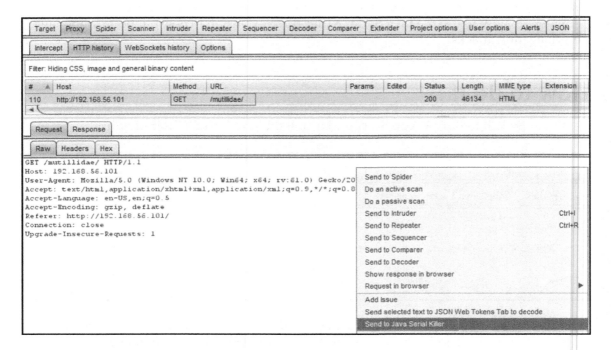

Unfortunately, there aren't any serialized objects in Mutillidae so we will have to create one ourselves.

5. Switch to the **Decoder** tab and copy the following snippet of a serialized object:

```
AC ED 00 05 73 72 00 0A 53 65 72 69 61 6C 54 65
```

6. Paste the hexadecimal numbers into the **Decoder** tab, click the **Encode as...** button, and select base 64:

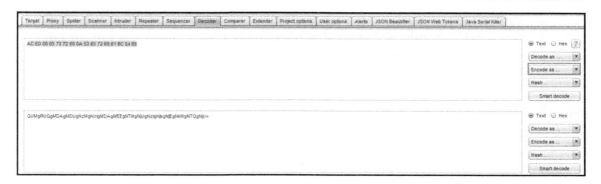

AC ED 00 05 73 72 00 0A 53 65 72 69 61 6C 54 65

QUMgRUQgMDAgMDUgNzMgNzIgMDAgMEEgNTMgNjUgNzIgNjkgNjEgNkEgNTQgNjU=

7. Copy the base-64 encoded value from the **Decoder** tab and paste it into the bottom of the request you sent to the **Java Serial Killer** tab. Use *Ctrl + C* to copy out of Decoder and *Ctrl + V* to paste it anywhere in the white space area of the request:

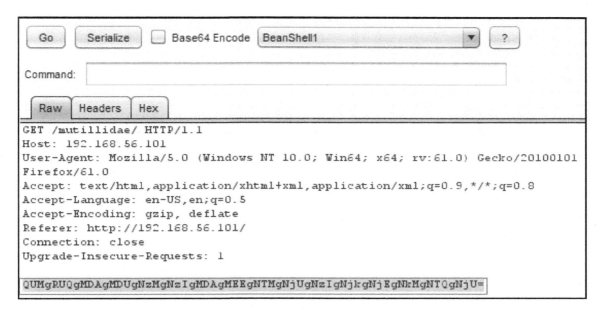

8. Within the **Java Serial Killer** tab, pick a Java library from the drop-down list. For this recipe, we will use **CommonsCollections1**. Check the **Base64 Encode** box. Add a command to embed into the serialized object. In this example, we will use the **nslookup 127.0.0.1** command. Highlight the payload and click the **Serialize** button:

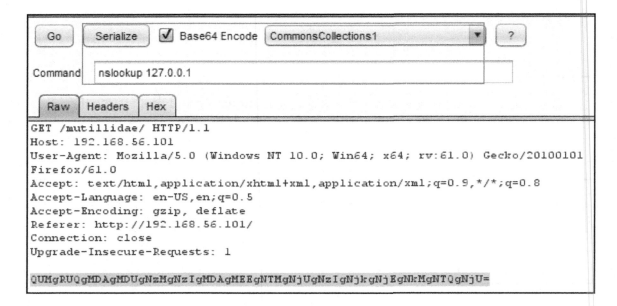

9. After clicking the **Serialize** button, notice the payload has changed and now contains your arbitrary command and is base-64 encoded:

10. Click the **Go** button within the **Java Serial Killer** tab to execute the payload. Even though you may receive an error in the response, ideally, you would have a listener, such as `tcpdump`, listening for any DNS lookups on port 53. From the listener, you would see the DNS query to the IP address you specified in the `nslookup` command.

How it works...

In cases where application code receives user input directly into an object without performing sanitization on such input, an attacker has the opportunity to provide arbitrary commands. The input is then serialized and run on the operating system where the application resides, creating a possible attack vector for remote code execution.

There's more...

Since this recipe scenario is a bit contrived, you may not receive a response on your network listener for the `nslookup` command. Try the recipe again after downloading a vulnerable version of an application with known Java deserialization vulnerabilities (that is, Jenkins, JBoss). Reuse the same steps shown here, only change the target application.

See also

- For more information about real-world Java deserialization attacks, check out these links:
    - **Symantec:** https://www.symantec.com/security_response/attacksignatures/detail.jsp?asid=30326
    - **Foxglove Security:** https://foxglovesecurity.com/2015/11/06/what-do-weblogic-websphere-jboss-jenkins-opennms-and-your-application-have-in-common-this-vulnerability/
- To read more about this Burp plugin, check out https://blog.netspi.com/java-deserialization-attacks-burp/

Other Books You May Enjoy

If you enjoyed this book, you may be interested in these other books by Packt:

Web Penetration Testing with Kali Linux - Third Edition
Gilberto Najera-Gutierrez

ISBN: 978-1-78862-337-7

- Learn how to set up your lab with Kali Linux
- Understand the core concepts of web penetration testing
- Get to know the tools and techniques you need to use with Kali Linux
- Identify the difference between hacking a web application and network hacking
- Expose vulnerabilities present in web servers and their applications using server-side attacks
- Understand the different techniques used to identify the flavor of web applications
- See standard attacks such as exploiting cross-site request forgery and cross-site scripting flaws
- Get an overview of the art of client-side attacks
- Explore automated attacks such as fuzzing web applications

Advanced Infrastructure Penetration Testing
Chiheb Chebbi

ISBN: 978-1-78862-448-0

- Exposure to advanced infrastructure penetration testing techniques and methodologies
- Gain hands-on experience of penetration testing in Linux system vulnerabilities and memory exploitation
- Understand what it takes to break into enterprise networks
- Learn to secure the configuration management environment and continuous delivery pipeline
- Gain an understanding of how to exploit networks and IoT devices
- Discover real-world, post-exploitation techniques and countermeasures

Leave a review - let other readers know what you think

Please share your thoughts on this book with others by leaving a review on the site that you bought it from. If you purchased the book from Amazon, please leave us an honest review on this book's Amazon page. This is vital so that other potential readers can see and use your unbiased opinion to make purchasing decisions, we can understand what our customers think about our products, and our authors can see your feedback on the title that they have worked with Packt to create. It will only take a few minutes of your time, but is valuable to other potential customers, our authors, and Packt. Thank you!

Index

testing for 149, 151, 152
Repeater
    using 33, 34
Representational State Transfer (REST) API
    account provision process, testing 127, 128,
    132, 135

S

Same-Origin Policy (SOP) 327
Scanner
    active scanner 84
    passive scanner 84
    using 84, 86, 89, 91, 93, 95, 96
Sequencer
    used, for testing session token strength 162,
    165, 167
serialization 330
session fixation attack 162
session fixation
    testing for 170, 173
session token strength
    testing, with Sequencer 162
session-handling macros
    creating 274, 276, 278, 281, 284, 286, 287
Spider
    Control tab 73
    Options tab 75, 77, 78
    using 73, 78, 81, 83
splash screen 19
SQL injection
    testing for 243, 244, 245
SSRF
    determining, with Burp Collaborator 318, 320,
    324, 326
    URL 326
    used, for determining Burp Collaborator 322
stored cross-site scripting

testing for 232, 234

T

Target Site Map
    setting up 26, 27, 29

U

UI redress attack 252
user options
    Display tab 69
    Misc tab 71, 72
    setting 68
    SSL tab 69
username enumeration
    performing, against target application 104, 107,
    110, 112

V

virtual machine (VM) 7

W

weak lock-out mechanisms
    testing 112, 113, 116, 118, 119
weak validation
    bypassing 200, 202, 203
web app pentesting lab
    setting up 11
    software tool, requisites 11, 14, 16
whitelisting 200
workflows
    circumvention, testing for 209, 210, 212, 213,
    216, 217

X

XXE attacks
    performing 306, 308, 309, 310, 311

Made in the
USA
Middletown, DE